SAM's EDISTO ISLAND PARADISE

"The Paradise God took two extra days to create"

Written by Sam Lybrand

Copyright © 2012-2015, Sam Lybrand. All rights reserved.
This book, or parts thereof, may not be reproduced in any form without the written permission from the author; exceptions are made for brief excerpts used in publication reviews.

Printed in the United States of America

10 9 8 7 6 5 4 3 2

Empire Publishing

www.empire-publishing.com

Contents

INTRODUCTION	1
EDISTO	4
CHAPTER ONE	13
A Photo Collection	23
CHAPTER TWO	84
CHAPTER THREE	151
CHAPTER FOUR	191
CHAPTER FIVE	230
CHAPTER SIX	243
CHAPTER SEVEN	249
CHAPTER EIGHT	265
CHAPTER NINE	280
CHAPTER TEN	308
CHAPTER ELEVEN	317
Dream Dreams and See Visions	322
DEDICATIONS	324
CREDITS	326

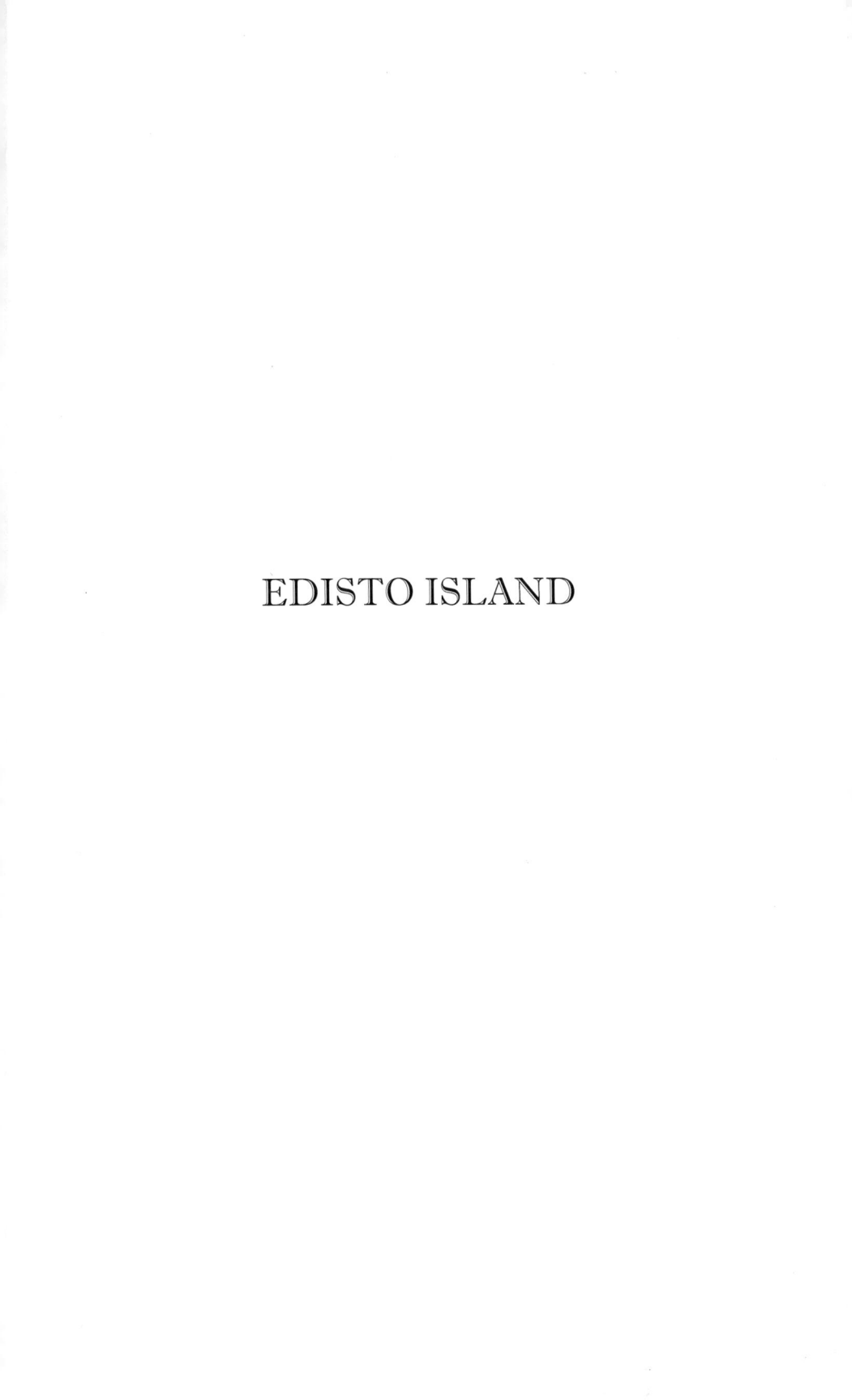

EDISTO ISLAND

INTRODUCTION

This book is about what interest me about Edisto Island and about some of the things I personally did coming up on Edisto. It is not written as a history of Edisto but as a number of facts and unique experiences I have had.

In my mind's eye, Edisto Island is all about the mysteries of life that can be enjoyed on this special place called "Ed-is-tow". Edisto is like a very enjoyable book that you have to read to its end so that your lasting memories will be recalled as warm and wonderful. While reading, if you get emotionally involved and relate to each character or event, it makes the book even more enjoyable. Therefore there is no table of contents for you to be able to pick and choose which chapters or sections you will read.

Have absolutely no doubt, and there is no apology, from the beginning, that this book is about Sam Lybrand and what interests him about Edisto Island. It also has as many pictures as I could take that would show off the character of Edisto and why I have loved it most of my life

This book includes pictures taken by me of scenes that I think represent Edisto. I am not a professional photographer; I just used a good camera and all I had to do was get the sun right and then push one button. The contents in this book are what interest me about Edisto and things I did or experienced while living there as a young child and as far back as I can remember.

Also, as a disclosure, I am not well versed in the English language and I am told I write in conversational English. But most people understand what I say when I say it. So, please excuse any misuse of the King's English. My wife, Joyce, has edited this book the best she could. I overrode her many times because I liked the way I said some things better than the way she thought I should have said them.

The pictures I present are to let see what you can expect to see and enjoy on Edisto. But I must warn you that you will not see Edisto in all its beauty unless you get off the main drag. Take a tour or two and read some of the great books written about Edisto and then go seek out the interesting places on Edisto.

The Edisto experience will reveal itself to those who seek its peace and tranquility. As I put this book together I realized more and more how fortunate I am to have lived on such a place which God took an extra measure to create. As I have said before, this is not a history book. It is about what interests me what I have experienced over the past three

Edisto's
"Old Man of the Sea"
Sam Lybrand

quarters of a century. Come join with me as I try to reveal what interests me about "Edistow". If you read this book and have not visited Edisto Island, you will come! Many come and never go home.

In the beginning was the Word, and the Word was with God, and the Word was God. The same was in the beginning with God. All things were made by Him; and without Him was not anything made that was made. In Him was life; and the life was the light of men. John 1:1-4 KJV

God bless all that read this book, every one of you! Granddaddy Sa

EDISTO

The fool hath said in his heart, there is no God. They are corrupt, they have done abominable works, there is none that doeth good.
Psalm 14:1 KJV

More to Write Home About

Edisto Island, SC has been occupied since before recorded history if you believe all the evidence found on Edisto in recent times. Therefore it must have held some fascination and worth to mankind over these many, many years. The more you read all that has been written about Edisto and the more you go out into its creeks, marshes and old plantation sites, the more it grows on you. It tends to make you want to stay on the ocean side of the Dawhoo Bridge and never leave. One fascination after the next keeps coming up and giving you another avenue of interest to explore. I honestly believe that one could not learn all there is to know about Edisto in one lifetime.

Each creek has its own story. Each plantation has its own story. You could spend a lifetime just sifting through piles of shells left on the beach by a passing storm and finding ancient trash in these piles of shells that one would not notice just walking by. Then you could spend another lifetime trying to figure out how it got in a pile of shells and what it really is.

As a child I spent many hours just sitting and looking at the clouds and watching local storms form and hearing thunderstorms coming down the Edisto River to where I lived. Since everything is so open you can see rain clouds forming way off and you can watch the way they are headed and thus be able to take cover or get ashore when needed.

Many spend many hours watching and looking for all the birds that call Edisto home. Some birds just pass through. Some come for a season and some call Edisto home and stay year round. Edisto has shore birds, sea birds, woodland birds and just about any variety of birds you can name. Every now and then a bird that is not supposed to be on Edisto shows up for no apparent reason and every Edisto bird watcher gets excited. Over the years birds that have not previously called Edisto home just come and stay, like the wood stork that one day just came and stayed.

Likewise some come to Edisto for its fishing, shrimping and crabbing. Like the birds, some fish stay in Edisto's water year round. Some, like winter trout, can be caught only certain times of the year. Some are caught in the many creeks Edisto has to offer and some are only caught offshore. Little fish, big fish, red fish, blue fish, you name it, Edisto has them.

This book will talk about a wide variety of subjects that have interested me over the years. I will tell a few stories and throw in this and that. I hope all this will hold your interest. So come along and dream a little with me.

The great bridge over the Dawhoo River that connects Edisto Island with the mainland.

Atlantic Intracoastal Waterway

It's a large bridge!

6

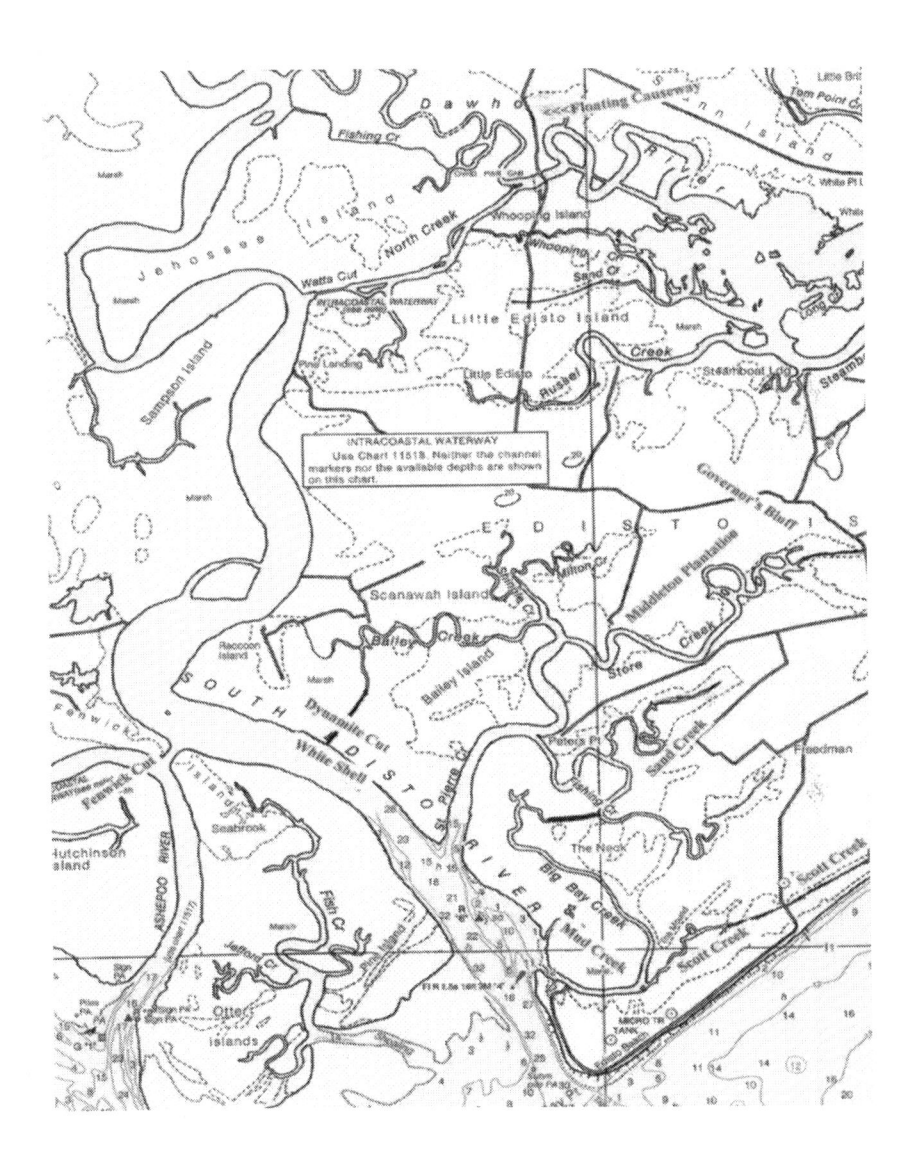

This Navigation Chart is a portion of Coastal Survey number 11521 which is put out by the U.S. Department of Commerce. The entire chart includes the Charleston Harbor and approaches. This portion is of Edisto Island and a few of the places talked about in this book. I have made a few ink additions and added some names in red so that when I mention these names in this book you will know approximately where they are located on this chart.

7

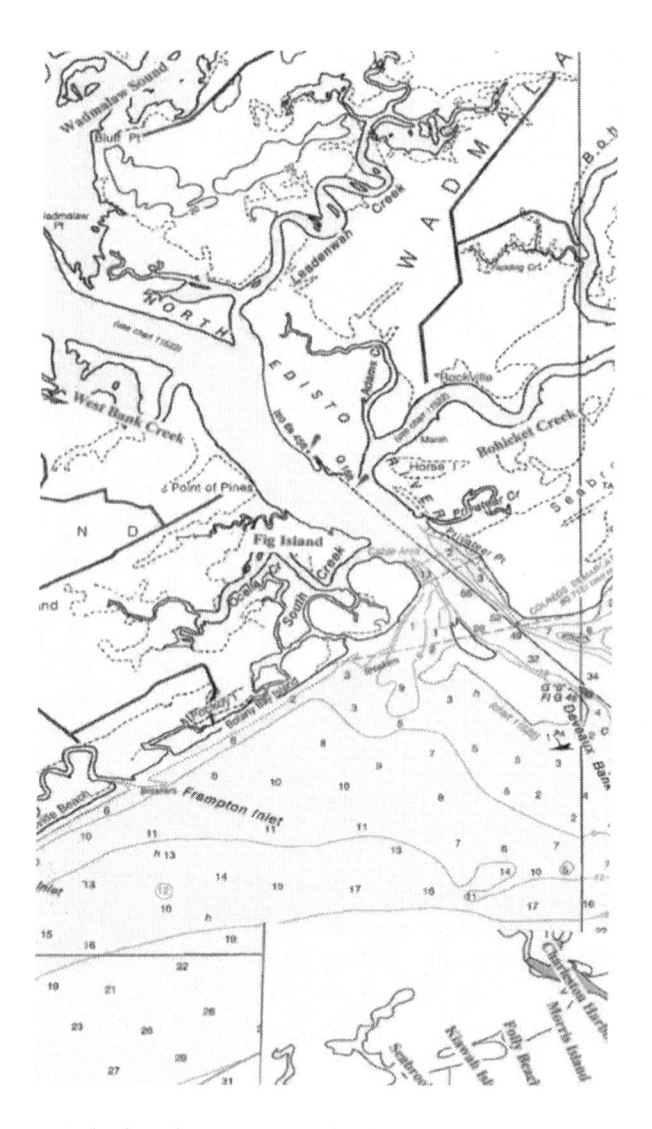

A chart is never completely accurate because the ocean and the creeks are constantly changing things. Therefore this chart is designed to give you a general idea of what Edisto's layout looks like with many of its many creeks and waterways.

The little numbers you see everywhere are how deep the water is at low tide. Edisto Island is about 8 by 7 miles wide. It is a small island for so much beauty and history.

Oak lined drives were common in Colonial days.

Homes and docks on Big Bay Creek.

Local Edisto shrimp boat docked on Big Bay Creek

Trinity Episcopal Church

Home built for Carolina Lafayette Seabrook Hopkinson in the 1840's

CHAPTER ONE

Awhile back, I began to think about how lucky I was to have lived on Edisto Island, SC during the early years of my life. I also thought back on my frequent visits to Edisto to visit my parents, Jennie and Harvie Lybrand, while I made a living for my own family in Orangeburg, SC; Hendersonville, NC and Columbia, SC to keep up with what was going on here on Edisto. During my dreams and visions of Edisto and how much it has meant to me, I began to think how nice it would be if I handed down to my children, grandchildren and others the joy and fulfillment Edisto Island has given me. Therefore this book began to form in my mind as I went about making a living. While driving here and there, ideas began to pop into my head until I knew what I wanted to leave for others to enjoy and even want to visit my little piece of paradise.

This book has been written in a lovely little house situated on the salt water creek called Store Creek. Sitting at my computer I can hear the sounds of the Laughing Sea Gull as they look for scraps on the creek left by fish eating fish, etc. I also hear the unique call of the ringed necked kingfisher and the splashes of the pelican hitting the water trying to catch its next meal. Every now and then I hear the distinct blow of the bottle nose dolphin coming up for air.

In addition to the creek sounds, the woodland birds constantly sing as if they were all singing in concert just for me. What a privilege I have just living and experiencing such sounds constantly.

In addition to hearing the birds, my eyes are constantly filled with the beauty of the ever changing colors of the creek we live on and the seasonal changes in color of the marsh grasses. We are fortunate to see beautiful sunsets as the sun goes down behind the maritime forest across the creek from us. Sometimes as the sun sets, it turns the creek red and even pink with a bright yellow line across the creek that you think you could walk on. As the sun rises in the morning, it turns the trees across the creek a brilliant and intense green as to say, "Look at me, ain't I pretty in all my glory?"

With all the emotions Edisto's sounds and beauty brings to mind, I often think about what a wise old man once revealed to me. He told me that he had a vision in one of his most memorable dreams that after God had finished His six days of creations on Earth and had rested for a day; He mustered up all His creative abilities and spent two more glorious days creating the South Edisto River and the surrounding areas of Edisto Island. We now call this area the ACE Basin, which takes in the parts of the Ashepoo, Combahee and Edisto Rivers from Highway 17 to where they flow into Saint Helena Sound and then into the Atlantic Ocean. The ACE Basin is one of the wonders of the world with all its beauty, wildlife and history.

When God poured out His spirit on the earth, Edisto is where He must have sent old men to dream dreams and young men to see visions. Get out amongst this natural area and while you are taking it all in, you will begin to dream dreams and see visions of how God meant this beautiful world to be kept and enjoyed. Man should be ashamed with all his quests for power and unmerited gain when he could be enjoying this beautiful world God created. The sea islands of South Carolina must have been one of those creations that the Bible recorded as, "And God saw that it was good."

Now clear your mind of your worldly cares for a time and allow me to paint a vivid picture of how I am now experiencing Edisto, how I remember it as a child, and all that it encompasses. Even if someone never is able to come visit Edisto in person, he will have peaceful and exciting memories of one of God's natural wonders called Edisto (Ed - is - tow) after he reads my tales of Edisto. Find a quiet place while reading this book and reflect on all the places, names and experiences it contains.

In God's great wisdom he created Edisto as an island on the east coast of North America, not too far north to have extremely cold weather and not too far south to get too hot or to have stagnant, sameness weather.

Rabbit Trail: (I'll explain what a rabbit trail is later.) While editing this chapter Joyce wanted me to add this about Edisto. She said that the weather is pleasant much of the year, especially in the spring and fall. Some years there are gray, cold days in the winter and the summers have many very humid and hot days. But often you can escape' to the rivers, creeks and beaches for a respite. The weather can be especially pleasant in the fall. While she was telling me this, Scott, Joyce's son, and his family came to use our dock to go over to a sandbar to allow their children to play on their own private beach right off our dock. I looked up and, lo and behold, Marie, Joyce's daughter, and her family came paddling down the creek from their house, up the creek, and joined Scott and his family. Joyce, seeing this, put on her bathing suit and joined them. There is fun to be had most of the year. Cooling off in the creek with children and 'grandchildren makes us forget how hot it is.

Most of the wildlife that call Edisto home stay here year round with a few exceptions, such as the striking black headed laughing gull that announces his presence each year in early March and leaves for Florida in October. Even many ruby throated hummingbirds and the multicolored bird of paradise, the painted bunting, stay here year round.

If you know where the holy city of Charleston, South Carolina is located and where historic Beaufort, South Carolina is located, you will find Edisto Island between the two of them. Edisto does not take a back seat to either of these two settlements because it used to be one of the richest places in the world. The spirit of this wealth is still felt by those who take the time to let their minds wander and create visions of how man has enjoyed Edisto for thousands of years. How about an ancient structure on Edisto that datesback 4,500 years? This structure was so interesting to one group that they wrote a 200 page research paper about it. One of South Carolina's well known naturalists once stated that when he died he wanted to wake up on Edisto. I once took a nature tour with him and he must have stopped 25 times in 100 feet to tell the group about interesting things along the way, such as the saw palmetto. I will not go in that much detail, but I may get a little wound up because I love Edisto so much and have spent a lifetime experiencing all it has to offer. There is no telling where this book will lead. Come join the ride.

Oh, as I go along I will go off on many rabbit trails. Some say I tell people more than they want to know about things. But everything about Edisto excites me and I cannot keep from sharing all I know with all who will listen. Many of these rabbit trails will be personal experiences to give this book a little color and personality. All of these rabbit trails will be indented so when you run across an indent you can say, "Here we go again. What is Sam going to talk about now?"

As mentioned in the introduction, some say I write in conversational English, whatever that means. But everyone seems to know what I am talking about. In high school I had the choice of taking Latin or agriculture in the last two years. Since I spoke loweountry English, I knew that I would not be able to pass Latin when I could not even speak the King's English properly. Therefore I took agriculture and still use what I learned in this course designed for those students were not planning on going to college. I did go to college and graduated. I got through college English by writing about Edisto and my adventures growing up here. The professors loved my stories and passed me. I now tell people that the three most useful courses I had in high school and college were agriculture, typing and public speaking. In all honesty, I probably would have gotten along just f'me in life if I had just taken these three courses. At age 75 I can still type as well as a secretary; I know how to grow almost anything. Additionally, I am comfortable talking to one person or over 100. It is my hope that this book will entertain and inform you about Edisto.

Rabbit Trail: Over my lifetime I have observed that we miss a great deal when we look down at people who don't speak the King's English as well as they should. I agree that everyone should be well educated in communication and the ability to speak properly. Some people's talents lie in the ability to build and create wondrous things. Therefore when we avoid these people and don't have a dialog with them we may miss something wonderful that we could use to improve our own well being and quality of life. I am not excusing my own lack of communication skills; I just want you to know that some of my most memorable experiences have come from those who many would consider less educated. I love to watch skilled cabinet makers and rock masons as they create beautiful things that can improve our quality of life.

This recording of an old man's memory will include how I envision Edisto. It will begin with how Edisto is laid out and what makes it an island and all that this includes. Next, I will talk about things I learned as a child living right on the Atlantic Ocean sitting on the beach, looking out to sea and wondering about the past and who took advantage of my paradise before me. The beach community where I lived as a child had many summer homes and not very many year-round residences. My family and two other families were the only ones to live full time on the beach.

In the winter, the beach was deserted. In the summer there were several thousand people living on the beach. The island people called us "Beach People." Since there were no children living on the beach, other than my two brothers and myself, during the winter I had hours upon hours to read, explore and learn about my wondrous surroundings. There was a four year difference between my brothers and myself, therefore I spent most of my time by myself. To this day I have no trouble entertaining myself and feel sorry for those who are bored when there is so much to learn and explore all around us. The other two families were the Holmes family and Fontaine family. Marion Whaley came to live on Edisto a year or so after we did. I will talk about them as my story unfolds.

After I have talked about who and what I know about the past on Edisto, I will talk about the beach which is what initially attracts most people to Edisto at the present time. How it evolved into a place that families have been coming to for generations is a whole story in itself. Once people come to the beach many of them discover that there is more to Edisto than just the beach. I think you will enjoy this section.

As I develop the mysteries of Edisto, I will mention many names and places that you will become familiar with. Then when you visit Edisto and pass the Presbyterian Church on Edisto Island, you will say to yourself, "I read about this stately old building in Sam's book on Edisto." You will remember that it used to be the richest church in the world and was first organized about 325 years ago partly because a ship was sunk off the harbor entrance to Charleston.

As I go along I will talk about the characters I remember growing up with and what I learned from them about how to live out my life in the most productive and contented way. Some of these fascinating people I will talk about will be Boy Rat, Cliff Bunton, Mrs. Murray, Judge Seabrook, Captain John, Mac Holmes, the Fontaines, Janie Parker, of course my parents and many others. Coming up in the forties and fifties there was no welfare thus everyone worked and everyone went to one of the 14 churches located on Edisto, an eight by seven mile wide sea Island. The churches and our community were the welfare system. I don't remember any murders and no one that was starving. Everyone had a garden. There were oxen on the island to cultivate these gardens. The houses were all neat with the trim painted blue to keep the evil spirits away. Many people used the creeks for much of their food. We still fill our freezer each year with shrimp, crab meat and fish of all kinds.

My favorite meal is shrimp and grits. My wife and I have a 16 foot flat bottom johnboat and 15 horse outboard motor and seldom go further than Store Creek to catch all the seafood we want and can use.

Once you get the hang of why I have grown to love everything about Edisto, I will talk about all the named creeks and other bodies of water in the section dealing with how Edisto Island is laid out and some of the experiences I had growing up on my special Island. I will include brief comments on the sand dunes on Edisto that are the highest point in Colleton County, which extends 40 miles inland. The height of these sand dunes is significant because Colleton County goes inland all the way past I-95. Of course, when talking about all the salt water tidal creeks on Edisto, I will include stories and observations of the plentiful wildlife and some of my own experiences.

 I will try to tell you where I got the information I present in this book but some of the facts and stories presented are just stories I have in the back of my mind and I have forgotten where I heard them. Local lore is where I have gotten much of my information. Therefore give me the benefit of doubt and enjoy my stories of Edisto as I remember them and lived many of them. This is like many mail order catalogs that have not included an index or table of contents. I have purposely not put a table of contents in this book so that you will have to read the whole book to get the best out of what I have to say. You might get the best out of this book by sitting in a rocking chair on a porch while you read my Edisto tales.

 I'll warn you that if you come to Edisto and just ride down Scenic Highway 174 and never get off it you will miss Edisto and all it has to offer. There are many books written about Edisto and I will refer to some of them as I go along. As you have probably already noticed I have put what I call "Credits" at the beginning of this book to remind me of how many people have helped me with this book and a list of books and resources I used in putting this book together. These keep me from having a big head and thinking I did this all on my own. There is also information on the internet. But be careful with all the material you find on the internet. I have already come across information on the internet that was wrong. For example, some information I looked up on Edingsville Beach say it was destroyed in the awful 1893 hurricane when in fact it started washing in 1850 and the 1885 storm actually took it out. The 1893 only took a few remaining homes off the beach. The 1911 hurricane took the sand dunes off Edingville and left only a narrow strip of land that the spring tides now cross into the marsh. If I am still around when you arrive on Edisto and want a tour of the island given by me personally, look me up in the Edisto Island phone book and find Sam & Joyce Lybrand who live at 1578

Creekwood Road and see if I am available. If I am we can negotiate a small fee for me to present Edisto to you like no one else on Edisto can. Keep in mind that I am not a professional tour guide, just an old story teller. Also keep in mind that I may talk your ears off and even show you my camellia garden with 100 different varieties of camellias and all that my garden has to offer.

The school experiences I had on Edisto were unique and I will spend a little time on my memories of being the only one in the seventh grade. I'll also tell you a little bit about my high school, college experiences and how I got into the U.S. Coast Guard.

This collection of stories and information about Edisto will include why many thousands of people spend their vacations year after year here. I will tell you how you can enjoy Edisto. The secret to enjoying Edisto is knowing its past and total surroundings and how you can enjoy it all. So come enjoy Edisto. Many who visit Edisto once come back year after year and some even just stay and live out the rest of their lives here. Once you have visited Edisto you will remember the experience the rest of your life.

Rabbit Trail. Joyce's family goes back to the 1700s on Edisto and more than 50 people is too many for her. I personally like Yankee money. So come on down to Edisto.

When you finish reading about God's special place remember that all this did not just happen and that Jesus Christ created it all for all of us to enjoy. All of nature is straining in anticipation of His return to set everything right like God intended in the beginning. Keep the two scripture passages presented below in mind as you enjoy Edisto as seen through an old man's eyes and memories.

The pictures included in this book were taken by me and I am responsible for them. Of course the section on my family and how we fit into the Edisto story are old family pictures I have saved over the years and wanted them published so that they will be easily kept for my descendants.

These two scripture passages are worth reading (The first has already been quoted but I think it is important to remember) to your grandchildren to give them some sense of what is important in life and who is responsible for the world we live in.

John 1:1-3 KJV

1. In the beginning was the Word (Jesus Christ), and the Word was with God, and the Word was God.

2. The same was in the beginning with God

3. All things were made by him: and without him was not anything made that was made.

Romans 8:18-23 KJV

18. For I reckon that the suffering of this present time are not worthy to be compared with the glory which shall be revealed in us.

19. For the earnest expectation of the creature waiteth for the manifestation of the sons of God.

20. For the creature was made subject to vanity, not willingly, but by reason of him who hath subjected the same in hope.

21. Because the creature itself also shall be delivered from the bondage of corruption into the glorious liberty of the children of God.

22. For we know that the whole creation groaneth and travaileth in pain together until now.

23. And not only they, but ourselves also, which have the first fruits of the Spirit, even we ourselves groan within ourselves, waiting for the adoption, to wit, this redemption of our body.

God created a perfect world. Man blew it. Christ gave us a way to get right with God. Christ will return to finally make the world right again. Next time God's creation will last for eternity uncorrupted. The knowledge of God is born in all of us, thus we all have no excuse for not living according to the will of God for our lives. When we live in the will of God for our lives we can enjoy places like Edisto to its fullest.)

If we don't lie, cheat or steal, we don't have to remember what we said in the past, we don't have to worry about who is knocking at our door or who is calling us on the telephone... Life is just more joyful and contented when we live a life pleasing to God and this is the truth. I can testify to this fact.

Life is fragile. The son of friends of ours just suddenly and unexpectedly died in the prime of life. On the other hand my father and grandmother lived to a ripe old age of 93 and 95. Both enjoyed life and were very productive. Therefore enjoy the days you have because no one except God knows what tomorrow will bring.

As you live out your ordained number of days here on earth, you are as successful, happy and contented as you decide to be. It is not what happens to you that determine your future life. It is what you do with it or how you react to what happens to you.

You will miss the real beauty in life if you do not stop and look for all the beauty that surrounds you in nature and in all the people that come into your life as you live it. Dream a little, love a lot and be kind to others and your life will be fulfilled.

Granddaddy Sam

A Photo Collection

"Beautiful Scenes of Edisto Island"

Old Presbyterian Church is getting new paint.

The church graveyard has grand tombstones. This one speaks of a life that is broken.

Grand live oaks draped in
Spanish moss are plentiful in
Church grounds

Small Frampton Creek is also beautiful.

Blue shutters and trim keep the evil spirits away

Marsh grass areas produce the most protein of any area on earth. When this marsh grass dies down in the winter its dead grass create rafts that float down the creeks to the ocean and make hiding places for young sea turtles. They also eat the insects that land on it and small fish that also hide under the rafts. When the marsh grass washes up on the beach it enriches the sand where sea oats grow and stabilize the sand dunes. Plankton also depends on it. Much of life on earth starts here.

House on the creek with Palmetto tree in

Oyster bed, pluff mud and marsh grass at low tide. Note all the thousands of mud snails.

Edisto has a top notch golf course. Duplexes overlook this golf tee.

Governors Bluff Hopkinson's plantation home. Built in early 1900's after 1st house was torn down and this house was built.

Coming home with the day's catch.

Look how many shrimp I caught.

Hauling Landing. Especially good fishing spot because of all the old concrete waste where little fish like to hide from big

Grill and Fishing tackle shed built by Sam Lybrand.

One day's catch!
6 Spot tail bass
2 Trout
2 Whiting
A bunch of small fish for crab trap.

Proud catchers of da fish!

You will find many different ways to show off our beautiful marshes and creeks.

Westcott Road – what all roads on Edisto used to look like. Imagine seeing a buggy coming down this road carrying the master and his wife on the way to church Sunday morning.

Egret looking for something to eat.

Middleton Plantation House overlooking Sore Creek. Built in 1820's.

Many Edisto yacht owners dock their boats at Edisto's marina on Big Bay Creek.

When I was coming up in the 40s & 50s the lawn in front of this building went out all the way to the beach. There were lifeguards that lived in this building that stood watch over the swimmers. Many times the lifeguards showed movies on the lawn in front of this building.

Old State Park bath house built by CCC boys in the 1930's.

In the 40's and 50's this picnic shelter was used very often for church outings. There were several of these shelters in this part of the park and also one over by the State Park cabins on Scott Creek.

State Park picnic shelter built by CCC boys in the 1930's.

State Park path from picnic shelter to beach.

Beach in front of State Park.

State Park rental cabin on Scott Creek.

State Park nature trial.
One of many.

Grandchildren are still the glory of an old man.

Edisto's creeks are inviting.

Daughter on the beach during a windy and rough surf day.

High tide and rough surf. But still beautiful.

Lady fishing off a Store Creek sandbar.

Some sandbars are long enough for a private beach for grandchildren to play on.

A johnboat is all you need to catch fish on Edisto.

Small creeks are where the most shrimp are caught.

House facing Dock Site Road. The other side faces Big Bay Creek.

Edisto Beach has around 30 accesses to the beach so all can enjoy the beach easily even if they don't own a house on the beach front.

Houses on Edisto Beach facing a small yacht basin.

My favorite lady doing what she likes best – taking care of her flowers.

Some of her beautiful flowers. Flowers grow great on Edisto.

Sea oats keep our sand dunes from blowing and washing away.

Cassia bushes are often seen growing well on Edisto.

Swamp Sunflowers are often seen along the roadsides and in many gardens on Edisto.

The town of Edisto Beach has a nice park used for special occasions on Big Bay Creek.

Edisto Beach has about seven miles of bike paths that are constantly being used.

White Shell – A unique oyster shell formation on the river bank of South Edisto River.

White Shell at the entrance of Dynamite Cut. Raccoon Island is in the background.

A Palmetto tree in full bloom. The Palmetto tree is the state tree and pictured on our SC State flag.

Palmetto Blvd on Edisto Beach is a four lane road. You don't feel boxed in while staying on Edisto Beach.

Another view of the wide Palmetto Blvd.

Jungle Road runs parallel to Palmetto Blvd from Hwy. 174 to Lybrand Street.

Live Oak covered King's Highway.

It is easy to catch Blue crabs with a chicken neck.

With a small four foot cast net you can catch all the shrimp you want.

Belser Plantation House on Store Creek.

Windsor Plantation House on Russell Creek.

Small creeks, johnboat and cast net equals dinner.

Second row beach houses on Palmetto Blvd.

Elegant creek house.

A grand house on Palmetto Blvd.

Another beautiful beach access with a nice boardwalk.

Houses facing the Atlantic Ocean on Edisto Beach

Edisto Beach has many nice homes for rent year round.

Edisto Beach is never very crowded.

Just Caught Creek shrimp & mullet. Creek shrimp make great shrimp & grits. Put mullet in crab trap and have a dozen blue crabs the next day.

CHAPTER TWO

"Let not mercy and truth forsake thee: bind them about the neck; write them upon the table of thine heart." Proverbs 3:3 KJV

As I began this section it was a pleasant cool evening with a full moon so bright you could clearly see the creek from our front porch. This particular evening the creatures that live in the creek seem to be having a reunion because of all the splashing and flickering going on. I guess a school of menhaden had come up the creek and all the bigger bass and black drum were feasting on them. Maybe a small shark or two had joined the fun. For someone that lived on the creek this was music to my ears because it would be unusual if there was not plenty of going on in the creek at night. I also love to sit on our porch and listen to the woodland night sounds. We live on the end of a street with a lot of wooded areas around us in which God's other creatures live. We often see raccoons come into our yard. They seem to come from the marsh area and run back into the marsh when they see you. Close to dark when we are coming back to our dock from fishing, we often see raccoons in the edge of the marsh. I guess there is plenty for them to eat in the marshes and they just come into our yard looking for an easy meal. When the wife is not looking, I often put out table scraps for them to eat.

After I had settled down and gotten myself something to drink I began thinking again about my unique island called Edisto and how it is laid out. As I mentioned earlier Edisto fronts on the Atlantic Ocean. Edisto's coast runs at an angle from the southeast to the northeast out into the Atlantic Ocean. If you drew a line straight across the ocean from Edisto to Europe you would run into the Rock of Gibraltar. On the north of the island is the North Edisto River which is more like a sound than a river because of its size and the fact that it goes no further inland than the inland side of Edisto Island. At the inland most part of the North Edisto River it forks into the Dawhoo River on the left, the Toogoodoo Creek straight ahead and the Wadmalaw River (most locals call it the Wadmalaw Sound because of its great width) to the right. Some say that the early settlers considered placing Charleston on the North Edisto River but the local Indians convinced them that Charleston Harbor would be a better place to put a settlement. The North Edisto is one-half mile wide at its entrance and is a very deep body of water as compared to the Charleston harbor shipping channel which is only about one-fourth of a mile wide.

Some say that the North Edisto River was first used some 30 to 40 years after Columbus discovered America. The way I look at it is that Columbus did not discover America because areas like Edisto had been occupied thousands of years before Columbus was even born. All Columbus did was let the Europeans know that there was a whole another continent across the Atlantic Ocean from Europe.

The first European settlers that came to the Edisto area soon realized that you could ride the North Edisto River tide in, go into the Wadmalaw Sound and then ride the Stono River tide out and be in Charleston by row boat in about six and a half hours. Therefore Edisto was settled right along with Charleston. On the south is the South Edisto River which by all accounts is the longest black river in the world. Its source is a swamp area north of Interstate Highway I-20 between Aiken, SC and Columbia, SC. It goes this far inland without any rapids or dams. Most rivers in South Carolina have rapids at the fall-line. It is called a black river because it passes through several swamps on the way to the coast.

On the inland side of Edisto Island is the Dawhoo River, North Creek and Watts Cut which are now part of the Intracoastal Waterway. There is a section that used to be part of Edisto called Jehossee which was a large rice plantation with approximately 800 slaves. It was cut off from Edisto by the digging of Watts Cut in the early 1700s to be able to get to the mainland easier. Some waterways on Edisto are called rivers and some are called creeks. All but the South Edisto River should be called creeks because they have salt water tides flowing in and out of them daily.

Rivers come down from the inland part of the state. I guess you could justify calling the North Edisto River a river because of it great size. In truth, all of Edisto's creeks should be called tidal creeks because the tide ebbs and flows in and out of all of them approximately every 12 hours. On Edisto you can figure about one foot of tide, in or out, every hour. On Edisto the tides rise between five and seven feet depending on the phase of the moon.

Pluff Mud, Marsh Grass, Oyster Beds and Tidal Currents

If you are going to visit Edisto or even if you live on Edisto you need to know about pluff mud. All creeks have pluff mud and salt water marsh grass growing on their banks. Oyster beds are scattered here and there in most tidal creeks. I mention oyster beds because marsh grass, pluff mud and oyster beds go together. The pluff mud has a distinct odor which some find offensive but old time residents love the odor because when they smell it they know they are home or near home. The pluff mud is formed by the sediments brought in and deposited each time the tide comes in. When the tide stops coming in and is still for a minute or two, called slack tide, it drops its silt that becomes pluff mud. Pluff mud is found in all tidal creeks on Edisto and is ten or more feet deep in some places. All creeks would eventually fill in by the sediments brought in by the incoming tide if it were not for our fast moving tidal currents which run about four miles per hour. These tides are to be respected because a man can only swim against these tides for a very short time. As stated above, our tides normally rise about five feet. During a full moon it can rise up to seven feet and maybe a little higher if the wind is blowing in the right direction. The current runs about four miles per hour and a little faster during spring tide or full moon tides. Therefore these currents are to be respected. The following Rabbit Trail gives you an idea of what I am trying to tell you about respecting these tidal currents.

Rabbit Trail: During college, at The Citadel, I took two other couples out in my sailboat with my date and me. We sailed out the Ashley River and anchored in Wappoo Cut to go swimming. I told the other cadets to swim against the tide and then float back to the boat. One of these cadets, who was a very strong football player, told me he was a strong swimmer and jumped in and swam with the tide to show the girls how good a swimmer he was. He swam down a way and then turned around to swim back and after a short way he wore out and start calling for help. I hollowed at him and told him to tread water and pulled up the anchor and floated back to him. Of course he looked like a fool in the eyes of the young ladies. This could have been a serious accident and we could have lost a friend because he underestimated the strength of the tidal current. But all learned a lesson that most people cannot swim against the tide.

The following pictures show our dock at low tide and at high tide to give you an idea of how low tide looks at our dock and how it looks at high tide. Sometimes during spring tide the tide comes over our dock about a foot.

The water in these tidal creeks looks muddy because of the sediment in the water and also all the plankton in the water, especially when the water is warm. Plankton is the larva or eggs put out by the millions by oysters, crabs, shrimp and every imaginable form of sea life and you cannot see it just looking at the water. There is so much plankton in the water that some fish and shellfish live entirely on it.

As you ride down any of Edisto's creeks in your boat there is pluff mud and marsh grass on both sides of the creek with oyster beds here and there. Many thousands of pictures are painted of these picturesque creeks but looks can sometime get you into trouble. If you were to get out of your boat and step onto one of these pluff mud banks you would sink up to your knees in a hurry. If you struggle much in this mud you may sink down to your neck in a few minutes. A snowbird (what we call people who live in the north during the summer and then come to live at Edisto when it starts getting cold) was recently riding down Bailey Creek and got stuck on a mud bank. Instead of taking a paddle and pushing himself off, he got out of the boat and tried to push his boat off the mud bank. Immediately he began to sink and struggled to get out, only to go deeper into the mud. Luckily for him the tide was going out. A couple came by in their boat and tried to help him but could not get him out. They finally had to call the U.S. Coast Guard to come with a helicopter and put straps under his arms and lift him out. If the tide had been coming in he would have drowned before any help could have come.

On the bright side, between the later 1700s and the middle of the 1800s, sea island cotton growers used one third pluff mud, one third marsh grass and one third barnyard manure to grown their famous sea island cotton. Each farmer had his own formula used in mixing these three elements together and kept it a secret.

It is a well known fact that an acre of marsh grass grown on pluff mud produces more protein that any other acre on earth. In the marsh you will find marsh hen (clapper rails) and marsh wrens that live there year round. You also find fiddler crabs, mud snails and periwinkles by the millions. Just before the tide goes into the marsh on the incoming tide, shrimp and fish gather at the marsh edge and rush into the marsh to feed. Raccoons also frequent the marsh to feed on clams, oysters and whatever they can find. I often find muddy raccoon tracks on my dock showing that they had just come out of the marsh and up on the dock to see what was left there.

Many times when you come across an old wooden boat up on the bank you will find hundreds of open clam shells that the raccoons have put there for the sun open so they can easily eat them.

My wife and I spend many hours in a johnboat shrimping and fishing in the creeks near our house. We carry two eight foot one and a half inch in diameter poles with a wooden four inch square on the end of it to push us off any mud bank we get stuck on. The pole by itself would be worthless but the square on the end gives enough surface against the mud to push us off.

There are many sandbanks in fast moving creeks where you can get out of your boat and shrimp, fish, dig for clams, or just sit and take it all in. We have a long sandbar in front of our house that is our private beach that our grandchildren spend many pleasant hours on. A few creek banks are sandy enough that you can get out of your boat and cast for shrimp. In fact, there are even a few clay banks along some creek banks. I tell you all this because even though pluff mud and the marsh grass that grows in it are beautiful they must be respected or you can get in big trouble in a hurry.

One of the delights of living on Store Creek is looking out our windows and observing the ever changing colors of the salt water marsh grass. In the spring it turns bright green and seems to say, "I'm back, look at me!" As the new grass matures it produces seed pods that the red wing black birds love to eat. Sometimes you see many of them in a group eating the seed of the marsh grass. In late summer and into fall the marsh grass turns a golden color and is beautiful as it waves in the wind as to say, "Look at me, ain't I beautiful!" After the first cold snap the marsh grass turns brown and stays that color until the next spring when it comes alive again. Many small sea creatures eat the dead marsh grass. You might say that the food chain for all the earth starts in salt water marsh grass. You see rafts of it floating down the creeks and out in the ocean. Many offshore small fish and turtles use these rafts to hide from larger fish and some bigger fish use them for shade.

You also find large quantities of marsh grass washed up on the beach during spring tides that provide places for sand to build up on and to help build sand dunes. They even help add to the nutrition of the sand for plants that also help hold the beach soil from washing or blowing away. These marsh grass areas are so important that many research papers are written about them and their importance to live on Earth.

Rabbit Trail: As I go along and talk about the many features and scenes you can enjoy on Edisto you may soon realize that I have put pictures of many things I talk about among the large pictures in the first of this book. From time to time you may want to look at these pictures again. For example, marsh grass, an oyster bed, pluff mud and mud snails are all seen on one picture.

Just looking at oyster beds you would not think that they play a very important part in the whole coastal scheme of things when in fact they play a very important part. Oysters live by taking in salt water and filtering out the material in the Water (plankton) as food. It seems strange, but oysters and even clams and other filter feeders constantly clean the tidal water as swamps clean fresh water but in a different way. Therefore these oyster beds you see up and down our creeks are needed to help keep our creeks clean. But these beds are also dangerous because the open ends of oyster shells are as sharp as a razor. One should not try to walk on an oyster bed without solid shoes on their feet. You should also not try to swim around oyster beds or try to climb out on them for the same reason. An oyster cut is hard to heal because the cut is usually ragged and may have mud in it. These beds have positive and negative sides to them. Another positive point is that some fish hang out around oyster beds because bottlenose dolphin will not try to catch fish on an oyster bed in fear of being cut or harming themselves while trying to catch a fish. This is why many fishermen fish around oyster banks after the tide covers them.

Sea gulls also help clean up the creeks as scavengers. They don't hunt fish and other sea life like pelicans, osprey, egrets, herons, cormorants and wood storks do. They clean up what sharks and bass leave behind while hunting small fish. If it were not for the gulls rotten fish and other dead sea life would be polluting our creeks. What amazes me is that there are enough scraps left over from what big fish leave behind to feed all the many gulls that patrol our creek. I should have known this by all the splashing that goes on in the creek at night.

Sea gulls are also opportunists. If you go out on a dock notice that a passing sea gull will stop and circle you to see if you have a fish you can throw to him or one he can steal. The other day my son, Jim, was cleaning a few whiting at my dock fish cleaning counter and had left one that he had cleaned to go help his wife get another

Fish off her line when a black headed laughing gull came swooping down and grabbed the fish and flew off with it. Almost every time we go shrimping, a gull will land on the mud bank near us as to ask us to throw him a fish if we catch a small fish in our cast net along with the shrimp. Another thing to look out for is when you see several gulls on an oyster free mud bank and dolphins are out in the creek nearby. Stop and see what will happen. Many times a group of dolphin will get close together and rush the mud bank, pushing small fish up on the mud bank. The dolphin will then wiggle up, catch the fish in their months off the mud bank and then slide back into the water. Of course the gulls are there to get the fish that the dolphins are unable to get before they slide back into the water. Maybe these gulls are smarter than we often give them credit for.

One last thing: if you have marsh grass growing in front of your creek property it breaks the waves caused by boats or wind that erodes your bluff. Lots that face the creeks that have marsh grass on the creek side do not wash and should be looked for before buying creek property.   Now back to talking about how Edisto is laid out.

Therefore Edisto is a real sea island by the fact that it is cut off or made an island by six separate named bodies of water, the Atlantic Ocean, the North Edisto River, the South Edisto River, Watts Cut, North Creek and the Dawhoo River. We often forget Jehossee but it should be considered part of Edisto Island. Before Watts Cut was dug the Dawhoo River separated it from the mainland and Jehossee was part of Edisto Island. Not far back from where the Dawhoo River goes into the South Edisto River, Jehossee's high land and the high land on the mainland are close to each other, only separated by the Dawhoo River. If it were not for having to cross the Dawhoo and Watts Cut this would have been the best way to get to Edisto with a simple bridge. I don't know why this was not done when as you will see later in this book the route that was taken to put a bridge across to Edisto Island was quite a difficult job.

Edisto is actually eight islands that are grouped together and called Edisto Island. When you come to Edisto down Scenic Hwy. 174, the first small island that you come to after you have crossed the large Dawhoo Bridge is called Whooping Island. There used to be a ferry that carried people from the mainland, across the Dawhoo River to Whooping Island. It was named Whooping Island because you had to stand on the island or the mainland and whoop for the ferry. When you leave Whooping Island you cross Whooping Island Creek to get to Little Edisto which is a little larger island that is on the inland side of Edisto Island and is known for being a little lower than the rest of Edisto Island. During the 1893 hurricane a large two mast schooner was brought up Sand Creek and stranded on the wood line. It remained there until it rotted down in the 1950s. When we came to Edisto in the 1940s you could see it clearly from Scenic Hwy. 174 as we headed for the beach.

Rabbit Trail: In the last couple of years Highway 174 was designated as a National Scenic Byway because of its beauty and historical significance. It begins at US Highway 17 where the signs point to Edisto Beach State

Park. It turns right in the village of Adams Run, goes through Sugar Hill, passes Toogoodoo Road on the left, passes over Toogoodoo Creek, passes Little Britton Road and then bears right at White Point Road toward the large Dawhoo Bridge. Once you cross the bridge you are on Edisto. Scenic Highway 174 ends on Edisto Beach when the road turns right onto Palmetto Blvd. The following is a picture of the sign showing that Highway 174 is designated as a National Scenic Byway.

When you cross over Russell Creek you leave Little Edisto and are on the main part of Edisto Island. There used to be a wooden hump back bridge over Russell Creek to allow barges and tugs to go under to carry cabbages from a packing shed on Russell Creek to a shipping dock at Meggett, SC off the Wadmalaw Sound. During the forties and fifties Meggett was known as the cabbage capital of the world. I once rode a cabbage barge from the Russell Creek packing shed to the Meggett dock where the cabbages were put on a train destined for New York City. It sounds a little strange but Edisto was planted in truck crops in the forties and fifties and most of its produce went to New York City.

Rabbit Trail: The wood bridge that crossed Russell Creek was so steep that when I drove the school bus in high school I had to stop at base of the bridge and have a student walk up to the top of the bridge to see if anyone was coming. If nothing was coming he would motion for me to cross the old wooden hump back bridge. We had to do this because the bridge was so narrow it was not safe for the school bus and another vehicle to pass on the bridge. It was known by everyone on the island as the hump back bridge.

One morning the fog was so thick that we could only see a few feet in front of the bus and thus had to turn back at the hump back bridge. When I got into the eleventh and twelfth grade and went to Charleston on dates I often had to follow the white center line to get back home because you could only see a few feet in front of the car because the fog was so thick.

Edisto is made up of a bunch of peninsulas. Point of Pines, Peters Point and the Neck are three of these peninsulas. I live on Store Creek across from the Presbyterian Church on Edisto Island's manse (Where our preacher lives). Since I live off Peters Point Road I have to go back to Scenic Hwy. 174, go up Scenic Hwy. 174 a ways and then down Manse Road to get to the Manse. I can clearly see the Manse across the creek from me but it takes about 15 minutes to get there by land.

On the ocean side of Edisto are three barrier islands named Botany Bay Island, Edingsville Beach and Big Island (now called Edisto Beach.)

- Botany Bay Island has the North Edisto River on the north, Frampton Inlet on the south, Ocella Creek, Townsend Creek and South Creek on the inland side. Of course it faces the Atlantic Ocean. One point of interest is that right off the north side of Botany Bay Island at the entrance of the North Edisto River is another island that the ocean has been building since around 1910. It is called Deveaux Bank and is now an island about one mile by one mile. One day it may be a large island in its own right. Presently it is a state protected bird sanctuary for many types of sea birds. In the 1960s I tried to buy Deveaux Bank and have wind fences put on it to make it larger for God's birds. The beaches along the front of Edisto Island were being developed and had displaced many of the nesting birds there. When I was coming up on Edisto Beach the area between the current camp sites and Jeremy Inlet had thousands of terns nesting there every year. If you walked through this nesting area all the nesting terns would fly off their nests and make a deafening sound that would run anyone away from the area. When more and more people started coming to the State Park the terns moved their nesting area out to Deveaux Bank. It turned out that I forced the State to keep it in reserve for the people of South Carolina as a sea bird reserve, which accomplished my purpose.

Shortly after this happened an attorney from Charleston tried to buy it from me since my name was all over the place regarding Deveaux Bank.

New Barrier Island being built by nature:

The next page is an aerial photograph of Deveaux Bank given to me by Matthew Kizer. In the background to the left is Seabrook Island and then further on is Kiawah Island. One day, if the hurricanes do not wash it away, it will be a large barrier island on its own. An island like this is built by the wind. At low tide, when the beach between the low tide mark and the high tide mark becomes dry, the wind will pick up the dry sand and blow it against the sea oats or any other fixed items and drop it. Bit by bit this builds sand dunes and thus makes the island larger and larger. Since it is very shallow around Deveaux Bank, the area between the low tide and high tide is large and thus there is a large area for the wind to pick up the dry sand and add it to the building of the island. As the dunes build and stabilize, other plants and shrubs are introduced by wind and birds. Over time, these plants will drop their leaves and sticks and start building humus that builds soil. Then soft wood trees will come and as the years go by you have an island that will stand a storm and continue to build.

•Edingsville Beach (one of my favorite places) has Frampton Inlet on the north, Frampton Creek on the inland side and Jeremy Inlet on the south. It also fronts on the Atlantic Ocean. For what it is worth I got engaged to my first wife in 1959 on Edingsville Beach. As a child I often swam Jeremy Inlet from the Edisto Beach side and collected fossils on Edingsville beach.

•Big Island, now called Edisto Beach, has Jeremy Inlet on the north, Scott Creek and Big Bay Creek that separates it from the mainland. The upper part of the island fronts on the Atlantic Ocean and the lower part fronts on St. Helena Sound.

Rabbit Trail: (Written by David Lybrand, my brother.)

Edisto Beach was known as Big Island during plantations days. I was connected to the main body of a 1000 acre plantation by a causeway and a small bridge. I suppose it was used for hunting and an occasional outing on the beach.

The plantation was known as Locksley Hall and was owned by the Edings family. After the war of northern invasion, there were so many

16

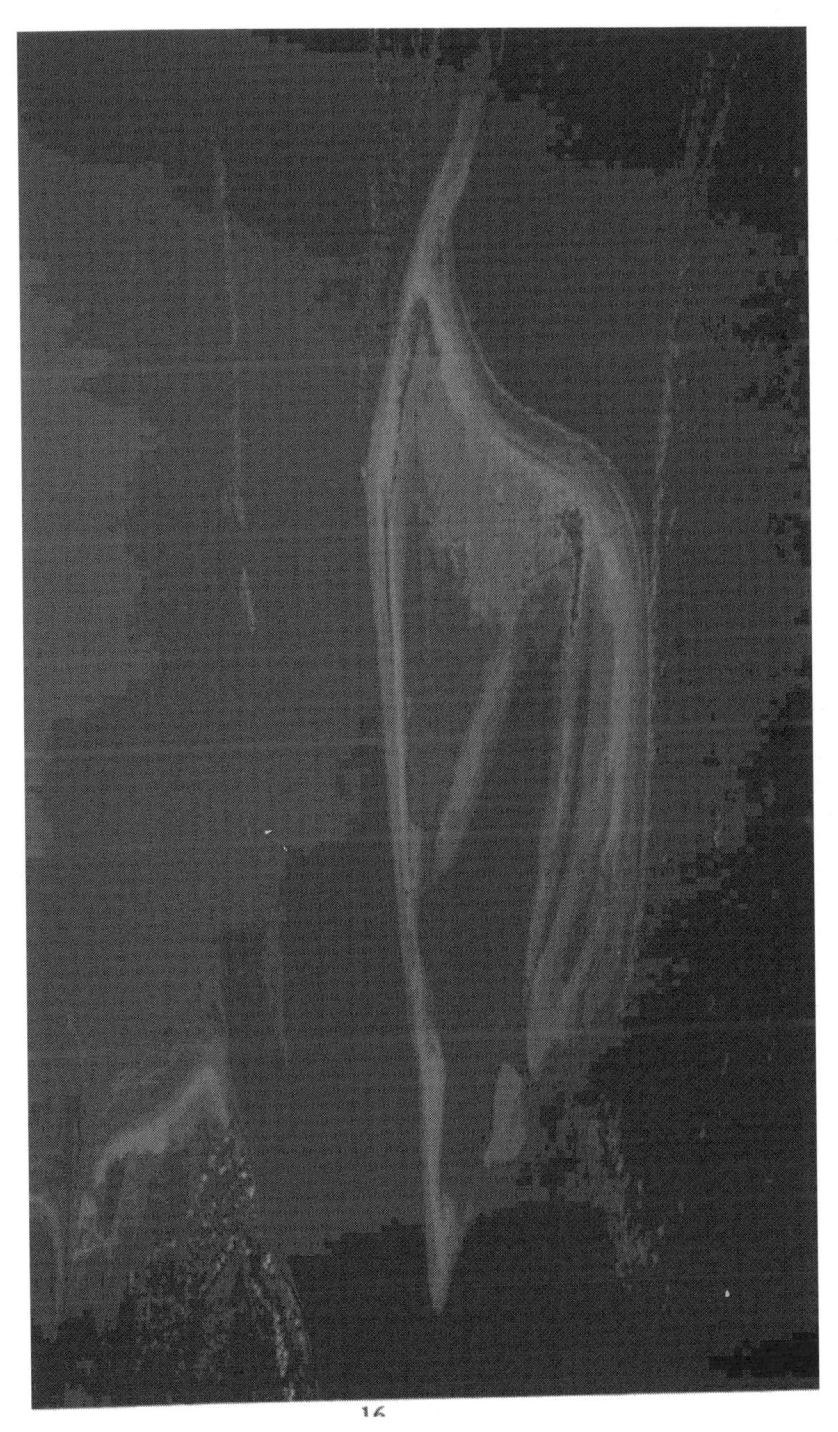

untimely deaths in the family before the war that they decided not to return to their Edisto plantation.

The property was offered for sale due to delinquent taxes and was purchased the first time by a Mr. Wright. He was unsuccessful as a landowner. The second tax sale went to John McConkey, a native of Ontario, Canada, sometime in the late 1800's. McConkey, not having the benefit of slave labor, decided to raise cattle on the open fields of the abandoned cotton plantation. On November 23, 1915, he was murdered in his home, presumably for the cash he had on hand from his cattle business.

The third beneficiaries from a tax sale were two Seabrook brothers. They changed the name of the plantation to Seaside. Now the story gets interesting, a well connected group from Sumter, SC purchased Big Island and 600 acres of Seaside plantation in 1925. They incorporated it as Edisto Beach, Inc. and changed the name of Big Island to Edisto Beach, Lots were offered in 1927 on the front beach for $500.00, the second row went for $250.00.

Apparently the depression required some original thinking in that the Sumter group persuaded the State of South Carolina in 1939 to pave the road from Highway 17 all the way to the Edisto Beach. The Sumter group successfully convinced the State to additionally include an unprecedented four lane highway with sidewalks on both sides of the strand parallel to the front beach.

According to the heirs of the Sumter group, the State received title to what we now know as the Edisto Beach State Park which includes the oceanfront north of the pavilion up to Jeremy Inlet and the 600 acres on the island that the Edisto Beach, Inc. company originally purchased. It is interesting to note that none of this transaction was ever written on paper.

Edisto Beach, Inc. sold their right, title and interest to Edisto Beach Development Company, a group from Augusta, GA (This group also included an attorney from Charleston and several local people, notably Harvie Lybrand and Steve Flowers) in 1954. In October 1970, Edisto Beach Development Company sold their right, title and interest to Sea Island Resorts, Inc. (As David put it,) "The company was owned by Sam Lybrand's brother who built the Golf Course which was originally named 'Oristo'".

For what it is worth, a barrier island is an island that is in front of a sea island and takes the brunt of storms that pound the coast from time to time. Edisto Island is a sea island that has three barrier islands protecting the main island. Over time these barrier islands have built up and have been torn down. If you live on Edisto Beach full time you will notice that the sand dunes are constantly being built up and torn down by the tides and wind. That is why the sea oats are important. They help hold the sand dunes together from the ravages of time.

I will talk more about these barrier islands in later chapters. On the South Edisto River side of the island there are two islands that have only been developed in recent times. They are named Scanawah Island and Bailey Island. They are now developed and have large private homes built on them. Another named small island that I do not think should be considered as a major part of Edisto Island proper is called Raccoon Island. It fronts on the South Edisto River closer to the South Edisto River than Scanawah and Bailey Island. In addition to these eight named islands there are many, many marsh islands that have no name. There is a marsh island worth mentioning called Big Island (not to be confused with Big Island now called Edisto Beach) that was part of the Peters Point plantation. A road has been built across the marsh to get to it. Sand Creek that comes off Fishing Creek circles around part of it. I believe this is the only marsh island that has been subdivided and now has houses on it other than the one off Scott Creek. A road was built to it during Sam Fox's developing of Jungle Shores. I'll talk about Jungle Shores later in detail. There are a few other marsh islands that have a house or two on them. As land becomes more valuable and used up on Edisto, I believe you will see more and more of the beautiful and isolated islands being built on. (According to my wife the proper name for a marsh island is "hummock."

There is a large hummock across Store Creek from where Joyce and I live. It has so much salt marsh around it that it is nearly impossible to get to. About the only time you could really get to it is on a spring tide when the tide goes over the marsh grass and then you'd only have a short time to explore the island before the tide goes back out.

Back in the days when the creeks and rivers were the main highways on Edisto there were three major canals or cuts dug or made. There are also several minor cuts made to shorten distances you have to travel down a creek or to create a place to put a dock. The first was Watts Cut, dug in the early 1700s, that was cut to get Jehossee's rice to the mainland easier. It connected North Creek and the South Edisto River. North Creek runs off the Dawhoo River. The second is a cut that connected Fishing Creek and Big Bay Creek. It has no name that I have ever heard of. You will find it on a chart right off the end of the Neck. These two creeks come close to each other and it made sense to connect them. The third is what is called Dynamite Cut which was blasted open by oystermen back in the 1930s as I am told. I really don't know exactly when it was blasted in. It connects Bailey Creek with the South Edisto River. As you will come to realize, the South Edisto River was used and still is being used frequently by all who have lived on Edisto and still live on Edisto. From time to time you hear of people putting in on the Edisto many miles inland and drifting or motoring to the ocean. I've personally been on the Edisto River at several different places in the state and found it to be a beautiful river. Many cities and towns in South Carolina get their drinking water from the Edisto River. It is still a clean river, free of pollution, and many in South Carolina spend a lot of time and money to keep this natural resource clean and useful to South Carolina.

Another unique feature of Edisto is that the South Edisto River creates a long and shallow group of sandbars that extend several miles out into the ocean in front of most of Edisto Beach. These are created from the sand and silt that the South Edisto River carries down from the upper part of the state. You might call this a delta area in which one day these sandbars may turn into islands of their own. You can see these bars from the beach because, even at high tide, you can see sea swells breaking on them as they come in from the ocean. Therefore these sandbars stop the sea swells from hitting Edisto Beach and stop most of the undertow. As a result Edisto Beach is one of the safest beaches on the Atlantic Coast with few or no drowning in the ocean off Edisto Beach.

Edisto has attracted many people over the years for many reasons. Some of these reasons are: It has a safe family beach. Fossils and many varieties of sea shells are found washed up on the beach. The scenery is beautiful and varied and attracts many artists. The creeks and rivers that crisscross Edisto attract many fishermen and hunters. The history of Edisto goes back to the creation of our nation and well before. Many come to just get out on the beach or in the creeks to watch the activities of all the fish and sea birds. If the real story was told most come to Edisto just to get away from the noise and constant to and fro of city life. Last year my daughter's family was sitting on the beach and observed 80 pelicans flying in formation heading back to Deveaux Bank to roost for the night. I recently saw a bottle nose dolphin wash a large spot tail bass up on a mud bank and then wiggle up on the bank, get the bass, and swim off with it. Many come to observe the bird life on Edisto with its approximately 200 plus varieties of birds. We have the sea birds, the shore birds, eagles and osprey, woodland birds such as the painted buntings and indigo buntings and, of course, egrets, herons and wood storks. The ringed neck kingfisher is one my favorites. Of course there many other reasons but this will give you a few reasons. The following are four pictures of some of my favorites. The first two are of the painted bunting and a nesting pair of bald eagles. These two pictures were taken by my good friend Susan Roberts, a professional photographer who lives on Edisto Island with her husband. The last two were taken by me. The one at the bottom left is of our local pelican that patrols our creek and the one at the bottom right is of the laughing gull which I have already talked about.

Many loggerhead turtles come up on the beach and lay their eggs. There is even a group that patrols the beach in the early morning to make sure no one bothers these turtles as they lay their eggs. It is a sight to see when a hundred or so baby turtles dig their way out of their sand nest and head for the sea. If they survive these same baby turtles will return after many years at sea to lay their own eggs on this same beach that they came from.

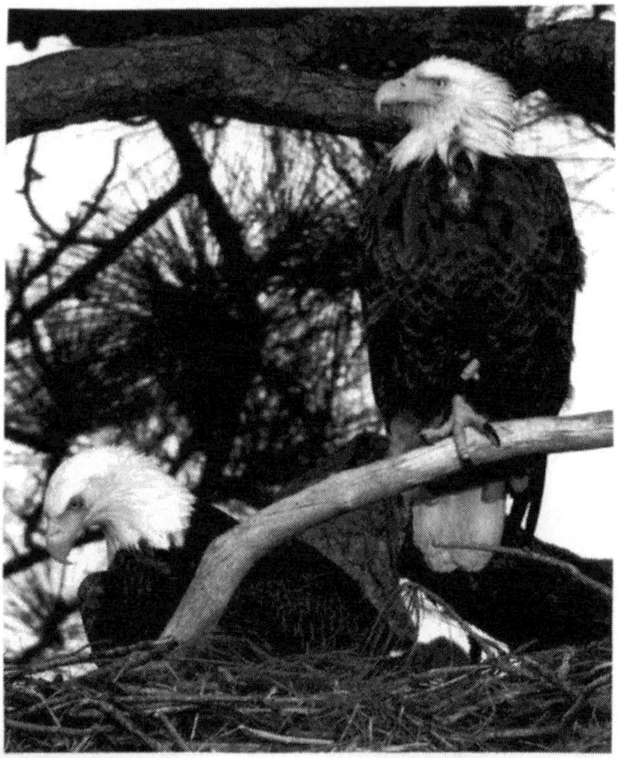

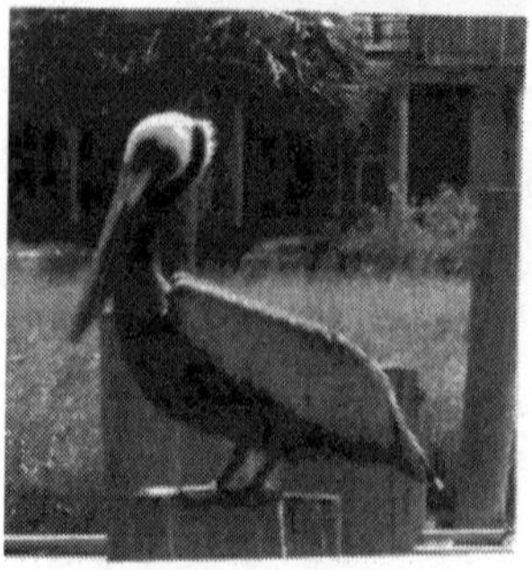

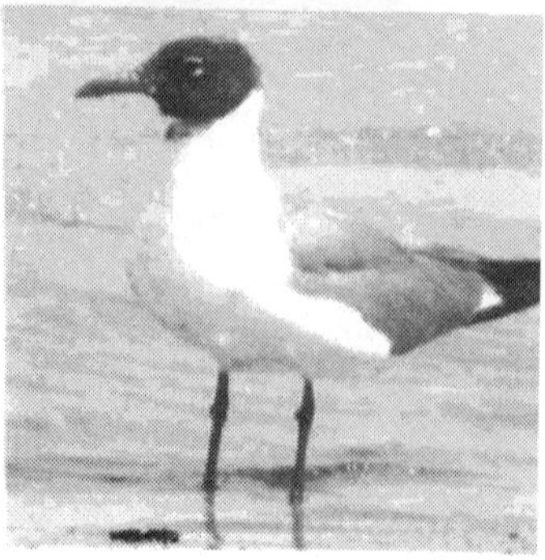

The following subjects give a little more interesting information about Edisto and its surroundings.

South Edisto River:

Where the Edisto River flows into the ocean, it is called the South Edisto River. But everywhere else in South Carolina it is called the Edisto River. A ways inland it splits into the North and South Edisto, not to be mistaken for the North Edisto River that is on the north side of Edisto. Some old plats show the Edisto Rivers as being called Pon Pon around the area of Jehossee plantation. The following is a portion of what I got off the internet from Wikipedia free encyclopedia.

The Edisto River is the longest completely undamned, unleveed blackwater river in North America, flowing 206 meandering miles from its source in Saluda and tributaries (North Fork and South Fork) from springs under the Sandhill region of and largest river system completely contained by the borders of South Carolina. Its Dawhoo River connects the Edisto to the North Edisto River, where the Wadmalaw the coast and the Dawhoo River, the river is known as the South Edisto River. The location of Edisto Gardens (on the North Fork). The river system being blackwater throughout its entire length flows through highly intermittent bottom channel, with its flow basin increasing to over a mile or more of total width. The bottomlands confluences with the Ashepoo and Combahee river basin.

A major tributary is Four Holes Swamp, which is unique in that it has no

I knew most of this information but the way Wikipedia put it was better than I could say it.

Therefore you will find the name Edisto used quite often around South Carolina.

One point of interest about the South Edisto River that has always been of interest to me is that so much fresh water flows down the river that you can place a pipe down close to the bottom of the river near where it flows into Saint Helena Sound and pump out fresh water.

On the next page are a couple of pictures of one of the most unusual places on Edisto. It is called "White Shell" by the local people. Large amounts of oyster shells are piled up along the bank of the South Edisto River from St. Pierre Creek and up past Dynamite Cut. From Bay Point they sparkle in the sun.

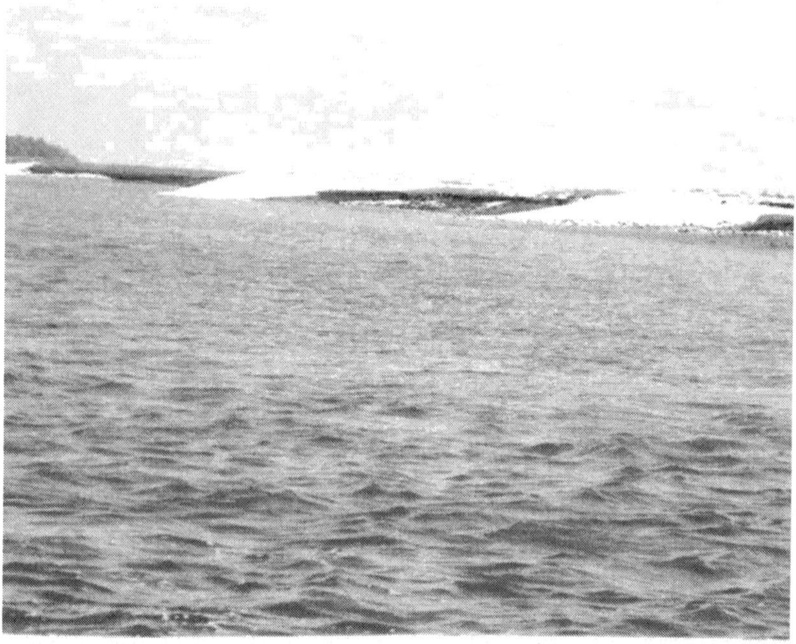

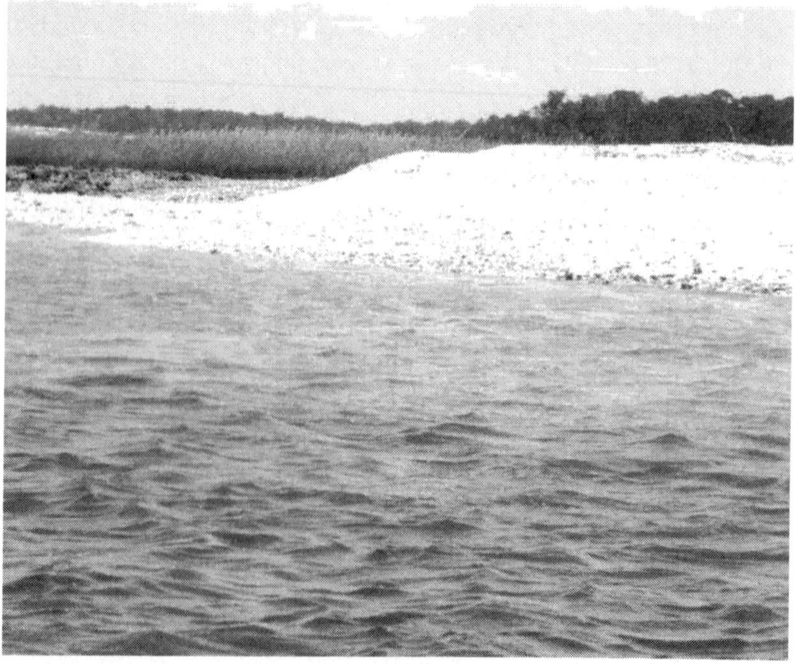

The Creeks, Rivers and Other Waterways Associated with Edisto Island:

Edisto probably has more of its area covered by water and salt marsh than it has dry land. At least it seems that way. These are the named and unnamed creeks and rivers on Edisto and the other bodies of water that are associated with Edisto. I have included a little bit about what I know about each of them with a few stories added. I have spent many hours of enjoyment on these creeks and still spend time on them filling my freezer with seafood we eat year round. I like to tease others by telling them that life is hard when you have to live on Store Creek with all its beauty and sea life. Many people that have been coming to Edisto for years have not been to all these beautiful places. As a teenager coming up on Edisto I believe I have been on all of them at one time or the other.

Bailey Creek is one of the creeks that St. Pierre Creek turns into and it continues around the back of Bailey Island until it turns into Dynamite Cut. It separates Scanawah Island from Bailey Island. There is a fairly recently built bridge over Bailey Creek which connects Scanawah Island to Bailey Island. My mother-in-law's favorite story was seeing her father have his cows swim Bailey Creek from the Laurel Hill Road area to Bailey Island to graze and then having them swim back in the evening. Of course this was long before the bridge was built. At one time he owned a large part of Bailey Island. When I married Joyce her mother was still getting money from a mortgage on a lot she inherited from her father and sold. If you stay on Edisto very long you will come to understand that Edist0's people and families are connected in many ways. I still have not found out all the connections and cousins Joyce has on Edisto. Every time I turn around I find out about someone else she is kin to.

Big Bay Creek is the most used creek on Edisto. It runs off the South Edisto River at the edge of St. Helena Sound. Where this large creek begins is called Bay Point. It has always been one of main creeks on Edisto Island. Big Bay Creek is at the back of Edisto Beach and it and Scott Creek separate Edisto Beach from Edisto Island. At the mouth of Big Bay Creek where it come off the South Edisto River and where Mud Creek comes off Big Bay Creek there is a deep hole caused by the currents of these three bodies of water. One time I measured it as being 70 feet deep. I saw a 13 foot long hammer head shark that was caught out of this hole.

Rabbit Trail: The way you catch large sharks that seem to like this deep hole is to put mullet and stingrays on a large shark hook and attach it by a small chain to a five gallon gas can and then run a half inch rope to Bay Point and wait. Sharks love mullet and stingrays. When a shark hits this bait he will hook himself and pull the five gallon can under. After awhile the can will come up and then the shark will take it under again. This will go on for about half an hour until the shark wears out. You can then haul the shark on shore. I've never done this but I have actually seen it done and have seen a very large shark caught out of this hole.

If you had been on Big Bay Creek as late as 1910 you would have seen clipper ships tied up along old wooden docks that have long since been eaten up by sea worms. The present Big Bay Creek is one of the gathering places for people who visit or live on Edisto. It is where there is a marina, shrimp boat docks and docks where sport fishermen leave to go out offshore to several man made reefs and to the Gulf Stream to fish. Since Big Bay Creek is near the Intracoastal Waterway, some boats traveling it come to Edisto Marina to refuel. There are expensive homes and condos along Big Bay Creek near the docks. As referred to there is also a marina located at the dock as well as a place to buy seafood and restaurants.

Rabbit Trail: When I think about shrimp boats I think of how seaworthy they are. Trawlers, as they are called, have deep chests and narrow waists. The deep chests keep them deep in the water and they are very unlikely to capsize. The narrow waists help in a following sea that will lift the boats in heavy seas instead of breaking over the stems or backs of the trawlers. As I will talk about later, I have been out in 20 foot seas in a shrimp trawler and felt safe. In heavy seas a trawler will throw you around but you feel safe because you know that it will take anything the sea throws at it. About the only kind of sea that will challenge the ability of a trawler to stay afloat is a very large rogue wave which is very rare and would be a once in a lifetime event.

My family owned a 50 foot lot with a boat dock in this area where I kept my sailboat, the only sailboat on Big Bay Creek when I was a teenager. A little further down, the State Park fronts on Big Bay Creek with a public landing called Live Oak Landing. Past the State Park you come to the Neck where large homes front Big Bay Creek. Big Bay Creek runs out where a cut connects it with Fishing Creek. One thing that I find interesting about Big Bay Creek is that as a young man I took many pleasant trips on Teddy

Bailey's and Mac Holmes' boats from docks they had built out of trees that were not treated. Now when you ride down Big Bay Creek there is no trace of these docks that were there in the 1940s and 1950s because the sea worms and other sea creatures have eaten then away and the pluff mud has filled in any holes left by these old docks. Of course there is no evidence of the fact that in times past clipper ships used Big Bay Creek as a port of call.

The present docks are built of concrete or treated poles and material. Of interest, in 1666 Lord Proprietor's explorers met Indians on Bay Point. When they met, as I am told, the Indians wanted them to stay because they recognized the fire power these explorers had. In those days there was constant fighting between tribes and the Edisto Indians wanted these people on their side.

Another Rabbit Trail: Say you wanted a new couch in colonial times. Here is what you would have to do if the one you wanted was not made on Edisto or close by. You would go down to the dock and tell the sea captain what you wanted and place an order. He would then leave Edisto on his clipper ship and ride the Gulf Stream up to the North Carolina Outer Banks, maybe stopping at a few other ports along the way. At the Outer Banks the trade winds blow from America to Europe. He would then square sail across the Atlantic Ocean and deliver his American cargo to the ports of Europe, riding a southward current down the coast, and stopping at Europe's ports. At one of these ports he would pick up the couch you wanted. After he had loaded his ship he would go down to about the Rock of Gibraltar and square sail back to North America because in this area of the world the trade winds blow from Europe to North America. He then would stop at Edisto to deliver the couch that was ordered. He would then lower the couch to a small barge and it would be pulled by a rowboat (most locals called a row boat a "Bateau" and this is what I called a homemade rowboat as a youth.) to a marsh bank where an ox cart would come down to the creek bank and have the couch loaded onto it. It then would be carried to the plantation owners who ordered the couch. This process would take about two years. What made all this possible is the fact that the trade winds travel in different directions in different parts of the Atlantic and the currents run up and down the coastlines. A clipper sailing ship was ideally suited for this kind of commerce. But you could forget just going down to the department store and taking home major items for your house. But they got it done and all demands will be met when a demand presents itself. For several hundred years clipper ships took advantage of these trade winds and currents to pick up and deliver their cargo until steamships came along. Man has been rowing and sailing thousands of years before modern times. As a teenager I learned to sail and how to row. If we run out of gas on Edisto I am equipped to get around anywhere I want to go on Edisto.

Blue House Creek is a small creek that runs off Russell Creek near Steamboat Landing. Some say it is a great fishing creek.

Dawhoo River has already been talked about. It connects the North Edisto River to the South Edisto River, running on the inland side of Jehossee Island. North Creek runs off of it and connects it to Watts Cut. At the present there is a public landing on the Dawhoo next to the current bridge that goes over the Dawhoo. There have been two other bridges that crossed the Dawhoo, built after the crossing was done by ferry.

The ferry on the Dawhoo: One of my favorite things to do is read about experiences of people who actually lived on Edisto in the past. Chalmers Murray lived on a small farm at the end of Botany Bay Road on Frampton Creek. He lived from 1894 to 1975 and wrote a small book of his experiences from the time he was a child until he got out of the service. This book is Turn Back 0 Time In Your Flight, 11 reminiscence of growing ug on Edisto Island. It was written in 1965 and published by the Edisto Island Historic Preservation Society of Edisto Island, SC. There are several parts of this book that I am including because they clarify or add to my attempt to tell my side of the Edisto Story. I am including several segments from this interesting book and will identify them as I go along as "Stories from Chalmers S. Murray's book."

The following is about the ferry that crossed the Dawhoo before the first bridge was constructed in 1918 according to Chalmers Murray. Here is how it goes.

Stories from Chalmers S. Murray's book

"At last I summoned up the courage to make the trip to Charleston, accompanied by a young Negro man. I could not tell how fast I was going since the car was not equipped with a speedometer but, it seemed to me, we were flying. Now thinking back over it I doubt I was making over thirty miles an hour. It was forty-five miles from our house to Charleston. It must have taken me all of three hours to get there. The roads were not paved in those days and time was lost waiting for the ferry across the Dawhoo River. That morning the ferry — a flat boat that could hold two cars — was on the other side. It seemed it was always on the other side. My companion and I whooped and whooped and, at last, we saw the ferry boat moving. It was a ticklish business driving onto the ferry since the boat and the loading platform never quite met but, at last, I made it. The boat was moved by the ferryman fitting a stick in a wire that stretched across the stream and pulling on it hard. If the wind was blowing hard it might take nearly a half an hour to cross. The ferryman was powerfully built and he invariably made the crossing, unless there was a storm brewing.

The mile and a half long cause way beyond the river was partially covered with water at high tide and exceedingly rough. I had to take it in low gear. Across on the mainland, I put on speed and made it to the next well, some fifteen miles away. This was the first watering station. One had to stop every now and then to fill the radiator and to cool the engine down. Between Edisto and Charleston there were nineteen railroad crossings."

While I was writing this book I came across an article written by Chalmers S. Murray when he was a writer for the News and Courier. The article did not have a date. Since it was about this same causeway I thought it would be interesting to include it in this section. Here is how the article looked and its content.

NON SINKING ROAD SOUGHT BY EDISTO

Dawhoo Causeway's History
Laden with Tales of
Bogged Vehicles

ROAD IMPASSABLE

Heavy Rains and High Tides
Made Situation Acute
A Few Months Ago

By C.S. Murray

Edisto Island, Aug 21. — Special: Now that reconstruction of the Dawhoo Causeway seems assured, the people of Edisto Island can afford to

107

laugh at some of the adventures they had when crossing the way during the worst moments.

The engineers had a tough assignment from the start. Here was a stretch of road that always had caused trouble,

Before the Confederate War, a causeway had been thrown up in the Dawhoo marshland to afford passage between Edisto and the mainland for the carriages, carts and wagons of the day.

Even in those remote days when heavy vehicles were unknown, the earth refused to stay put. Many a time a carriage or wagon bogged axle deep in the mud and was hauled out by man power .Shortly before hostilities the causeway was abandoned.

In1914 the road through the marshes was rebuilt. It was a mud road for several years, much to the discomfort of everyone who crossed it. Often motorists were forced to build a sort of road out of the loose puncheons (discarded loose boards) along the way before they could proceed.

Mosquitoes Bad, Too It is recorded that a party of young men from Charleston essayed the crossing and, finding they would have to shove the car for about a mile through the pluff mud, removed everything but their underclothes. The mosquitoes set their skin on fire, but they would not dress, fearing injury to their suits. They rode the rest of the way to the southern end of the island in their scanty attire. The automobile was shipped back by boat the next day.

The shell road was considered a great improvement, even though the shells occasionally cut holes in tires and made riding rough. Soon the causeway began sinking and it was not long before every spring tide covered the entire road. Every year more shells would be dumped on the low spots, but this did not help matters much.

A Floating Road No one seemed to realize then that the causeway was a floating at least a road that floated on a bed of mud. It felt solid enough, but later developments proved there were only a few feet of shells and dirt surface between traffic on the road and unexplored paths of decaying vegetable matter. 'I know that brackish water marsh well,' remarked an old resident of Edisto once when the causeway was being rebuilt for the third time. 'There simply is no bottom. I have seen a mule suddenly slip down through that mud until only his ears were showing.' As soon as construction work began in the spring of 1937, the elements started misbehaving. Until this year, Edisto generally had experienced droughts in the spring. This season was the grand exception. For days it rained --- hard pelting rain that reduced even solid roads to a quagmire. The causeway did not have a chance.

Engineers are Puzzled Contractors were puzzled. They expected the roadbed to sink. It seemed, but did not believe such big holes would develop. The local people called these holes 'mud bubbles', explaining that once in a while air would get mixed with the mud and a bubble would form. When weight was added, the bubbles would pop, and the road would sink to a depth of five feet or more.

Other people held the old creek beds under the causeway responsible for the trouble. Earth placed above these 'dead' creeks would sink as rapidly as it was dumped, they said. In some instances this proved true.

How to keep the road passable while adding earthen weight to the roadbed was a knotty problem. And when it rained the weight was increased again. Heavy motor trucks added their hit. Just about the time the contractors thought the road would hold for a spell, along would come a high spring tide, and the whole thing would have to be done over again

Everybody Talks About It During a most memorable week in the late spring, when the road became totally impassable, the Dawhoo cause way was a universal subject of conversation among the island folk. One man estimated that he mentioned the work fifty times a day, and though he grew to detest the name, he could not stop talking about it.

Enough suggestions were made about the proper way to construct the causeway to fill five or six fat volumes. Some of the amateur engineers advocated the building of a steel bridge, others a wooded bridge. Some said the road should be piled, 'Dump old automobiles and stumps in the mud, that will hold it,' volunteered one individual. Several people proposed the building of an out and out floating road constructed of mattress work. It is safe to say that everyone who crossed the Dawhoo marshes made a suggestion.

Walking it was Fun Engineers said earth fills would go down in a wedge shape. A number of islanders said that they would spread out. And so the battle was fought furiously with words. The mud kept its own counsel and acted in the most peculiar ways. When compressed too suddenly, it would slip from under the bottom of the road and pop up several yards away. Today banks of black mud, caked by the sun, stand as mute evidence of the unpredictable behavior of the substances.

When the causeway was declared officially impassable on one occasion, the islanders at first thought walking the muddy road was out of the question, but one or two people started a fashion of hiking across to meet waiting cars. Others followed. It became quite the thing to do. In fact, there were some people who considered a walk of a mile through thick sticky mud a real lark.

However, after the islanders had crossed without serious mishap for several months they did not want to go back to walking when a hole developed recently and blocked traffic for around forty hours.

'It used to be fun at first.' Grumbled one, 'but now the fun has worn off. It's entirely too monotonous.'

Crossing the causeway next year on a hard smooth all-weather surface will give the islanders the keenest satisfaction — a feeling of satisfaction that cannot possibly be appreciated by an outsider."

Note that when I was talking about when Edisto Beach was being developed, my brother, David's story stated that the Sumter Group got the State to pave the road from Highway 17 to Edisto Beach in 1939. This road had to cross the Dawhoo causeway and is where Chalmers Murray found out that the causeway would finally be fixed permanently. I have loved the way that different stories confirm the truth of each other's details. My estimate is that the new road was begun in 1937 and finished in 1939. Another interesting thing that I found out is that one of my distant cousin, Mike Lybrand Smith, helped construct this new road.

Over the years I have been told several times that when the first settlers wanted to put a road across a marsh area they cut logs and placed them one after another and then put oyster shells and dirt on top of the logs and thus made a passable road. It was called a floating causeway. I imagine that the Dawhoo causeway began this very way, but I have no record of this happening.

Again, the first bridge was built in 1918, according to Chalmers Murray, and was a wooden bridge that sounded like it was going to fall in when you crossed it. It had a turn section in the middle to let boats through. To open the bridge the bridge keeper had to put a large crank handle with a small gear on it in a hole that connected to a large gear wheel. When he turned the small gear that was slipped in place next to the large gear the bridge would open as he turned the crank handle. When a boat blew three blasts on a horn, the bridge keeper, who stayed in a small room over the turn section, would lower two gates on each side of the turn section of the bridge to stop traffic and then proceed to open the bridge for the oncoming boat. Many young people used to love to help the bridge keeper open the bridge if they got there just as the gates were lowered. They would stay on the turn part until it was closed. This old bridge was replaced in 1954 by a concrete bridge. I know the date because the school bus I drove was the first vehicle that was allowed to cross the bridge when it was finished. This bridge also had a turn section but it was run by a large electric motor. The gates that stopped traffic were also run by electricity. A portion of this second bridge is still there and is part of the public landing. When they tore the second bridge down they took the parts and made an artificial reef off Edisto. It currently has a buoy that marks the spot and many fishermen from Edisto visit this reef to fish. I have personally been to this reef with my younger son. The current large bridge is about 50 feet above the Dawhoo River and looks like a wonder of the world it is so big. I personally think we lost a part of the Edisto lore when the old wooden bridge was replaced. I even like the idea of having a ferry to cross the Dawhoo.

Dynamite Cut was blasted through from Bailey Creek to the South Edisto River by oystermen to make it easier to get from Bailey Creek to the South Edisto River. I am not sure when it was done. I believe it was blasted through in the 1930s. At the entrance of Dynamite Creek is part of White Shell of which I have already shown pictures.

Fishing Creek is the first major creek off St. Pierre Creek on the right. It begins at the tip of Peters Point Plantation and goes almost to Scenic Highway 174. Sand Creek begins off its left between Peters Point Plantation and where Fishing Creek turns to the left at the Neck. It connects with Big Bay Creek by a cut at the tip of the Neck. It continues past Fishing Creek subdivision on the right. Across the creek from Fishing Creek subdivision there used to be an Oyster Factory. Now there is a major Edisto road named after the old Oyster Factory. In the 1940s and the 1950s, maybe earlier, there was a large operation run by the Flowers family where they brought oysters, to a large building to be shucked from the shell and made ready to ship. Many times I went with my father to the Oyster Factory to buy oysters. I loved to go and watch about a dozen local ladies shuck oysters and listen to their gullah (the low country way of speaking). You had to listen closely to understand what they were talking about. The ladies sat behind a concrete ledge with a sharp chisel-like metal bar imbedded into the concrete ledge. They would put the open end of the oyster on the sharp bar and hit it with a metal oyster knife. This would cause a small opening in the end of the oyster shell. They would then put the oyster knife inside of the opening and cut the oyster's foot and remove the oyster from the shell. They would then throw the shells aside to be taken back to the creek. These ladies were supplied with unopened oysters from a coal type shoot from the outside. The empty shells would then be put on a barge and taken back to a creek bank to create another oyster bank. These opened oyster shells would attract oyster plankton that would attach themselves to the oyster shells and in a couple of years you would have oysters you could harvest. Oyster plankton will attach themselves to any hard surface in the creek. If you leave your boat in the water during the warmer months over about a week you will get small oysters that attach themselves and are nearly impossible to get off your boat. When the Oyster Factory was closed, the land was cleared, subdivided and sold for building sights. Now there are several large houses overlooking Fishing Creek where the Oyster Factory used to be. As you will see in another chapter, "The Lord giveth and the Lord taketh away." What you learn from this is that nothing stays the same and we all should be prepared for change. I have come to believe that the only thing you can count on is change.

Now one of the most popular things to do at an Edisto gathering in cold weather is have an oyster roast. People will place a large flat piece of metal over a fire and put live oysters on it. If the metal is very hot the oysters will open very soon and you can easily take the oysters out with an oyster knife and eat them. The trick is not to get the oyster too hot because it dries out and you lose the real salty taste of a nicely roasted oyster. Some people like them raw. With a good oyster knife I can easily open a live oyster. You put the oyster knife where the two halves hinge together and pry it open. This takes a little practice. But when you begin to love oysters you learn fast. Some people who first go to an oyster roast see people eating raw oysters and say, "Who in their right mind would want to eat a slimy raw oyster?" Eating raw oysters is an acquired taste like Yankees eat cream of wheat where southerners eat grits. My wife Joyce, especially likes raw oysters that are fresh out of the creek. When you live on the coast there are certain things you have to learn in order to enjoy all its bounty.

There is one more thing about oysters you need to know. It is not recommended that you eat oysters from creeks where there is a lot of motor boat activity because oysters take in the water in these creeks and there may be oil in the water they take in. But there are creeks where there is little or no boating activity where you can safely get good oysters. Or just go out and buy them from professional oystermen. We have a few of these professionals on Edisto who sell safe oysters.

Frampton Creek begins at Frampton Inlet and continues behind Edingsville Beach. You have to cross a small wooden bridge over Frampton Creek to get to the fairly new subdivision of Jeremy Cay. It also runs behind Cowpens which will be discussed in a section on the Edingsville Village that no longer exists. Many people consider Frampton Creek a good fishing creek.

Rabbit Trail: I once went out in Frampton Creek at night with several other people to try to see if mullet would jump at a fight at night.

Once we were in the creek we put up a white sheet and shined a bright light on it. The creek came alive with mullet jumping everywhere and, as expected, many jumped into the boat I was in. In a short time we had all the mullet we wanted and turned around and came home.

From time to time I have been out on the dark of the moon to gig for flounders. The creek will come alive if you shine a bright spotlight on a shallow area next to the bank. Shrimp and small fish will go wild as if a big fish was trying to catch them when the spotlight is shined on them. It almost looks like the water is boiling with all kinds of sea life. There is enough protein in these salt water creeks to feed an army if you are willing to go out and get it. Up until the advent of welfare many local people got much of their protein from all the creeks on Edisto.

There is a story that has been going around for years that says an Edisto man decided to leave Edisto and go to New York to seek his fortune. When winter came and work got scarce he started looking for the creek to live off until he found more work. When he did find one he came back to Edisto where he knew he could live off the creek when there was no work. This is an experience not soon forgotten.

Back to ------ --

There is a private landing that you can get to via Botany Bay Road called Mead's Landing. Ten years ago when I was sparking Joyce I once took her over to Botany Bay paddling down Frampton Creek from Mead's Landing in a canoe and sang to her as we went along. The young people could learn a thing or two from us old guys. I also wrote her an original poem once a day for 60 days until I got her to agree to marry me. The young guys know all about electronic things but us old fellows know how to court and keep our ladies happy. Guys, it is called courting or sparking as I like to call it. Pay attention to us old guys and you will be happily married for many years. Even when you are married 50 years still call you wife your bride and you will be rewarded handsomely. Ladies like to be courted. Ladies, men like to be petted and fed good things. Feed your man well and he will stay home.

Frampton Inlet is one of the two ocean inlets on the front of Edisto Island. It separates Botany Bay from Edingsville and is the beginning of Frampton Creek.

Jeremy Inlet is also one of the two ocean inlets on the front of Edisto Island. It separates Edingsville Beach from Edisto Beach. The point should be made that both of these inlets are beautiful, especially as the outgoing tide spills into the ocean. At low tide you can walk across Jeremy Inlet where it meets the ocean. But if there is any tide at all the current coming and going out of this inlet is strong and should be respected. As a teenager I used to walk from where Scenic Highway 174 ends on Edisto Beach down to Jeremy Inlet looking for fossils. When I got to Jeremy Inlet I would go a little inland and then swim the inlet and continue looking on Edingsville. I usually took our little dog Peabody with me. If there was any significant tide I'd go upstream a little bit and pick up a sizeable piece of driftwood and start swimming across the inlet. If the tide was going out I'd put Peabody on the inland side of the driftwood while I swam on the ocean side of the driftwood so he would not be dragged out to sea. Peabody would paddle his little heart out trying to stay up with me. But I always made sure he was upstream and staying up with me. He seemed to enjoy the whole process. Sometimes I'd get a ways up Edingsville Beach and have a load of fossils and look back and see where I had left from. It looked far away and I'd think to myself, "How am I going to get back." It always worked for me to not think about the mile or so I had to walk and just take one step at a time.

It felt heavenly when I got back to the car and had it take me back home with my load of ancient trash.

Manse Creek runs off Store Creek and makes a circle and comes back into Store Creek across the river from Creekwood subdivision where Joyce and I live. The chart show it as a large circle, but the fact is that at the north end of it, where it comes back into Store Creek and up by the bluff where the Presbyterian Manse is located, it is silted in and cannot be navigated at low tide. It takes a fairly high tide to now travel the full circle. I am not sure why the current no longer freely flows through Manse Creek. Manse Creek is open until it reaches the bluff on the south side, then it becomes silted from there on until it reaches Store Creek. Sometimes during storms or when there are several real high tides, the channel of certain creeks will change. If a strong current does not continue to flow through a creek it will silt up and if the creek gets too shallow marsh grass will begin to grow in the creek until it completely closes off. Rabbit Trail: There are generally two types of creeks on Edisto Island. They are referred to as deep water creeks and tidal creeks. Deep water creeks usually have at least four to five feet of water at a dock at low tide and you can come and go with your boat at any tide. Tidal creeks are those that go dry at low tide and you can only get to your dock when you have several hours of tide. All are referred to as tidal creeks but when you hear tidal creek people are usually talking about creeks that go dry at low tide or sooner. Back to ---- --

Milton Creek is one of the branches of St. Pierre that runs behind Middleton Plantation. It is said that it got its name because when referring to it the people at the time used the slang for Middleton or Milton when referring to this creek. Another creek: Between Store Creek and Milton Creek there is another right large creek that runs around part of Middleton where there is a community dock that is not shown on most charts. It has no name that I am aware of. There is a bluff on this creek that has a great view of St. Pierre Creek and on out to the Sound. One of the interesting things about Edisto is that once you think you have seen it all you find another breathtaking view or another fishing hole you never heard of or experienced. Most fishermen will not tell you where they caught their last big catch. Recently my wife and I went to our favorite fishing hole and found that we were not the only ones that knew about this fishing spot.

Mud Creek runs off Big Bay Creek close to where Big Bay Creek comes off the South Edisto River across from Bay Point. It runs out into a vast area of marsh across from Edisto Beach's dock area. The Neck is on one side of this large marsh area and Bailey Island is on the other side. There are thousands of acres in this marsh area which is actually an island by itself.

Rabbit trail. One of my fondest memories is going marsh hen hunting out in this area with my oldest son Jim. The marsh hen is actually the clapper rail and is only found along the coast of the Gulf of Mexico and the East Coast. It is a noisy bird and makes a loud series of unmusical ticks. One will sound off and then you will hear another and then another or about five or six before they stop making their presence known. They are good to eat and are easy to kill because they fly very slowly. The point is that they are hard to get to because they live. out in the salt water marsh and are very seldom seen, only heard. You can get to them during a spring tide when the tide covers all the marsh grass. You can then see them swimming around because there is no marsh grass where they can hide. When you get close to them they will flush so you can shoot and kill them. You are allowed to hunt them in the fall but are not allowed to use a motor on your boat and have to pole yourself along to try to get to them. I use my 16 foot johnboat to get to them. One early misty morning on a spring tide when my son was a teenager we went out in this area to hunt marsh hens. We were having fun shooting marsh hens but misjudged the tide and stayed longer than we should have. Before we knew it the tide started out and we almost got stranded out in the marsh. We would have had to wait 12 hours for the next tide to be able to get back to the dock if we had not gotten out before the tide went down. We had to get out of the boat in the cold water and push the boat as fast as we could to get it into a small slew to get back into Fishing Creek near Peters Point Plantation. We had entered the marsh off Big Bay Creek and ended up in Fishing Creek. If you look at a chart we had gone entirely too far for the time and tide we had. So when you are cruising down one of our many creeks and hear a loud strange bird call, it is probably a marsh hen telling you that he is there and you are in his territory.

We have a marsh hen that usually stays under our dock. Every now and then when I walk out on our dock I will scare this marsh hen and he will make a lot of racket and scare my pants off as he flies or swims off. Even up close when he goes off in the marsh grass near our dock he is hard to see. It is a rare time when you actually see a marsh hen out in the open or along a creek bank.

North Creek is a short creek that connects the Dawhoo River and Watts Cut.

North Edisto River is a very wide river on the north side of Edisto Island and is really not a part of the Edisto River system. From earliest times the North Edisto River has really been a sound more than just another tidal creek.

Pirates used it to get into Bohicket Creek to a pirate port now called Rockville which is across the North Edisto River from Edisto Island.

Pirates also brought slaves into Rockville to sell them. They came into Rockville because they were renegades and could not go into a large port like Charleston for fear of being captured and even hung.

Rockville got its name from the fact that large river bottom rocks were once found on the bottom of Bohickit Creek.

I understand that explorers visited Edisto about 30 to 40 years after Columbus discovered the new world. In earlier days, before there was a bridge across to Edisto, people used to come from Rockville to get to Edisto Island. Or they used two large boats that left Steamboat Landing that carried people back and forth from Edisto to Meggett and Charleston. There were shipping docks on the North Edisto River off Point of Pines. As the clipper ship docks on Big Bay Creek have disappeared by the ravages of time, so have these old docks disappeared.

The first permanent settlement built on Edisto was on Point of Pines. The story goes that the pirates burned it down soon after it was built because they did not want anyone to know about their comings and goings. Steamboat Landing is also off the North Edisto River on Russell Creek and was used for many years to catch a boat to Charleston. At the present there is a public landing where Steamboat Landing used to be. This is one of three public landings on Edisto. The William Seabrook plantation house is located on the North Edisto River near Steamboat Landing.

Rabbit Trail: I have included pictures of Edisto's three public landings. The first, on this page, is the one at Steamboat Landing. The top one on the next page is the Dawhoo Landing and the bottom picture on the next page is the Live Oak Landing on Big Bay Creek.

Note that the large bridge that crosses the Dawhoo River is right next to this landing. Back to:

Dawhoo River Public Landing

    A while back a large sunken sailboat was found in the North Edisto River with its mast cut off. It was later found that some people brought in a load of drugs and landed them on the shore of one of the small creeks off the North Edisto River. They then took the boat out in the river and sunk it after they cut the mast off. It must have been high tide when they sank the boat and they had not figured that it would be seen at low tide even with its mast cut off. The sailboat was salvaged but the drug dealers were never found.

The Live Oak Public Landing on Big Bay Creek

There is something else interesting that I have seen on the North Edisto River and nowhere else. Very large, six to eight feet wide stingrays were jumping out of the water and landing back in the water, sounding like cannons going off. Some tell me I was actually seeing mantarays. In any case they looked like stingrays and they were as big as I have ever seen. Stay around Edisto very long and there is no telling what you will find out or experience.

The Social Event of the year

During the first week of August one of the oldest coastal events of the year is held off the North Edisto at Rockville. It is a sailboat race to justify a week long party. Here are a few descriptions of this event given by others.

The first description of the Rockville Races comes from Edisto, A Sea Island Princigaligg, by Clara Childs Puckette, published by Seaforth Publications of Johns Island, SC.

"An annual event long enjoyed by boaters on the coast is the Rockville Races. organized in 1890 by Edisto and the neighboring sea islands. Today it is among the oldest social gatherings island people still carry on. The chief feature, of course, is the competition between sailboats of the several islands. Edisto's first competing boat was the Infant, soon replaced by the Minnie Ha Ha. Just as it was at the beginning, the races today are a three-day celebration. In past years the enthusiastic onlookers from competing islands came in pleasure boats that comprised a veritable fleet. Now most arrive in Rockville on the North Edisto by automobile. The program, past and present, remains about the same. After each exciting day of racing there is a dance in the evening at the Club House, for which event an orchestra is brought out from Charleston to make glad the night. Few occasions are so packed with excitement and fun."

Stories from Chalmers S. Murray's book

The second description of the Rockville Races comes from lI1_n1_ Backward 0 Time in Your Flight by Chalmers S. Murray, printed by Edisto Island Historic Preservation society.

"The great event of each summer was the Rockville Yacht Races in which boat, from the various islands vied for the coveted cup. The course, started at the village of Rockville on the Bohicket River, ran to the buoy between Seabrook and Botany Beaches, then up the North Edisto River to a point almost opposite Edisto Island, and back to Rockville.

In the early days, the boats were small yachts, all built by the islanders. Later, they were of the swallow type and carried (besides a mainsail and a jib) a spinnaker. The Regatta was always held during the second week in August, a time noted for its thunderstorms. At first there were only two yachts competing - James Island and Wadmalaw. Later, Charleston, John's Island and Edisto Island were competing. In the last race, the Regatta was open to perhaps fifty yachts from various places along the coast near Charleston.

I think I was at least fifteen before I attended the races. We got aboard a freight boat at Point of Pines Landing on Edisto Island and proceeded to Rockville where we spent three days. I was not old enough to go to the three balls held in Rockville, but I was content. Three or four boys about my age passed the night in a tent under a big oak tree where we cooked our meals over an open fire. We were already interested in girls, and there were plenty to choose from. Most of them went to the balls, much to our disgust.

The races started, as I remember, at three o'clock in the afternoon and usually ended long before sunset. The yachts were very swift in even light breezes. We boys would climb aboard one of the river steamers that followed the races and off we would go full steam ahead. None of us could afford binoculars but our eyesight was keen and we took it all in. Before we left the dock the yachts had jockeyed for position and, when the start gun was fired, they got under way.

We kept our eyes peeled for the Edisto boat, the Minnehaha, which was usually in the rear. She was skippered by Washy (Washington) Seabrook who was, I think, not a very skillful navigator. In later years when McGowan Holmes was skipper the Minnehaha came in first, to the great jubilation of the Edisto Islanders. That was after World War I, in which Holmes had served as a Captain in the infantry."

The following is a part of a real estate newsletter I wrote and published in August of 2008 dealing with Rockville.

"When I was growing up on Edisto during the 40s and 50s the Rockville Races was the social event of the year. To this day when I smell burnt diesel fuel it brings back fond memories. Before I was old enough to participate in the sailboat races, I went on several trips with others over to Rockville on a shrimpboat to watch the races. I can still remember the shrimp boat going from the Dawhoo River toward Rockville and seeing and hearing huge stingrays jumping out of the water and making a gun-like thundering sound as they hit the water. The trip from the docks on Big Bay Creek on Edisto to Rockville was exciting because there was always something going on along the way. Since I was in my early teens this was especially exciting and I took in all that I saw along the way. During the races the shrimp boat would take us alongside the racing sailboats. We watched the various boats tacking back and forth trying to get the windward position and beat the next boat around the buoy marking the course. The races started in front of the Rockville Yacht Club. The boats sailed out around the Bohicket Creek entrance marker and to the next buoy and then returned the same way. The small sailboats went inland to the next buoy and the larger sailboats went out toward the Atlantic Ocean. When all the boats were underway, Bohicket Creek looked like one mass of white sails. The first time I went over to the Rockville Races, I never knew that there were that many boats in the world. Everyone that sailed in the races or was a spectator seemed to be having a great time. To this date the Rockville Races is one big party.

The Rockville Races is an annual event which was begun in 1890 by Edisto and the neighboring sea islands. Many of the people that were kin to each other or knew each other from James, Johns, Wadmalaw and Edisto Islands looked forward to getting together every summer. Edisto's first competing boat was The Infant, which was later, replaced by The Minnie Ha Q and then the Dog House, which I was familiar with.

Since we knew about the Rockville Races that were held each year during the first week in August, my brother and I decided to enter the races. The races were held Thursday, Friday and Saturday. The sailboats raced by class. I remember the largest class was the Moth class with many sailboats competing against each other. The Moth was a small boat about 10 feet long with a huge sail that looked like a moth off in the distance. Of course there was the Lighting class in which we were to compete. Then there was the Sea Island One Design. As I remember there was a Sea Island One Design from each of the islands south of Charleston down to Edisto Island. The race of the Sea Island One Design class was always the talk of the race and the one that created the most interest. Edisto's sailboat was called Dog House, James Island's was named Cygnet, Johns Island's was named Marcheta and Wadmalaw's was named Undine. The Sea Island One Design was a 24-feet long scow with a large mainsail and a jib. A scow is a sailboat that looks like a bottom and deck that were only about a foot apart. From a distance a scow looks like a big sheet of plywood with a sail on it. It has no cockpit, at least to speak of. Of course there were other classes of sailboats racing but I was only interested in the Sea Island One Design and the Lightning classes of boats. Back in earlier day my wife's father, Billy Hills, Marion Whaley, Sr. and other islanders sailed the Dog House. Oh, I remember that Edisto's sailboat was red. Many years have passed and I don't remember who won the races or what happened to these old boats."

Last year (August 2010) there was a large Article in the Post and Courier out of Charleston, SC about the big party that was going on at Rockville. Therefore the 1890 party is still going on.

Recently I was standing on one of Edisto's docks and a ways down a shrimp boat was getting ready to go out. I smelled the burnt diesel fuel and memories came to me of the days of my youth, sailing and having fun at Rockville. What a joy it is to have such wonderful memories of one's youth. As an adult I have visited the Rockville Race as a spectator from time to time and each time memories come flowing back.

As you can already tell, one of the highlights of the summer during my teenage years was the Rockville sailboat races. We owned one of the first Lighting class sailboats that was made of wood. It was 19 feet long and about six feet wide and could seat six people. It took three to sail it. One was the skipper, one worked the mainsail and the other worked the jib and centerboard. Since I was the oldest and my brother and I owned the boat I was the skipper. I cannot remember how many times we raced in the Rockville Regatta. Since our sailboat was made of wood and the others were newer and made out of fiberglass, we never won a race but we always had fun just being in the race. One race stands out. As we rounded the Bohicket light, the bottom padeye that held the rudder in place broke off and we lost control of the boat. I had to think fast. We always kept a six-foot oar in the boat for pushing off sandbars when we grounded by mistake. I grabbed the oar and lashed it to the back stay and used it to gain control of the boat. In the meantime the boat began to fill up with water through the hole that the padeye left. I then got one of my crew to climb under the seat and stuff a shirt in the hole. This stopped the water from coming in so we could bail the boat. Believe it or not, we finished the race and did not lose our position during all this. All this happened in a matter of less than a minute. When I came back from the service and the old boat had seen its last, my mother kept the old oar and had an artist paint river scenes on it. To this date I have this old now 60+ year old oar hanging on the wall in our back room. Every time I pass it I think of the fun days I spent in Rockville.

Here is how we spent our time at the Rockville Races. We pulled our sailboat over to Rockville with a small motor boat on Wednesday afternoon. That night there was a dance. After the dance we wrapped up in the sails and spent the night on the boat. Thursday we raced and repeated what we did on Wednesday night. We repeated this on Friday and Saturday and then came home on Sunday morning. Therefore we had four parties and three days of racing. As a sideline, I learned more in one race than I learned in two years sailing by myself around Edisto. From other more seasoned sailors I learned how to get the most out of my sails and how to keep the least drag on the water by keeping the "bow" and stern out of the water as much as possible. Therefore with efficient sails and the least drag from our boat we got the maximum speed the boat would allow.

The following are some pictures my brother, David Lybrand, recently took of the Sea Island Yacht Club at Rockville and some sailing scenes of the Sea Island One Design which are still of interest to me. From the original Sea Island One Designs I understand that several more have been added. I am not totally sure but I think the original ones were built around 1947. In the 1980s I understand that the Privateer, the Bohicket II and the Grey Ghost have been added to the Sea Island One Design. I am not sure what kind of sailboats the local islands used to compete since the 1890s until the Sea Island One Designs were built.

It was suggested that I not put this story in but it will give you some idea of what goes on in Rockville besides sailing. Buck Fisk and I were buddies since our early years. One day during college I said to Buck, "Let's go over to the Rockville Races party tonight." He agreed and I took our whaleboat over to Oak Island Plantation's dock and where Buck met me. We then went over to the Sea Island Yacht Club's lodge or club house, docked our boat and began enjoying the libations or whatever you want to call what we began drinking. About two AM I began to feel a little unstable and told Buck it was time to go home. He agreed and we began our way home down Bohicket Creek toward the light where it comes off the North Edisto River. As I rounded the light, the two sides of the banks began to close in on me. I got scared and after a little while called for Buck to come help me find the way. He came back to where I was steering and passed out on the seat. Thank goodness I had enough good sense left to cut the motor and throw out the anchor. Then I went to sleep on some fishing tackle. About first light some sea gulls woke me up and I began pulling up the anchor. I did not get any tension until I reached the chain on the anchor that protected the anchor rope from getting cut by oyster shells. Then I realized that what I had seen the night before was one river bank when I was supposed to be looking at two river banks. Instead of making a 90 degree turn I had made a 45 degree turn and was headed straight for the far bank. Another 30 seconds and our 28-foot whaleboat would have run up on the bank and we would have really been in trouble. I guess the good Lord watches after drunks and fools.

I got home around six AM and was going to bed when Daddy came in and thought I was getting up and put me to work. I did not get away from him until about 11AM. By this time my head felt about as big as a large watermelon. When I had time to really think about the ordeal, I realized that if I had turned left toward the ocean instead of turning right toward our landing we may have never been heard from again because the ocean was not very far away from Bohicket Creek. As a result of this adventure and one in the service I don't keep hard liquor in my house.

I got off the track telling stories. Here are the pictures David took for me.

The Sea Island Yacht Club in Rockville, SC

Close-up of the Dog House

Sea Island One Designs at the starting line.

The race is on.

A picture from the Post and Courier that I thought was a good likeness of the Sea Island One Design.

All nine of the Sea Island One Design sailboats participated 42 in the 122th Rockville Regatta, put on by the Sea Island Yacht Club, on Saturday. The weekend event marks the end of the summer sailing season.

126

Ocella Creek runs off the North Edisto River and is the first creek you come to on the south side of the North Edisto River as you come into the river from the ocean. It runs behind Botany Bay Island. It continues into the main part of Edisto about halfway across it. The headwaters of Store Creek and Ocella Creek would come together except for a small strip of land that separates them. It is a pretty creek and has many small creeks running off of it. A friend of mine recently told me that he and another guy went all the way to the end of Store Creek on a very high tide and pulled their boat across this small strip of land and continued on Ocella Creek to the North Edisto River.

Rabbit Trail: When my children were younger I would put a small johnboat in at a private hard mud landing at the head waters of Ocella Creek off Point of Pines Road. We would take the creek over to Botany Bay Island to look for shells. During one of the hurricanes Botany Bay was cut in half and created a new ocean inlet. It has since filled back in by the sea. One time we took the channel that was cut by this storm to get to Botany Bay. On the way back in this channel we got stuck because the tide had gone out faster than I expected and left us high and dry. We had nothing to do but wait on the tide to come back in. We were lucky because we only had to wait about an hour for the water to get deep enough for us to use the motor. At this time I was visiting my parents and had promised them that we'd be back about noon. But of course we were not going to make it. At about four PM we were on our way back when my brother came looking for us. Mother had sent him to look for us. He asked if we were lost. I told him I knew exactly where I was and I had just misjudged the tide. He got mad because mother had panicked and had called out the troops to find us. The point of this story is that you are always your parents' children as long as they live. Mothers don't worry about you as much when you are not living under their roof. But when you are staying with them you become your mother's child again. You should be aware of that and tell them when you are going somewhere and when you will be coming back.

Russell Creek also runs off of the North Edisto River and it and Sand Creek occupy a large part of Edisto Island up closer to the Dawhoo River. There seems to be an endless supply of small creeks going off it. Russell Creek is to the North Edisto side of Edisto as Store Creek and Big Bay Creek are to the south side of Edisto. You cross Russell Creek when you leave Little Edisto and come onto the main part of Edisto. When you cross Russell Creek going off the island you can see one of the large plantation houses on the right. It is a sight to see when the sun shines brightly on this stately old home. With Russell Creek in front of it, it is a picture perfect low country scene. Many pictures are taken of this scene as an example of Edisto in its glory. From time to time I have seen artists sitting on the side of the road across the creek from this old house painting their hearts away. I took a picture of this scene and have presented it below.

Windsor Plantation house on Russell Creek

Sand Creek is one of the two creeks on Edisto called Sand Creek. The first one branches off Russell Creek and you cross it as a small creek on Little Edisto. It is in this creek that the 1893 storm stranded a large two masted schooner that was still there in the nineteen forties.

Sand Creek is the second Sand Creek. It branches off Fishing Creek and runs parallel to Peters Point Road almost to Red House Road. It goes around one of the marsh islands that is now occupied called Big Island, not to be confused with Edisto Beach, which was also once called Big Island. It was part of the Peters Point Plantation. Before all the environmental regulations a one lane dirt causeway was constructed over the marsh from Shell House Road to Big Island. Then Big Island was cut up into lots and sold. Today it would be nearly impossible to get a permit to put such a long causeway across any marsh area.

One of the prettiest seascape views on Edisto is from the side of Big Island that faces Fishing Creek. From there you can see across the vast area of marsh I talked about earlier and as far out as St. Helena Sound. The sunsets from there are out of this world.

One of the advantages I have in writing this story of Edisto is that I have actually seen and experienced most of these places in person. Many people would give a lot to have experienced what I have experienced in my 75 years. I had a paradise coming up and took advantage of it.

School House Creek is one of my favorite creeks to fish in. It runs off Store Creek across from the Sunnyside Plantation and in front of Governors Bluff Plantation. It runs behind the old two room school house where I went to grammar school and almost up to the Episcopal Church. It has many sandbars to play on if you don't catch a fish. Last fall I caught a large trout trolling with an electric chicken plug. This creek is not named on some of the charts but is well known to anyone that fishes in this area.

Scott Creek is where I spent many hours as a teenager because it ran behind the beach where I lived. Scott Creek is in a long narrow strip of marsh that runs from Jeremy Inlet to Big Bay Creek. When you ride across the causeway that connects Edisto Beach and the main part of Edisto you can see down this narrow strip of marsh on both sides of the causeway. As you come onto the beach on the right you can see all the way to the docks on Big Bay Creek. On the left you can see all the way to Jeremy Inlet. The causeway between Edisto Beach and the main part of Edisto used to have a bridge to allow Scott Creek's water to flow from each section of this long stretch of marsh. I am not sure who took this bridge down and filled the area in so Scott Creek's water could not flow through. Maybe it was filled in during the building of the new paved road in 1937. As a result Scott Creek is now silting up on both sides of the causeway. There is a remnant of an old Indian mound on Scott Creek that at one time was large enough to be seen from the ocean side of Edisto Beach. Some charts show it as Spanish Mound. But Scott Creek has almost washed the old Indian mound away over time. The State Park has preserved what is left of it. It is believed that the people who built this mound were the same ones that built Fig Island which I will talk about at length later on in this book. Currently there is a nesting pair of bald eagles on Scott Creek.

Rabbit Trail: As a teenager I rowed a twelve foot dingy from our dock on Big Bay Creek up Scott Creek, past the old Indian mound to the causeway that divided Scott Creek and takes you from the main part of Edisto to the beach. I can still row any small fishing boat with ease, even at 75. My children say the oar locks don't work but they do and with the right rhythm you can row for hours. On one occasion I was rowing from the docks up Scott Creek with our little dog Peabody sitting on the back seat. I was wearing a new suede leather jacket and got hot after rowing a while. I took the jacket off and put it on the back seat with Peabody and kept on rowing. The next thing I knew Peabody (he was named Peabody because when he was young, Daddy said he was the peeingest little body he ever saw) was sleeping on my jacket with his muddy feet. I was never able to get the mud out of my new jacket. For what it is worth, I keep oars in our johnboat and can easily row it if our outboard motor breaks down. Back to - There are two marsh islands along Scott Creek that I loved. One was in the marsh directly behind our house. I would leave our house on the beach, walk through the woods a ways and cross some hard mud when the tide was out to get to this marsh island. There was a small creek that came off Scott Creek about where it branched off Big Bay Creek that came up to this little island. Sometimes I would keep the small boat I rowed around on this island. If I left the boat on the island unattended for more than a couple of days, the raccoons would put many, many live clams in it so the sun would open them with its heat. The raccoons would come back and eat the clams in a day or so after the sun had opened them. Before I took the boat out again I had to throw out all the empty clams shells. Now there is a low tide road out to what I called My Island.

There is another marsh island that is up Scott Creek some distance from the Indian mound where I often went to explore and even spent several nights camping out on. On one side of this island the creek made a big loop. Over the years the woods behind my house were developed and the developer put a single lane causeway out to this island and built a house on it. It now has several houses on it. Since there was really no good place to put a dock on this island the homeowners cut through the loop near the island and built a dock. Now the loop is about filled in with silt because the current no longer goes through this loop.

Here is another point of interest. Just past the Indian mound there used to be a landing where rum from Cuba was brought in during the Prohibition times. This area was seldom visited at this time and it went on undetected for some time before they were found out.

The State Park has some cabins they rent along Scott Creek that are in high demand.

When the beach started washing in the 1950s the State brought a dredge up Scott Creek and down a small creek across from the State Park cabins. I was present when they began dredging the creek and placing the dirt near the island I just talked about with the new cut. When the dredge got close enough they began pumping sand onto the beach. They dug a very large and deep dredge hole which is now called the Yacht Basin. This so called Yacht Basin is also filling in because the current of Scott Creek does not run through it to keep this area open. Before too many years there will be no trace of this dredge hole and marsh grass will have reclaimed it. Sadly, the people that built on the so called yacht basin, thinking they would always have deep water in front of their house, will end up with nothing more than a great marsh view. Scott Creek is so far from these houses that it would be impractical to build a walkway and dock on Scott Creek from their property.

You see, when most people see Scott Creek, all they see is a pretty creek; I see all that has happened to Scott Creek over the years. Knowing about Edisto and all that has happened to it is what makes Edisto come alive. Think about it. There is real evidence that 4500 years ago there were people in and around Scott Creek. Who knows, there is no telling how long human beings have been enjoying Edisto and all it has to offer.

As I dream dreams and see visions of what can be and what was, I can imagine an Indian brave in a dugout canoe on a moonlight evening paddling his young girlfriend down Scott Creek singing sweet melodies to her as he smiled in delight at her. Scott Creek is a peaceful and protected creek that would lend itself to such an event.

South Creek is a small creek that runs off Ocella Creek and runs behind Botany Bay Island.

South Edisto River (Edisto River & Pon Pon River) is already talked about enough. It will come up over and over again because it is a major player in the life of Edisto.

Store Creek is another of the creeks that branches off St. Pierre Creek. Some old maps show its name as St. Pierre Creek. It is the longest creek on Edisto and has several plantations facing it. As mentioned about Ocella Creek, it goes almost half way across Edisto and just about connects with Ocella Creek. One day a good hurricane might actually connect these two creeks and make it possible to take your johnboat all the way across Edisto in one creek.

In the plantation days it was a major highway for getting around Edisto. The plantations facing Store Creek are Peters Point, Pine Barren, Middleton, The Manse, Cypress Trees, Sunnyside Plantation, Governors Bluff, Westcoat Plantation and the old Bailey house. It is called Store Creek because there was a store near where Scenic Highway 174 crosses Store Creek or just before you get to Peters Point Road. It is where my wife and I live and has great crabbing, shrimping and fishing. It also has some very large sandbars that are quite often used as a place many families with boats will gather and enjoy the outdoors and a quite beautiful deep water tidal creek. These sandbars are also a good place to gig flounders at night on the dark of the moon. You can also dig clams on these sandbars.

Rabbit Trail: From time to time as teenagers, a bunch of us kids would get together and float down or swim down Store Creek from Joyce and Dottie Hills' house on Scenic Highway 174. I vividly remember that on one of these occasions I was sort of walking down a shoreline off Store Creek that was sandy enough to stand up on and notice a bleached out human backbone with five white buttons lying on top of the backbone exposed on a bluff a few inches from falling in the creek. Over the years Store Creek had washed into this old graveyard. While working on this book it has amazed me what I remember and what I don't remember. This backbone story is true. Back to ----- --

Steamboat Creek. The chart I have names the entrance of Russell Creek off the North Edisto River Steamboat Creek. Maybe this is called this because Steamboat Landing is located on it.

Saint Pierre Creek is one the widest creeks on Edisto and runs off the South Edisto River. (I've already talked about White Shell earlier but here is a little more.) From Bay Point you can see an unusual bright white area that rises above the marsh grass running for quite a ways up the South Edisto River on the Bailey Island side from St. Pierre Creek. This unusual formation runs from St. Pierre Creek all the way up just past Dynamite Cut. Therefore this shell bank runs for quite a ways. The locals call this area White Shell. It is a strange formation because the river just keeps piling worn out oyster shells along the bank. Every time I pass it there are many birds resting on it. This is one place I seem to always see oyster catchers. The oyster catcher is beautiful bird with black on top and white underneath with a long red bill that sets him apart. Several times I have pushed up on this shell bank to get out and fish and have seen horse shoe crabs laying their eggs. From Bay Point White Shell stands out like a brilliant white monument when the sun shines on it just right. As St. Pierre Creeks goes into the main part of Edisto it has Fishing Creek running off to the right in front of Peters Point Plantation and then goes up a little ways further and forks off into four major creeks in their own right. To the left are Bailey Creek and Shingle Creek. To the right are Store Creek and Milton Creek. If you will look at a chart of Bailey Island you will see a marsh area right across from Fishing Creek that indents into Bailey Island. This marsh area does not show a creek but there is one. I have caught the biggest and most spot tail bass I have ever caught in this creek that goes up into this area of marsh. The creek is longer than you would expect and is deep enough to get a boat into even at low tide. An old map that I once saw showed slave cabins on Bailey Island on this creek. I have been told that these were the slave cabins for the Peters Point Plantation. There is no sign of these slave cabins that I know of now. At a very low tide there is old brick work close to the entrance of this small tidal creek that may have had something to do with these slave cabins. This mystery is one reason I love Edisto because there is always one more mystery to investigate. What I am trying to do in this book is to wet your interest in also learning all there is to know about my wonderful paradise called Ed — is — tow.

Shingle Creek as mentioned before is one of the branches of St. Pierre Creek and it goes past Teddy Bailey's old home and the marsh area that it floods goes all the way up to Laurel Hill Road. After Teddy Bailey died the old plantation house was used as a boy's home called Brookland after the name of this old plantation.

St. Helena Sound is not a creek or river on Edisto but plays a major role in the life of Edisto. St. Helena Sound is a large indent between Edisto Island and Hunting Island. It is about ten miles across and is where the Edisto, Ashepoo and Combahee Rivers reach the Atlantic Ocean. On a clear day you can see the Hunting Island Light House. I have included a picture of this light house that I took while showing this area off to some of my grandchildren. Between where The Edisto and the Ashepoo and Combahee rivers come into St. Helena Sound there are two small islands called Otter and Pine Island. Otter Island was used during the Second World War as a bombing range. You can still find old bullets from this area because it was used so much. It also played a major roll during the Civil War. When I was coming up the Fontaine brothers took a small barge with a tractor on it over to Pine Island and cut timber which they brought back to Edisto Beach. They used the lumber they had sawed from these logs to build a nice house. Pine Island and Otter Island are actually a group of small islands grouped together with Fish Creek running between them. In the front of Otter and Pine Island are sandbars that run all the way out to where the South Edisto River finally becomes part of the Atlantic Ocean. During a strong inshore wind these sandbars have been seen to come out of the water all the way to the South Edisto River channel. There is real evidence that the South Edisto River was used during the old sailing ship days because some shrimpers tell of picking up cobble stones in this channel. Cobble stones or river rocks were used to ballast sailing ships when they did not have a full load. They were left behind when a sailing ship had a load of cargo. Several streets in Charleston are built out of these cobble stones.

Growing up I soon learned to respect St. Helena Sound because it can become very angry when a strong wind comes up. You will see what I mean as I try to expound on this sound.

As I was going through the material I had collected that interested me I came across an additional story at the back of Rumbling of the Chariot Wheels by I. Jenkins Mikell and published by R. L. Bryan in Columbia, SC. This story is 26 pages long and too long to include. It is written well and is very descriptive of the era and how people got around. I particularly like its description of St. Helena Sound, which I have included. I have read this story called Beyond The Breakers many times. The story is about four hunters, with four oarsmen and a handy man plus four hound dogs who left the Peters Point Plantation in a large canoe, as passenger boats were known at the time, designed to be rowed by six oarsmen. This trip to go hunting on Hunting Island in the middle of winter took place a week or so before Christmas. At the time Hunting Island was not occupied and was a hunter's paradise. The hunting party left the point where Fishing Creek comes into St. Pierre Creek, went into the South Edisto, passed Bay Point, and then crossed St. Helena Sound in front of Pine and Otter Islands. They had to cross many sandbars and ended up in a small creek behind Hunting Island called Johnson Creek. The boat was designed for six oarsmen but the party only took four. These four oarsmen rowed all day from early in the morning until about dark to get from Peters Point to Hunting Island. It is hard for me to imagine such endurance which seemed commonplace at the time. I. Jenkins Mikel] mentioned in passing that his father's pride and joy was a similar passenger boat that took twelve oarsmen to row it.

As the story unfolds, the morning after they arrived on Hunting Island they began hunting deer by having their dogs drive the deer past the hunters who were spaced a safe distance apart. The first day the dog ran a deer into the ocean and while the hunters waited for the deer to come back ashore a shark got it. After several tries they finally got a deer. About the time they started back home a storm came up so that they were not able to come back across St. Helena Sound for several days. During this time, waiting on the weather to calm down, all they had to eat was half cooked deer and oysters because they had used up all their supplies. After this ordeal they were able to row back to Peters Point.

Because I love this story and thought you might like it, I am including several passages from this very wonderful story. The first is I. Jenkins Mikell's description of St. Helena Sound. He make St. Helena Sound sound like a real live spirit ready to catch any unprepared seaman. Later on I have described an experience where St. Helena Sound caught my brother and me off guard and could have ended up disastrous.

This is the first selection from Beyond the Breakers:

"This sportsman's paradise (Hunting Island) is separated from Edisto by a stretch of water, "grand, gloomy (at times) and peculiar" — St. Helena's Sound. It was as though a prehistoric monster had come out of the sea and with a Gargantuan mouth had bitten out of Carolina a jagged mouthful of some eight miles in length by four in width, leaving the wound ever raw, resentful, treacherous and dangerous. The waters of the Edisto, Ashepoo, Coosaw and Morgan Rivers, with their sand and silt, levied from a thousand miles of territory, emptied themselves into this unsettled inland sea. Their outgoing tides meeting the incoming flood from the ocean cause swirls, currents and counter-currents that deposit the sand brought down in shallows, banks and quick sands a few feet beneath the surface. However harmless and inviting to the mariner may appear these long, sensuous swells rolling in from the ocean, and suggesting the perpetual baths of the mermaid, death and destruction awaits the boat and crew who here may get aground, and not speedily release themselves. These smooth and deceptive swells, opposed by any obstacle to their onward motion, break into combers, white- crested and cruel, soon filling any vessel so unfortunate as to be in their way or at their mercy."

Continued from Beyond the Breakers:

"At length we started in earnest. The men gave their cleanest stroke, their most lugubrious 'Spiritual.' In all my experience with colored oarsmen, I have never heard them sing (and singing is their chief inspiration) any but religious songs. True these may be distorted, almost unrecognizable, and far oof the mark, but nevertheless they are meant to be sacred hymns."

Continued from Beyond the Breakers:

"The tide was very low, though the Sound was smooth, which lowness of the tide made it necessary to go father out in the ocean than usual. We had to go outside some banks on which the swells were showing their teeth — shallowness of water the cause. We were about half over, the more numerous of the submerged banks had been left behind toward the Edisto side. Mostly deep waters were ahead of us."

Continued from Beyond the Breakers:

"But the worst was over, deep water the rest of the way and the sun leaning toward the west hastened us toward our destination. We entered a creek back of the island and rowed some three miles up toward the center or halfway the length of the island, where the only path existed, running from the back toward the center or half way the length of the island, where the only path existed, running from the back beach to the front."

Continued from Beyond the Breakers: (I have included this small section because it deals with bottlenose dolphin. When I was coming up we called dolphin porpoise and most of the locals still call them porpoise. A porpoise is a small dolphin that lives in schools, far out to sea. This small bit describes commonly seen scenes on Edisto as dolphin herd fish into a corner and eat their fill.)

"---then the sound of many waters as a number of porpoise succeed in 'cutting out' a school of mullet from its only protection -- an oyster bank — driving them, frantic with fear, into a kind of cul de sac — any mud flat — and rushing them with such vim and impetuosity that their very momentum caused the projection of their whole body out of the water onto the soft surface of the mud, fish in month. With the shake of the head, like a sea lion, they swallowed the fish and slid back into the water, and repeated the charge again and again until the now frenzied fish, leaping high in the air over the drum fire of living artillery, scattered into deep water."

Another interesting thing about St. Helena Sound is that on the south side of the sound, where the Ashepoo and Combahee flow into the sound used to be a busy seaway in the late 1800s where ships came off the ocean to get to Beaufort. During the 1893 hurricane a ship was sunk off Hunting Island. They say that part of this old ship can still be seen at low tide. Recent navigation charts still show this shipwreck. One thing that fascinates me is all the activity that went on in the 1700s and 1800s around Edisto and the nearby Sea Islands.

It is said that Edisto Beach has two beaches, the Ocean Beach and the River Beach. About a mile of Edisto Beach is on the South Edisto River side of St. Helena Sound. This part of the beach has smaller waves and is preferred by people with smaller children.

Rabbit Trail; One Thanksgiving day when I was in high school my brother David and I decided to go over to Otter Island to hunt. We told Mother we'd be back by four in the afternoon for our big Thanksgiving dinner. There is a creek named Fish Creek that runs between Otter Island and Pine Island and has a channel running through the sandbars out in St. Helena Sound and into the South Edisto channel. We got into our 28 foot navy lifeboat with its ten horsepower outboard motor in a well and went on over to Otter Island with no trouble. About noon we decided to head back because the wind was blowing hard from the inshore and we were afraid we'd get stranded on the sandbar as mentioned earlier. We headed back and sure enough we got off the channel and got stuck. Lo and behold, the wind started blowing harder and harder and the tide went out so fast that we had to take the motor out of the well to keep the foot of the motor from breaking off. By this time we were high and dry. It was very cold and we tried to start a fire on the sandbar with gun power, gasoline and whatever we could think of but were unable to start any kind of fire. Therefore we got back into the boat and wrapped up in some canvas thinking the tide would be back in soon.

After a while we looked out as far as we could see and all we could see was sandbars. In the meantime we were late for Thanksgiving dinner and my father came looking for us. He saw us across the South Edisto River stuck on a sandbar and saw that we were okay. About dark the tide came back in with a vengeance with waves breaking on us. The action of the waves, as it came in, broke the large rudder off the boat.

Not wanting to lose the rudder I took off all my clothes and got into the water because it was still shallow. I got the rudder and put it back into the boat and put my clothes back on. I took off all my clothes because I knew that if I got wet and could not get warm soon I might die from hyperthermia. About this time the tide came in deep enough that we could put the motor back into the well and try to head home. But we had no way of steering the boat because the motor well was next to the keel and one rib back from the center and therefore would not steer the boat with the motor and we had no rudder. I remembered that we had a large oar in the boat. I lashed it to the back stem of the boat and could only turn the boat about one or two degrees in the rough water. We headed across the South Edisto River to try to reach the beach on the Edisto Beach side. In the meantime my father and Marion Whaley came out in a right large inboard motor boat to try to get a line on us but the waves were so big by now that they could not get anywhere close to us. I finally got the boat close to shore on Edisto Beach, took off all my clothes again, got in the water and turned her toward

Big Bay Creek. I then got back into the boat, put on my clothes back on and headed home. When we got to the mouth of Big Bay Creek the water became calm enough that I could steer the boat very easily with the large oar. We got home safely and ate Thanksgiving dinner at ten that evening. The point of this story is to know your rivers and creeks and know what is possible at all times. Enjoy our creeks and rivers but do not be foolish. If a strong wind is predicted stay in the small creeks and don't go out in the sound with a small boat and watch the tides. As I was telling this story to someone earlier he asked me, "Sam how did you learn about hyperthermia?" I answered and told him that when you live on the coast and are constantly in and about the water you very early learn the dos and don'ts around water. You learn that cold water will kill you and that even wet cold clothes will kill you by stealing your body heat. You learn early because you don't get a second chance or can say, "I am sorry", because the creeks, rivers and ocean are unforgiving even though they are beautiful to look at and fun to explore.

As I was remembering this event I thought about how I. Jenkins Mikell described St. Helena Sound. She is beautiful and wonderful sunsets are seen behind the trees across the sound. But this beauty is deceiving when one is not prepared.

Another Rabbit Trail: A while back a couple with two children went out in a small boat to one of the sandbars that was out of the water at low tide. This sandbar was one of the ones the South Edisto River has created. They pulled their boat up on the sandbar and did not secure it with an anchor. They began having a picnic lunch and enjoying the sun and ocean breeze. After a while they looked back at their boat and it had floated off because the tide had started back in. The husband and one child swam out to get the boat and disappeared. The wife and other child were left alone on the sandbar with the tide coming in. These sandbars are not far off the beach so she started calling for help but she was out of voice range. In the meantime the tide kept coming in. She picked up the child that was left and kept waving her hand. Thankfully someone on the beach saw her and got a boat and went out and rescued her and the child. The husband and other child were never found. There are two lessons to learn from this true story. First, always secure your boat when you get out of it on any sandbar because the tide will float it off without making a sound. Secondly, be aware of the stage the tide is. If it is coming in you can get separated from areas of dry land you came from if you walked over to a sandbar at low tide. A few feet of tide can also create a tidal current that will easily get you in trouble.

One More Rabbit Trail: There is an island not far off St. Helena Sound on its south side called Morgan Island. I had been told that there were hundreds of monkeys on the island used for medical research. Therefore I had to see them for myself. A buddy of mine and I went over to Morgan Island and went into Morgan Back Creek off the entrance of the Combahee River and stopped by a dock where we thought the monkeys were kept, anchored and cut the motor off. At first there was nothing to be seen but a bunch of trees and an old house. We said to each other that we guessed we had been told a tale. But all of a sudden little heads started coming out from the palm branches of the palmetto trees and out from every branch of every live oak tree facing the creek. There looked like there were thousands of monkeys and they started running up and down the trees and putting on a show for us. Some people came out on the dock and told us to look all we wanted but not to come ashore. Therefore awhile back there were thousands of monkeys on Morgan Island; I don't know if they are still there. If they are still there this would be a nice venture from reality on a sunny, calm day while on Edisto. A trip by waterways that get you there from the inland side would be a better route than going in front of Otter Island and Pine Island because the weather can change very rapidly and you could be in trouble before you know it. Back to -------- --

On the next page I have included a picture I took some years ago of the Hunting Island Lighthouse while visiting the Hunting Island State Park. My grandchildren and I climbed to the top via some narrow steps. From the top you could see for miles as it was well above the tree tops. This was a great View of a typical marine forest. On a clear day you can see this lighthouse from Edisto Beach's river beach. It can be seen looking across the St. Helena Sound to the left sticking up over Hunting Island.

Hunting Island Lighthouse.

Townsend River is actually a small creek and should be named Townsend Creek. It is also one of the small creeks that cuts Botany Bay off from Edisto Island proper.

Watts Cut is the cut that was cut in the seventeen hundreds to connect the South Edisto River with North Creek and Dawhoo River so that the Jehossee Plantation people could get to the mainland easier.

West Bank Creek run off the North Edisto River and runs in front of Oak Island Plantation.

Whooping Island Creek is the creek you cross when you leave Whooping Island and come onto Little Edisto.

Fenwick Cut is not on Edisto but if you live on Edisto or fish or hunt much on Edisto you will know about Fenwick Cut. This cut is located on the South Edisto River across from Raccoon Island. It was cut so you could get from the South Edisto River to the Ashepoo River where they come very close together. Otherwise you would have to go out into St. Helena Sound and to the other side of it to get into the Ashepoo River. This is also part of the Intracoastal Waterway. If you continue down the Intracoastal Waterway a little further you will come to Beaufort. It is not unusual for someone to leave the dock on Big Bay Creek and ride over to Beaufort for lunch in a relatively small outboard motor boat. I am retired from 41 years selling real estate. Several years before I retired I had a client that wanted to see a piece of property on the Ashepoo River and wanted me to show it to him. From Edisto we had to go back out to Highway 17, go through Jacksonboro, go toward Beaufort, turn back toward the coast, go through Bennetts Point and then over two old handmade wooden bridges to get to the property which was close to Fenwick Cut. I could have gotten there faster if I had taken them over by boat from the docks on Big Bay Creek. After we had looked at this beautiful property on the Ashepoo, my lady client looked at me and told me it would take her two hours to go the convenience store and there was no way she would live that far out. Therefore they bought a piece of property on Scanawah Island and built a beautiful house there. Even though Edisto is a bit out from town she thought she was in downtown versus buying out by Fenwick Cut.

I hope the information I have expounded on about all the bodies of water on Edisto wets your appetite to come to Edisto and experience all their beauty and adventure for yourself.

One more rabbit trail before I leave the creeks. A couple of years ago I was slowly riding down Store Creek taking it all in going to my favorite fishing spot in my johnboat when a bottlenose dolphin put his head out of the water with a flounder in his mouth. He looked at me and then threw the flounder about 20 feet as if to say, "Can you do that?"

Marine Forest: One of the unique features of Edisto Island is that our forests are known as marine or maritime forests. Our forests are mainly dominated by Spanish moss covered live oaks that do not grow very tall because of the wind from the ocean. Instead of growing tall they may have branches that go out 40 feet or more. As you leave Highway 17 and travel down scenic Highway 174 you will begin to see these majestic oaks limbs hanging over the road.

There are also palmettos and magnolias which are the other two main trees found on Edisto. Therefore when you look back at the wood line from the beach the trees look swept back with an occasional tall pine sticking up above everything else.

Rabbit Trail: When I was coming up on Edisto Beach I had a 500 acre undeveloped marine forest all to myself from 1947 to 1954 when civilization came to my paradise. I'll tell you about one of the joys of my life exploring these 500 acres in another chapter.

Sea Islands: Edisto Island is a sea island. Wikipedia free encyclopedia describes Sea Islands like this. "The Sea Islands are a chain of tidal and barrier islands on the Atlantic Ocean coast of the United States. They number over 100, and are located between the mouth of the Santee and St. Johns River along the coasts of the US states of South Carolina, Georgia and Florida."

As far as I can count, there are 33 Sea Islands along the coast of South Carolina. Another item found on the internet stated that the islands have a humid, subtropical climate, with hot summers, warm winters and rain throughout the year. Another fact that I found stated that these islands take up 300 miles of the South Carolina, Georgia and Florida coasts.

I have personally been down the Intracoastal Waterway from Edisto to the Florida coast and can report that you have an island, then a sound or major river flowing to the ocean between each island with a few Sea Islands being behind other sea islands, but cut off from the mainland also by a major river. Therefore there is a sea island, body of water, Sea Island, body of water, etc. for approximately 300 miles. Some of the prettiest landscapes I have ever seen are found in and around these majestic Sea Islands. You will have to travel far and wide to find more picturesque settings. A few of these islands have so much salt marsh between them and the mainland that so far it has not been practical to build a bridge over to them. Some are currently being developed by using ferries to take people and supplies back and forth to these islands. Therefore when you refer to the Sea Islands you are talking about a very unique and beautiful landscape that is only found in the Deep South along the Atlantic Ocean.

Gulf Stream: The Gulf Stream flows off the coast of Edisto about 50 miles out. I understand that when you get where the water is 250 to 500 feet deep you are in the Gulf Stream. The Gulf Stream is visited often by sport fishermen that leave from the docks on Big Bay Creek. I have been offshore and as you get off Edisto for a ways you begin to see albatross and flying fish which you do not find close or around Edisto. My father believed that the Gulf Stream moves closer to Edisto in the winter. Sometimes during a cold spell, you could leave the beach while it was raining and as soon as you crossed the causeway leading to the main part of Edisto, you would begin to see icicles hanging from the trees. My father believed that there was a five or ten degree difference between the beach and the main part of the island. A proof of this is that my mother had a garden on the beach year round. Therefore there must be some truth to this fact. On the other hand there are years when it freezes all the way to the ocean and on a rare occasion it has been known to snow on the beach.

ACE Basin: It feels good when you know you live in a paradise and have enjoyed it to its fullest all your life and find out that other people from the state and the country think so also. The extended area in which I live really did not have a name until someone named it the ACE Basin. When you visit Edisto you cannot escape being told about the ACE Basin. It is approximately the area between St. Helena Sound and U.S. Highway 17 and includes where the Ashepoo, Combahee and the South Edisto Rivers begin to spread out and meet the Atlantic Ocean.

Let me tell you how the story goes on how this vast area was put under conservation. There were these duck hunters that hunted the Edisto River up around Willtown Bluff and Jacksonboro, SC. Over time they became aware of more and more people coming into the area to hunt and even to develop their duck hunting areas. Being smart "good ole boys" they got together and decided to do something about it. Therefore they called in the do-gooders involved in the environment in the state and federal government and told them they needed to do something to protect this prime untouched area for all its wildlife, etc. Well, the do- gooders jumped right on it and formed the ACE Basin. This is only a tale but I am told it is true. Many things that seem to be begun by well meaning people actually get started by some "good old boys" like those that duck hunted on the Edisto River. Now these duck hunters have their hunting area protected and they can hunt to their hearts' content.

Now let me tell you what I know about the ACE Basin and how others think or see it. The following is one of the best descriptions of the area that I could find on the internet.

"The Ashepoo, Combahee and South Edisto (ACE) Basin represents one of the largest undeveloped estuaries on the east coast of the United States. The ACE Basin consists of approximately 350,000 acres of diverse habitats including pine and hardwood upland, forested wetlands, fresh, brackish and salt water tidal marshes, barrier islands and beaches. The basin's unique estuarine system, the largest of its type in the state, provides invaluable habitat for a rich diversity of finfish and shellfish resources. The Basin hosts a wealth of wildlife resources, including such endangered and threatened species as bald eagles, wood storks, ospreys, loggerhead sea turtles and shortnose sturgeon, and offers a variety of recreational uses.

In the mid-1700s tidal swamps bordering the rivers were cleared and diked for rice culture. After the rice culture declined in the late 1800s, wealthy sportsmen purchased many of the plantations as hunting retreats. The new owners successfully managed the former rice fields and adjacent upland acres for a wide range. This tradition of land stewardship has continued throughout the 20"'century. Because of their importance to waterfowl, these former rice fields have been identified for protection under the North American Waterfowl Management Plan. The Ace Basin also has been designated as a world class ecosystem under The Nature Conservancy's Last Great Places program. In 1988, the ACE Basin Project was launched when Ducks Unlimited (DU), The Nature Conservancy (TNC), the South Carolina Department of Natural Resources (SCDNR), the U.S. Fish and Wildlife Service (USFWS), and private landowners formed a coalition known as the ACE Basin Task Force. Westvaco Corporation, the Lowcountl_'y Open Land Trust (LOLT) and Nemours Wildlife Foundation joined the Task Force in 1998. The mission of the Ace Basin Project is to maintain the natural character of the basin by promoting wise resource management on private lands and protecting strategic tracts by conservation agencies. A major goal of the protection efforts is to ensure that traditional use such as farming, forestry, recreational and commercial fishing and hunting will continue in the area."

Can't you just see all these agencies jumping at the chance to conserve this area not knowing that a bunch of duck hunters started the ball rolling? You will see covered in this book a similar ball that got rolling on Edisto Beach when Harvie Lybrand came to live on Edisto Beach.

The ACE Basin has 23 public landings to make the area accessible so the public can enjoy all it has to offer. Three of these public landings are on Edisto and have already been mentioned.

One place worth visiting is the Edisto Interpretative Center located at 8377 State Cabin Road, Edisto Island, SC 29438. You can call them if you wish at 843- 869-2756. You can easily find this center by turning right on Palmetto Road just past the U.S. Post Office on Scenic Highway 174 and go until you see the Interpretative Center signs. I often have taken my grandchildren and friends that visit me to see it. It has much information and exhibits on what you can see in the ACE Basin. It even has a short film you can watch that gives pictures and a short description of the ACE Basin. You can walk to the remains of the 4500 year old Indian mound on Scott Creek from this center. I am led to believe that some of the oldest pottery ever found in America was found on this mound.

I have always been interested in the wild birds that live in the ACE Basin, whether they are passing through or coming to nest. A bird check list shows that there is a possibility of seeing approximately 260 different kinds of birds; of course all are not here all the time. From our supper table tonight my wife and I saw two painted buntings at a special feeder I have set up for them with a special bird seed they like. I have several feeders up close to our dining room window and sometimes it looks like bird grand central station. The American goldfinch shows up in the fall and then leaves as it begins to get a little warm in the spring. Some painted buntings stay all winter but most go south to Mexico in the winter and show back up in the spring. We have red winged black birds by the hundreds from time to time. A flock of them will light in the top of our live oak trees and sing their heads off. Chickadees, tufted tit mouse's, nuthatches, purple finches, red bellied and downy woodpeckers, blue jays and cardinals are at my feeder year round, to mention a few. My birds will eat five gallons of bird seed a week. I don't think we have 260 types of birds coming to our feeders but if you take a walk in the woods around us, visit the creeks and our beaches we have too many to count. Where else can you see 50 to 80 brown pelicans flying in one line headed back to their nesting island?

Bennetts Point is about three to four miles up the Ashepoo River from Fenwick Cut and is sometimes known as the center of the ACE Basin. Several people I know go up there by boat from Edisto to buy large quantities of shrimp. It has a processing area for several shrimp boats that consider it as their home port. You can get to many places in the ACE Basin from Bennetts Point. I have been there several times and found it to be a quaint little settlement.

Bear Island Wildlife Management Area is located on the way from Highway 17 down Bennetts Point Road to Bennetts Point. Bear Island is actually many different islands and marsh areas that are full of birds. I've been there and I have never seen so many ducks and water birds in all my life. You can ride by some of these wet areas full of birds and they just keep doing what ducks do and seem to not worry about us. I understand that this area has around 12,000 acres under conservation. I have even seen two bald eagle nests in the area from a distance with bald eagles actually on the nest doing what bald eagles do.

The Donnelley Wildlife Management Area is another area near Bear Island that is run by the state that is also a place to check out.

The Grove Plantation House, built in 1828, is located on the road to Willtown Bluff off Scenic Highway 174 and is Headquarters of the ACE Basin. 1 say one of the headquarters because the ACE Basin seems to have several places you can enjoy and learn about my paradise. I've been to the Grove Plantation House and it is worth going to see. The view from its front porch is worth the trip. As you can see The ACE Basin is full of all kinds of state and federal agencies in the name of conservation. Those duck hunters did a good thing when they decided to try to see what they could do to stop the development of my paradise. Again, it is nice to know that someone else thinks my paradise is really a paradise worth preserving for generations to come.

I believe I have given enough information on the ACE Basin. As I mentioned before, I knew I lived in a special place that God took extra time to create and all the fuss over the ACE Basin proves it. To my wife's and my good fortune we actually live on one of the creeks that shows why someone would want to visit or come live in an area with so much going for it. Thanks to many people, Edisto and the ACE Basin have been preserved for many generations in the future to enjoy. With all the work that has gone into its preservation it would take a great natural disaster to destroy it. Praise the Good Lord.

With a little observation, study and imagination, Edisto is a place you can spend a lifetime and never be bored. For example, you can ride down any small creek on Edisto and see egrets, herons, wood storks, and sea gulls. If you are lucky you will see oyster catchers and even skimmers. It is not unusual to see a whole school of menhaden covering most of the creek, and bottlenose dolphin. Most of the time you will see mullet jumping out of the water trying to escape from being eaten by some big fish. A splash on the bank will reveal a stingray catching a small fish or shrimp.

Awhile back I was sitting on our floating dock. A large head suddenly came out of the water and looked at me as if to say, "No, I can't use him for my dinner." It was very large loggerhead turtle just passing by looking for a meal. These turtles have such a strong beak that they can crush a large knobbed conch and eat it. When you find pieces of these colorful conch on the beach a loggerhead turtle probably broke the shell and ate it not far off the beach.

If relaxing is your thing, Edisto has a wonderful beach with not too many people on it so that you think you have your own private beach with normal size waves or small waves. Hire a tour guide and go see some of the old churches and the grounds of plantation homes built in the 1700s and 1800s.

You cannot ride through Edisto Island and keep on going like you can ride through Charleston or Walterboro. The road comes to an end on Edisto. When this happens you have a choice. You can stop and explore all its wonders or turn around and miss an adventure of a life time. I can hear Ed-is-tow calling you now, "Come on down and let me show you where God sends the stressed out ones who go to and fro and never stop and smell the pluff mud, hear the call of marsh hen or even hear the creek come alive at night.

While writing about the natural wonders found on Edisto, this old hymn came to mind. Listen closely to the words and then I will explain why I think it applies to what I have just written.

What Wondrous Love Is This

1. What wondrous love is this, 0 my soul, 0 my soul, what wondrous love is this, 0 my soul.' What wondrous love is this that caused the Lord of bliss to bear the dreadful curse for my soul, for my soul, to bear the dreadful course for my soul.

2. What wondrous love is this, 0 my soul, 0 my soul, what wondrous love is this 0 my soul.' What wondrous love is this that caused the Lord of life to lay a- side his crown for my soul, for my soul, to lay a-side his crown for my soul. Amen.

This verse goes along with this hymn in my mind.

John 10:10 KJV

The thief cometh not, but to steal, and to kill, and to destroy. I (Jesus Christ) am come that they might have life, and that they might have it more abundantly.

You can find love and the abundant life anywhere you look. Even in a busy sinful city you will find the love of a mother for her children. When you get out among all that Edisto has to offer you cannot but be in awe of the love God must have had for us to create such a place for us to enjoy the abundant life. As God said to the rich man in Luke's story of Lazarus and the rich man who was worried that his live brothers might also be sent to hell, "They have Moses and the prophets; let them hear them. " Luke 16:29 KJV

Therefore learn what God has to say about how we should live and then try to live a life pleasing to God. Then you can enjoy the wondrous things found on Edisto with a clear conscience knowing that all its beauty and mysteries were put here by God for us to enjoy.

When I ran out of steam telling this part of my adventures, someone that I know said, "Sam, where in the world did you find all this material?" I answered him by saying, "Many miss the wonders God created by spending all their time on cell phones, in front of the TV or on the go all the time and not taking time to see and experience all the beautiful and exciting things God created for us to enjoy. When you have spent a great deal of your life taking all this in you remember what you saw and read about as a natural way of enjoying life and living it more abundantly." My friend said, "Amen."

CHAPTER THREE

Naked came I out of my mother's womb, and naked shall I return thither; the Lord gave and the Lord hath taken away; blessed be the name of the Lord.
Job 1:21 KJV

To begin this chapter there is one constant in life, change. We are born and we all die; we start school and we graduate; we get married and have children. The children leave home and, in this day and age, we work at several jobs during our working career. We are fooling ourselves if we think things will stay the same for very long. Therefore this chapter is about some of the changes that have happened to Edisto as far as I can determine. Of course there are many others. I chose these just to get you thinking about the past glory and destruction that has taken place on Edisto. The only constant that we all need to make sure we know is how we will spend eternity. An older friend of mine told me that we were on this Earth to get ready for eternity.

From my earliest remembrance I have often sat on the beach on Edisto (Ed- is-tow) and wondered what happened before me and who walked on this beach before me. Come with me and let us explore what is known about what happened in the past on Edisto. I find it fascinating and you could spend a lifetime gathering information about this. In this book I am trying to relate to you the things I know about Edisto. I am trying to back up what has been told to me or what I have read in the past, although I have forgotten where I received some of the information. I have begun to understand that your own experiences are not the best teachers. Other people's experiences are the best teachers. In trying to verify what I know about which people and animals occupied Edisto over time going back thousands of years, I have found more information about the past than I want to know and especially what I want to put in this book. But all this information does paint a good picture of the past when you read the different accounts of what has gone on in the past. Some I believe and some I do not believe. In reading this book I have written down what I believe. When my children were growing up I made up all kinds of stories to make them think and question everything they heard. They would often say, "Daddy, tell me the truth!" This book is the truth as far as I can determine. But if you do not agree with me then study the subject and find the truth as you see it. If you do not stop long enough to dream dreams and see visions then you will miss the wondrous pictures and stories your mind can create. As a child I had plenty of time to sit and look up at the clouds and see all the landscapes and figures of who knows what passing by. I also had plenty of time to sit on the beach in front of my house and wonder what is on the other side and who sailed these waters over the eons of time and where they were going. Therefore if you come to Edisto, plan on setting aside some time to dream dreams and see visions of the past and what is to come.

Off the cuff, here are a few things I know personally. First, for a while I lived outside of the Lexington, SC area which is situated on the fall line. There is a place called Peach Tree Rock that looks like a big washout where a pond or lake's dam had broken and caused the large washout. There is evidence that a pond or lake could have once been there because there is a small stream and waterfall that still flow through this washout. It is called Leach Tree Rock because there is a rock that is sort of pink in color and when you first look at it, it looks like one of the many peach trees that are grown in this part of the country. When you go down into this area you find large sea bottom slabs of rock with sea shells imbedded into them that looks like they have been that way for a long time. All I read says that the ocean once went up to this area. Of course I was not alive when this happened but it must be true because at one time sea creatures lived and died in Lexington County, South Carolina. The general elevation on the fall line in the surrounding area is around 300 feet above sea level. But this area is approximately 500 feet above sea level. Way back then something pushed this area up. The more you look into these things, the stranger things seem. But I have walked this area and the following pictures are proof that this is a real area where sea bed rocks are located.

If you are ever up in the Columbia, SC area it would be worth your while to go see the Peach Tree Rock area. From I-26 get off at Hwy. 302 toward South Congaree and go though South Congaree until you see where Hwy. 6 comes onto it from the right. Follow Hwy. 302 until you see where Hwy. 6 leaves Hwy. 302 to the left and follow it. It will take you cross a railroad bridge and a short distant on the left you will see a Peach Tree Rock road sign on the left. Go down that road a short distance and you will see a sign telling you that you are at the path that takes you down to Peach

Tree Rock. Park and take the path. At the first path intersection take a left and the washout with Peach Tree Rock and the small waterfall will come up shortly. The path to the right will wind around and you can see other outcroppings of interest. When you get down to where Peach Tree Rock is, it will be cooler because it is down in a washout. When I've been up in this area I have been to this location several times because it seems like you are in a different world here as compared to the general surroundings.

Secondly, some people mine shell sand on Edisto to use on roads. When it is put on roads and packed down it almost turns into concrete and makes an excellent road bed. The strange thing about this is that there are new looking sea shells mixed in this shell sand. It appears that something happened in a hurry or over a very short period of time because normally the shells you find on the beach are slightly rounded from being rolled over and over in the ocean before they are washed up on the beach. Could the ocean in the past have come in very quickly with large enough waves to wash up all this sand, taking the live sea shells with it? Or did an earthquake cause this to happen? I have found lettered olive shells in this shell sand that looked new. Thirdly, local tradition tells us that the Edisto River, or at

Small waterfall in Peach Tree Rock washout.

least a part of it, used to go through Caw Caw Swamp and then through Rantowles and into Wadmalaw Sound. Caw Caw Swamp is a very large swamp located on the Edisto River between Ravenel and Summerville, SC. Therefore there must have been a large earthquake or a large storm to cause this. I have nothing to back this up. It is just what I have heard and it makes a little sense since the Edisto River has such a large flood plain. The present creeks where it is said that the Edisto River once flowed do go a long way inland in this part of the low country. The upper end of these creeks still comes close to the Caw Caw swamp area. Therefore tradition may have some truth in it. I cannot find proof that the Edisto River was diverted through this area. Maybe there is some proof or research done on the subject. I just could not find it. Going down the present Edisto River shows no indication of this other than it still has a large flood plain along this part of the country.

Rabbit Trail: An interesting thing about this area of the Edisto River is that there once was a secret community of runaway slaves, pirates and Indians that lived in Caw Caw Swamp from around the late 1800s until the early 1920s, as far as I can find out. No one knew anything about them until the first airplanes started flying over the area and saw the smoke from their fires. The local people then began to investigate and this contact caused them to start coming out of the swamp. This is where the term "Brass Ankles" came from, because these people were a little darker than the people that lived in the local area. My first wife's first cousin married one of these young men and the family got up in arms because these "Brass Ankles" were looked down on at the time. I got to know Herbert and really liked him. He was an excellent carpenter and his ancestors had been out of the swamp for 40 to 50 years by then. Back to ----

One of my favorite things to do coming up was to go on the beach, especially after a strong northeaster and look for ancient trash. All mixed together in piles of sea shells were fairly new sea shells, old worn out sea shells, sea shells that were black or brown and maybe were petrified after being buried for ages. I would often find pieces of rusty iron and pieces of broken glass that had all kinds of shapes. I wondered what the caked rust was covering up and where the broken glass had come from. Mixed in with these shells were fossils that I especially looked for. Sometimes all you would see was a black or dark brown object that sparkled in the sun, giving me a clue that there was something for me to investigate. Many times only a small tip of a large bone would be showing and when you dug around it you found a large enough fossil to identify. I would box up the larger ones and send to the Smithsonian in Washington, DC to identify. Some of my finds were a large rib of a camel, a large mastodon tooth, and plenty of horse and bison teeth, just to name a few and to whet your appetite. Fossils are still being found on Edisto Beach.

Therefore Edisto is widely known for the fossils found on its beaches. I have in front of me on a shelf above my computer table a portion of the jaw bone of a mastodon. It is about 18 inches long and has a tooth as big as my two fists still in it. Note that I said a portion of a jaw bone. It is no telling how big the full jaw bone would have been. All I can think of is "big". In front of it I have the tooth of a mammoth. It is six inches long by four inches wide and three inches thick. Both were found on Edisto Beach. Therefore I think it is worth spending a little time talking about the animals that used to live on Edisto. Further on I will talk a little bit about the people that lived on Edisto 4500 years ago and speculate on humans that have been on Edisto for eons of time. Sorry, but I was just not around to give you a first hand account. But in my dreams I can imagine who these people were and what they looked like.

Below I have included a picture of the mastodon jaw bone I just talked about. This was provided by my brother, David Lybrand. Note how big it is and this is only a portion of the jaw bone. Just think, at one time animals like this were walking around Edisto.

On the next page I have included a picture of a portion of a mammoth leg bone. Note that I said a portion. This portion of a bone was heavy to carry and it is only a portion of this creature's leg bone. Tide Elliott, Joyce's grandson, found this on Edisto and gave me permission to take a picture of it.

Under it is one tooth of a mammoth. Also note how large it is and it is only one tooth. Also note that the mammoth and mastodon looked

somewhat alike but from looking at their teeth you can see that they are totally different species. Marie, Joyce's daughter, gave me permission to take a picture of it. It was also found on Edisto.

Whereas Edisto was once under water at least 300 feet as evidenced by the sea bed rock found in Peach Tree Rock, its shore line once went out around 50 miles or so. This occurred during the Pleistocene period, which is supposed to have run from a million years are so until 10,000 years ago. (It is my opinion that when some scientists cannot explain what happened they give it a long period of time as if time would solve or justify anything they cannot explain.)

Rabbit Trail: Let me stop right here. The first thing I am going to ask God when I get to heaven is how old this earth is and why He would give a guy like me free will. I personally believe God created our planet ready to live on and do not believe it is billions or millions of years old. Therefore I believe in a literal interpretation of the Holy Bible. But there is real evidence that the ocean did go up to the Lexington area because there are sea shells in the river bottom rock in Lexington and I have seen them. On the other hand I have seen an island being formed off the North Edisto River that has grown from a little or nothing sandbar to a mile by mile island. Deveaux Bank has grown from a small sandbar in my lifetime Therefore I think it is worthwhile to question how long it takes for things to change. Another example is the Bad Lands out west which were once thought to be thousands of years in the making. But recent discoveries have determined that the area was washed out in a few days. The Peach Tree Rock area also looks like it was washed out in a short period of time and I have actually seen this area first hand. I also know that it does not take thousands of years to fossilize animal bones. It may take as little as a few years. The determining factor is if water or oxygen got to the bones after they were buried. I guess what I am saying is that we should all keep an open mind as to how old this old Earth we live on is and just obey God and everything will all work out. Back to ------ --

During this period the temperature of the earth went from being very hot to very cold several times. When it was very cold the ice caps held much of the earth's water and thus the sea level went very low. Some say the sea level dropped 100 to 150 feet off Edisto and exposed the continental shelf as much as 50 miles out from the current coast line.

Rabbit Trail: Local fishermen tell me that out 50 miles the depth is about 250 feet deep. If the continental shelf went out about 50 miles off the present shore line and was about 300 feet below the current elevation, then what is thought to have happened seems to work out in current ocean depth readings. Again, at least this is something to ponder. Back to ------- --

Since this was a gradual slop the area was swampy. I could not verify it, but some say they have found evidence of an old cypress swamp off the coast of South Carolina that also somewhat verifies what I have become to believe about the continental shelf during one of the colder times. The way you get petrified is to fall into a mud bog or have a cliff bank fall on you. To get petrified the oxygen must be cut off from your bones and very little water gets to flow across your bones. For example I personally know of a man that was buried in a sandy area of the state in 1929. His wife died in 1972. When they came to bury his wife they found that the grave of her husband was caved in. Out of respect for her husband the funeral director was told to dig up the remains of the lady's husband and put them in a new casket and bury it beside his wife. When they dug down all they found was stained dirt. There were no bones, remains of the casket or even the metal handles and hinges. The point being is that if water gets to your body after you are buried the water will dissolve everything over a relatively short period of time. Therefore because there are so many fossils from the Pleistocene period washed up on Edisto's beach, there must have been many swamps or low areas that the animals of this period could have gotten trapped in and thus petrified over time. Since several beaches near Edisto have no fossils found on them, it must have been particularly swampy and low off Edisto. There was a die off around this period of time. You now find many bones of the large animals that died during this period on Edisto Beach. The bones that have been found on Edisto Beach were of such animals as mammoths, mastodons, bison, saber-tooth cats, giant sloths, horses and camels, to name a few. I am told that in limestone quarries close to Four Hole Swamp, the most common fossils found are from camels. I could go on for several hundred pages about fossils found on Edisto's beaches, but this should increase your interest about this period in Edisto's history.

Rabbit Trail: I have a third cousin living on Edisto who told me that she found a petrified part of a human skull on Edingville Beach as a teenager and took it home to show to her mother. Her mother took it and used it as an ashtray. She did not know what happened to it. This makes sense because people have been on the North American continent for a long time, maybe as far back as 12,000 to 20,000 years ago. These Paleo-Indians, as they were called, hunted mammoths and other big animals. Therefore it is possible that 10,000 years ago or earlier Paleo-Indians were running from a saber-tooth tiger not far off the present shore line of Edisto Island. Maybe one was caught by a saber-tooth tiger and the saber-tooth tiger dropped a part of him in a bog where it was petrified and later washed up on Edingville Beach. How about dem apples? Dreaming dreams and seeing visions are still good ways to pass the warm days of spring and summer. Back to:

There is a large dead coral reef about a mile off Edisto Beach which is a great fishing spot. After college and before I went into the service, I got a six passenger license and took fishing parties out to this old dead reef to fish. We caught fish on any tide when we went out there fishing. Therefore at one time the ocean off Edisto was warm enough to support a coral reef. You can often find pieces of this old coral reef washed up on the beach. The fossils found on Edisto speak of a cold period and the coral reef speaks of a warm period. Therefore no matter what the time table is there is real proof of changing times on Edisto.

Fig Island: (Pig Island) is one of the most fascinating places I have ever visited.

When you sit looking at any creek or river on Edisto you may have thought of how long men have been using these creeks and rivers to get around and find their next meal. The average person, not knowing about the past history of Edisto, might not even give it a thought. The fact is that men have been seeking shelter and their next meal on Edisto for thousands of years. There is one such place on Edisto that shows proof that men have been present on Edisto for a time even before the pyramids were built. This place is called Fig Island. Some say that originally it was called Pig Island. I have not been able to find out why it was called Pig Island. Some say it became Fig Island because of a misprint way back when.

Not long after you come into the North Edisto River from the ocean and pass Ocella Creek, you will see a rather large marsh island off to the left. At first glance it looks like any of the other marsh islands found on Edisto. If you look closer, you will notice that it has upland trees on it because of its elevation and maybe deserves a closer look.

About 4500 years ago this Indian chief was being paddled down Ocella Creek when the mosquitoes started eating him up something awful. He said, "Boys, you have got to get me out of these mosquitoes." So they build him a shell mound and built him a house on top so the sea breeze would keep the mosquitoes away. The whole tribe liked the idea so much that they built a huge donut shaped shell mount (ring) off the North Edisto River right in the middle of marsh grass to live on. This worked out so well that they built a huge shell ring mound next to it where they could have parties. Maybe this is how this shell ring got there.

I guess I should have put this made-up story as a rabbit trail. In all seriousness, there is one of the largest circle shell mounds (called shell ring) ever found mostly untouched and in the original condition. It was built on the North Edisto River not too far from where the river empties into the ocean. Dating shows that it was built around 4500 years ago. It is thought that the Paleo-Indians built it but there is no real proof of when those that built it came and went from the area. This large ring is called Fig Island and is the most studied place I have ever run across. Because of its uniqueness, it is now under conservation and no one is allowed on this ring in order to preserve it for further investigations and discovery of how people lived back then. Before it was put under conservation protection I personally visited it several times and found it impressive. There is endless material written on Fig Island and most of it can be found on the internet.

In my early years I personally visited this area. There is a landing of a sort a little way up a small creek which runs off the North Edisto River. You can only go up in the small creek after the tide has come in several hours. The mud at this landing is hard enough to walk on. As I remember walking up on this landing, I saw on the left what looked like an unfinished structure made of oyster shells. To the right was a large ring of oyster shells about 200 feet in diameter and wide enough to walk on. It came above the high tide mark several feet. There was a lot of debris in the middle that appeared to have been washed in during a storm. Not too far from it was a large shell ring that was not automatically seen as made out of shells because it had trees growing out of it. It appeared to be about 500 feet in diameter and 15 to 20 feet high above the high water mark. It was in the shape of a donut with the inside open with some type of grass growing in the middle. At first it looked like any other marsh island until you realized that it was higher than the normal marsh island. Then I realized that it did not have regular marine forest trees and instead had trees you'd expect to see further inland.

Rabbit Trail: Being interested in how things come into being I am told that everywhere would have the same trees, etc. if all the conditions were right for a particular tree. Seeds are dispersed all over the place, but if they don't land in a place where they can grow, the seeds will not sprout or if it they sprout they will shortly die. Therefore Fig Island must have had seeds from way off landing there and finding the conditions right for them to grow. Back to:

I understand that by the time this large shell ring was built the ocean had come back in to the present shore line. There is some evidence that even in the last 4500 years there have been rises and falls in the sea level. I have not done enough study of the evidence available to tell you more about the rise and fall of the ocean during this time. Fig Island is definitely one of the areas I recommend you spend a little time reading about. I still find it interesting every time I pick up all the material I have gathered about it over the years. In 75 years of being interested in Edisto, I have gather almost too much information to remember.

One more thought: what happened to the people who built Fig Island? In reading about the people that occupied America I learned that they were mostly hunter gatherers. The people that built Fig Island may have run out of enough oysters and game to support them and just left. Or some disease may have come along and wiped them out. I guess you just have to remember that God gives and God takes away; praise be the name of God.

I found on the internet the following pictures put out by the National Register of Historic Places program at the S.C. Department of Archives and History. They gave me permission to use these pictures. These pictures do not give the real feeling of what these people long ago accomplished but they give a general idea of the scope of the work that went into building Fig Island, for whatever purpose.

Aerial View of Fig Island

Interior View of Fig Island

As I continue this theme of what God has given Edisto and what he has taken away, the next place that I often visited as a youth is Botany Bay Island. In fact one of my first girlfriends and I often walked on this place called Botany Bay Island.

Botany Bay Island In talking about what has come and gone, Botany Bay has been ravaged by the sea over the years but it remains a beautiful place. It has washed greatly over the years and one storm even cut a new ocean inlet that was called New Inlet for awhile until the ocean decided to fill it in again. Like the scripture verse at the beginning of this chapter says, "The Lord giveth and the Lord taketh away." From time to time I have visited Botany Bay and I especially like the river beach. Many times I looked across the North Edisto River and saw a big lodge on Seabrook Island and people walking on the beach. The river was so wide it was hard to see what the people were doing. This was one of those times when you just had to use your imagination. Later as an adult and married I spent a weekend with my wife at a retreat at Camp St. Christopher and actually saw that it was as beautiful as I had imagined. Seabrook Island is named for William Seabrook who once owned it. He was a wealthy plantation owner whose plantation was also on the North Edisto River.

The following Letter to the Editor is a newspaper article written in The Post and Courier in 1979 that my wife had tucked away in one of her

FIG ISLAND EXTRAS

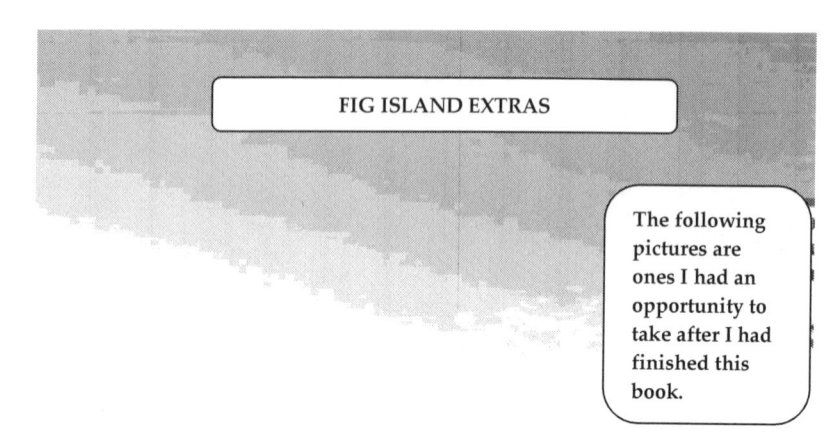

The following pictures are ones I had an opportunity to take after I had finished this book.

Duane Asbill took me over to Fig Island for a brief time to take pictures knowing it was under conservation and needed to be protected. These pictures give a truer representation of what Fig Island currently looks like.

This is what Fig Island looks like from a small creek off the North Edisto River.

This is another smaller Shell ring behind Fig Island.

Once on Fig Island, you will see how big it is and that it was made of oyster shells.

72 B

This gives an idea of how wide this shell ring

This is how it slops down toward the open center.

This is how it slopes down toward the marsh.

This gives an idea of how steep it is in some places.

scrap books. It mentioned her grandfather, Harry McTeer. Therefore I thought it might put another slant on Botany Bay Island. If you remember I told you that Otter Island off St. Helena Sound was also used as a bombing range during the Second World War. Edisto was an active place during this war. I'll talk more about living on Edisto during the Second World War. Here is how it reads. Botany

Bay Island

"Reading the article on Botany Bay Island reminded me of the five times it was my privilege to visit this beautiful spot during the early 1940s.

It was owned at that time by Dr. Greenway. He also owned other property, including farmland on Edisto Island, not far from the beach. During the early years of World War II the federal government leased Botany Bay Island from Dr. Greenway for use as a bomber target range for the Liberator bombers stationed at the Charleston Air Force Base. If those who have visited this island since that time think it is a beautiful place, you should have seen it before it became a target range. About 300 acres of it was high, dry land and at least 75 percent of the trees were live oaks. Its only inhabitants were wildlife, including a large population of deer. That was my reason for being there. I was pastor of the Osborne Baptist Church and several families living on Edisto Island including the Harry McTeers and the Kenneth Prices were members, Mr. Simmons was superintendent of Dr. Greenway's property and he told Mr. McTeer, possibly the island's leading sportsman, to get his friends together and go to the island and get some of the deer, because once the target practice began the deer would be slaughtered and no one would benefit. The boat belonging to the contractor who was clearing half of the island and setting up targets would take us to the island. The cutting of the trees and clearing the land for the targets had already begun, but only on the end opposite Seabrook Island. A few targets were already in place. The deer were as fat as fat could be and their main food was the abundant supply of acorns under 300 acres of trees. During the five hunts it was my privilege to have part in, we killed 34 deer. On the first hunt R.F. Harrell killed the biggest and heaviest deer I have ever seen covered with fat an inch thick.

On one of the other hunts one of the group shot a good-size buck but did not see the doc on the other side of the buck. When the buck fell, the doe turned and headed out of the woods for the water about 50 feet away. The fellow who killed the buck walked to the edge of the woods to see where the doe went. He saw nothing. She had disappeared. The skipper on the boat told him if he was looking for that doe he would find her where those bubbles were coming out of the water. The hunter removed his shoes and pants, waded to where the bubbles were, felt the deer with his foot, got hold of one leg and dragged her out. One pellet had hit her in one lung, and where she went in the water, the air escaping from her lung caused the bubbles."

THE REV. W.J. KENNEDY
6240 Old Point Road
Hanahan (SC)

Edingsville Beach/Village

The next area that has come and gone that interests me is Edingsville Beach. Back in 1824 the plantation owners noticed that if you could keep a constant breeze on you, you would be less likely to get yellow fever and malaria fever. Therefore the Edings Plantation started leasing lots on Edingsville Beach that was part of their plantation. About 40 to 50 plantation beach houses were built on Edingsville. Most plantation owners built their summer homes out there. They would take their families out there in the spring and they would return to the plantation homes in late fall. The Espiscopal and Presbyterian churches also built chapels out there. Even a pool hall was said to be built out there. This was a beautiful location with a wide sandy beach with large sand dunes in the back of the beach. They took their farm animals with them and kept them on a small peninsular called Cowpens located on Frampton Creek just behind Edingsville Beach. At the time, living on

Edingsville village was said to be just one big party. The plantation owners would leave Edingsville each morning to survey their plantations and then return in the afternoon leaving the head man or foreman to run things for them. I have even heard it called the Riviera of the South because of all the good times that were had there. In 1850 it began to wash badly and the 1885 storm took out most of the plantation beach houses. A few of them were moved to the main part of Edisto. The 1893 storm took out the rest of the remaining houses. The 1911 storm even took out the large sand dunes behind Edingsville. Now the footprint of the village is said to be several thousand feet out in the present ocean. Most of the sand that washed away is now on Edisto Beach.

Rabbit Trail: Many times over the years I have gone over to Edingsville to look for fossils and old ballast brick that were used to build summer house foundations and cisterns. It became one of my favorite places. When I decided to ask my girlfriend to marry me I took her over to Edingsville to pop the question. On the way there we had to cross a small creek that has about one foot of water in it. I put the ring in a small box that looked like a sandwich among the picnic lunch items we were taking to eat after we had explored Edingsville. Of course I gave her the sandwich that had the ring in it and told her I had made that one especially for her. Thankfully she was excited about the ring and said yes. I had measured the ring size by my little finger but it was still too large. On the way back, the small creek we crossed was about three feet deep. I almost had to carry her across this slippery mud creek but finally got her to get wet and cross the creek. I offered to keep the ring in my pocket until we crossed the creek but she would have nothing to do with that. She held the ring in place with both her hands and held her hands over her head until she was safely across the creek. We got married in December of 1959 after I graduated from the U.S. Coast Guard's Officer Candidate School. My first assignment was in San Juan, Puerto Rico. Edingsville was a special place for both of us until she died of lupus in early 2000. Edingsville is still a special place to me. But as Job said, "The Lord giveth and the Lord taketh away. " Just looking at present day Edingsville you would never know that a thriving community once existed there. Now all that is left is a small strip of sand between the marsh and the ocean. During spring tides or storms the ocean washes over this small strip of land and into the marsh behind it. If you were inshore looking at this area during a spring tide event you would not even realize that a rather large community was once located on this location. It is my opinion that one day a storm will create a small bay that will take in the marsh behind Edingsville and the remainder of Edingsville beach. Back to :

The following is an account of Edingsville as told by Chalmers S. Murray in his book Turn Backward 0 Time in Your Flight that I have already mentioned.

A Chalmers S. Murray Story

"I will never forget my first sight of the ocean. My father had rowed the family over to Edingsville Beach, the site of a little village which years before, had been wiped out by a series of hurricanes. The breakers there were probably no more than two feet in height, but to me, they seemed the height of mountains. They frightened me so much that I ran back up the beach as fast as my feet could move and I refused to even go wading.' I think my father, dressed in an old pair of pants, went into the surf and seemed to enjoy it thoroughly. Ina only shut her eyes and started to cry. It must have been at least two years afterward that I ventured to put my feet in the ocean.

In those days there were tall sand dunes and a heavy growth of trees on the little island. It was a wild but lovely place. Now all of the dunes and trees have been washed away, leaving only a narrow strip of sand which is covered by water during spring tide. At one time, sixty dwellings, a schoolhouse, a saloon and two churches stood on the strand. Erosion had exposed old creek beds, and fishing now is poor sport.

According to my father, my Uncle Eberson and other oldtimers now lying in the churchyards, the village of Edingsville was a sort of Garden of Eden. All of the planters of Edisto Island had summers houses on the beach to which they moved around the first of May, staying there until frost in the fall. Some of the planters even brought their hogs and cows with them. Since there was no standing water, the beach was free of mosquitoes. The people then thought that malaria was caused by the night air of summertime. They never let dark catch them on the mosquito-ridden main island. The village was quite a gay place with dancing, charades and much visiting back and forth. Everybody went to church on Sunday and paraded the strand in the late afternoon. The boys had lots of fun. The late Cecil Westcoat told of how he and several other youths used to ride their horses nude in the moonlight and go swimming in their birthday suits on the end of the beach reserved for males. They hunted birds' eggs, shot crows and sometimes mockingbirds with their bows and arrows and went sailing in the creeks, using burlap sack sails.

In those times women and girls bathed on one end of the beach and the men and boys on the other. The men went in the water nude, while the women wore nightgowns. Uncle Eberson said that when he was three years old he went with the women and girls. When asked what they did in the surf he replied that they just jumped up and down and screamed.

Cecil Westcoat told us it was pure heaven on Edingsville Beach in his boyhood days. 'Nobody ever died on Edingsville, and nobody really got sick,' he said. He painted pictures of the gentlemen walking on the strand with their gold- headed canes, the women in their Sunday fmery riding in carriages, and he also told of moonlight dances in the Hall that lasted from nine o'clock in the evening until sunrise. Uncle Eberson said that Mr. Westcoat was a big liar. 'I don't think anybody owned a gold-headed walking cane and there were no carriages on Edingsville,' he said. 'And what's more, there wasn't any Hall. Dances were held in private homes.'

Strangely enough, the children on Edingsville Beach attended school in the summer, and I have never found out the reason why, unless it was to make up for time lost in the fall and winter. The Rev. States Lee, pastor of the Presbyterian Church on Edisto Island, conducted the school, and my father said that he was an excellent teacher.

The last houses in the village of Edingsville were swept away in the hurricane in 1893 and no one dared to rebuild. It is impossible to mark out the place where the village stood, for the site is under water now."

Another Chalmers S. Murray passage:

"During my childhood days, the annual Sunday School picnic, attended by both Episcopalians and Presbyterians, was a memorable event. In earlier times it had been held at Cowpens Point, a small neck of land behind Edingsville Beach. It was shaded by hundreds of palmettos and cassinas and was situated on a salt creek. When time came for lunch, all buggy seats were removed and placed on the ground. Each child had a seat. After refreshments we would replace the buggy seats and go for a ride on Edingsville Beach. To me it was a most romantic setting for a picnic and I enjoyed every minute of it."

Of all the stories I have read about Edingsville, the following, also written by Chalmers Murray, is the one I like best. We are indebted to Mr. Murray for all he has written about his life on Edisto and the stories he has left behind. This is a newspaper article written in The News and Courier on December 25, 1955 by Chalmers Murray.

A Chalmers S. Murray Story

Life In The Lost Village of Edingsville
By: Chalmers S. Murray
Edisto

"A few very old people living on Edisto Island recall the last house left standing on Edingville Beach after the storm of 1885, but some apparently remember the lost village itself.

Here on the barrier sand reef locally called 'The Bay', planters of Edisto Island in 1825 built a pretty little hamlet along the crescent shaped sand, and before many years had passed it had grown to a village of some 60 houses.

By 1886, however, the encroaching Atlantic had already taken its toll, for a map in the possession of the South Carolina Historical Society, drawn by the firm of White and Gourdin, bearing the date, July 1886, shows only 41 houses, including two church building and a 'billiard saloon.'

LOWCOUNTRY NAMES

Lot owners then included such well know Lowcountry names as Middleton, LeGare, Edings, Bailey, Seabrook, Wilson, Whales, Beckett, Mikell, Jenkings, Murray, Clarke, Wescoat, Baynard, Owen, Street and Hanahan. Many of them had bought more than one lot, on speculation probably, for in spite of the constant threat from the sea, the fame of Edingsville as a salubrious summer resort was firmly established.

It was from my uncle, Eberson Murray, who died in 1938, and from several other old timers, that I learned something about life on Edingsville Beach in the 1870's and the early 1880's.

This is taken from an unpublished manuscript written by my uncle at my suggestion the year before his death.

TWO-STORY BUILDINGS

'Most of the cottages, as I recall, were substantial two-story buildings with wide verandas facing the ocean. They were spaced far apart and stood in two long rows; one row overlooking the East, and the other the marshland and creeks laying between the beach and the main island of Edisto.

'Although we had gardens in the village, much of the vegetables were brought from the plantation. Many hogs were raised on the beach for they could run wild and feed whenever they liked.

'We boys had the time of our lives. When we were not fishing or feasting on raw palmetto cabbages, or making bonfires, we were doing our school lessons --- that is if the weather wasn't too warm and the surf not too tempting.

'Yes, we went to school in the summer --- spasmodically. Our first teacher was Mr. Robert E. Seabrook, afterwards the principal of Craft's School in

Charleston. Teaching was a labor of love with Mr. Seabrook since his salary was exceedingly small. Later Miss May Lee, a daughter of the Rev. States Lee, taught at the village school.

TWO CHURCHES 'There were two churches in Edingsville --- a Presbyterian and an Episcopal. I remember the Rev. William Johnson, rector of the Episcopal Church, especially well. I have a picture of him now hauling his firewood in a little wagon on which he had rigged a sail. 'When the wind was right he would hoist sail, and with his firewood aboard, would go skimming over the hard white sand at a fine rate of speed. 'I suppose it is just such incidents that a boy remembers best.

CROWDED STRAND

'The strand was always crowded with people from mid afternoon until late evening. The only use the villagers had for their houses were places in which to eat and sleep. Nearly every night the younger set held a dance. The favorite dances were quadrilles, lancers, the old fashion waltz, the Virginia Reel, and a swift two-step whirl called the 'gallop.'

'Washy (Washington) Jenkins was perhaps the liveliest boy in our crowd. One day the notion struck him to rig up a baby carriage as a land sail boat.

'He had been watching the minister's wagon, and he thought he would contrive a speedier craft. While his parents were not watching he stole his little sister's carriage and the buggy umbrella.

'Rolling the carriage near the surf, he climbed inside, hoisted the umbrella, and away he sailed. Everything went all right until the carriage reached Frampton's Inlet.

HIT THE WATER

'Washy saw the water loom up in front of him and he turned the umbrella loose, but not soon enough. He and the carriage were driven into the inlet while he was thinking what to do next.

'He came out sputtering, dragging the vehicle after him. The umbrella had disappeared.

'You can imagine how warmly his parents received him when he sneaked into the house late that evening.

'Life on Edingsville seemed one long happy holiday. Illness was almost unknown, and as far back as I can remember, there were only one or two deaths.

'And it was such a beautiful setting for a village. The houses were shaded by oaks and cedars. Behind the big sand dunes rose an impenetrable jungle of cassina, chinaberry vines, honeysuckle and yucca; in front was the blue Atlantic.

Unfortunately, however, Edingsville was too good to last. As the storms ate away the sand dunes year after year, the planters abandoned their summer homes and started spending the year around on the main island. The beach dwellings were bought up by Negro farmers and moved off.

FEARSOME SPECTACLE

'When the storm of 1885 broke I was working up in the island about five miles from the village, Becoming alarmed about my people, I shut up shop and made my way to the beach afoot through a raging gale.

'At last I reached the village. The spectacle that met my eyes filled me with terror.

'The high tide that morning, driven by hurricane winds, had carried away the porch of our house and had undermined the foundation. Members of the family were hastily moving the furniture to the back beach. Our next door neighbor had also lost his porch.

'The water was swirling around our feet and the worst was yet to come for another tide was racing in.

'We had moved just in time. The water rose higher and higher and that night both of the front beach houses collapsed --- Mr. E.A. Bailey's and ours. That was the end of Edingsville.' (End of Uncle Eberson's story.)

One or two houses remained standing for several years, it seemed, but they were only used by picnickers and fishermen.

The late Cecil Wescoat, Edisto Island's well known primitive artist, painted numerous pictures of scenes on old Edingsville Beach. The pen and ink drawing accompanying this article is based on one of his oils.

ARTIST VVITH WORDS

Westcoat was also an artist with words. During his latter days he told many fascinating stories of life in the lost village, but I did not write them down and most of them have faded from memory.

'Oh, it was a grand and glorious place,' he would say over and over again. 'I never hope to see another like it short of heaven.'

Then he would go on to romance a little:

'How well do I remember sitting on our breeze swept verandas Sunday afternoon watching the afternoon parade. I can shut my eyes now and see old gentlemen walking by earring gold headed canes, young ladies in flowered muslins, arm-in-arm with their frock-coated escorts; old ladies out for an airing in their gleaming black carriages, and young men astride their prancing steeds, while the sand dunes threw purple shadows on the strand and the surf sung a deep low song.'

ALL GONE NOW

'All is gone now — the two rows of pretty houses, the fine old oaks, the high crested dunes, and the happy people I watched pass by in the Sunday parade. Nothing is left but the surf.'

Once Wescoat fixed his eyes on me and said: 'Did you ever hear band music on the Bay, my boy.' I answered that I had heard strange sounds on the beach, but no band music.

'I've heard that music many times,' he said dreamily, 'and others people have heard it too.'

'Right after the war a company of Yankee soldiers was stationed at Edingsville, and almost every afternoon they would give a band concert for the villagers. Now on a calm day, if you listen very carefully you will hear the bandsmen playing their sweet music.'

SOUNDS LIKE MUSIC

Afterwards I did listen very carefully when I went on the beach. Once or twice I did hear something that sounded very much like music, but it was always when the breeze was blowing strong.

Then there is the story of the Lady in White who is said to walk the beach on bright moonlight nights. Both my father and Uncle Eberson admitted after much coaxing that they had seen the ghostly. form once, but

Mr. Wescoat talked as though she were almost an old friend. This story will have to be related another time."

There are many other stories floating around about Edingsville. But God gives and God takes away. We will only know God's mind when we get to heaven and see God's plan for mankind.

I have included two pictures of paintings that have been in circulation around Edisto for some time. I understand that they were originally painted by Cecil Wescoat. My brother David gave these to me for a presentation I made to the Home Owners Association of the present subdivision in the back of what was once Edingsville called Jeremy Cay.

I have also included an old photograph that was taken by Eddie Hopkinson about 1911. It shows Ella LaRoach and Julie H. LaRoach in a horse carriage on Edingsville Beach with the old sand dunes in the background. It had to be taken before 1911 because the 1911 storm finally took these sand dunes out and left the beach as it is today. David also provided this picture.

The final thing that I have included is a layout of Edingsville Village. I have included a page showing who owned which lots. I understand that these lots were leased to these individuals by the Edings family starting in 1824. David also gave this plat and the owners' names.

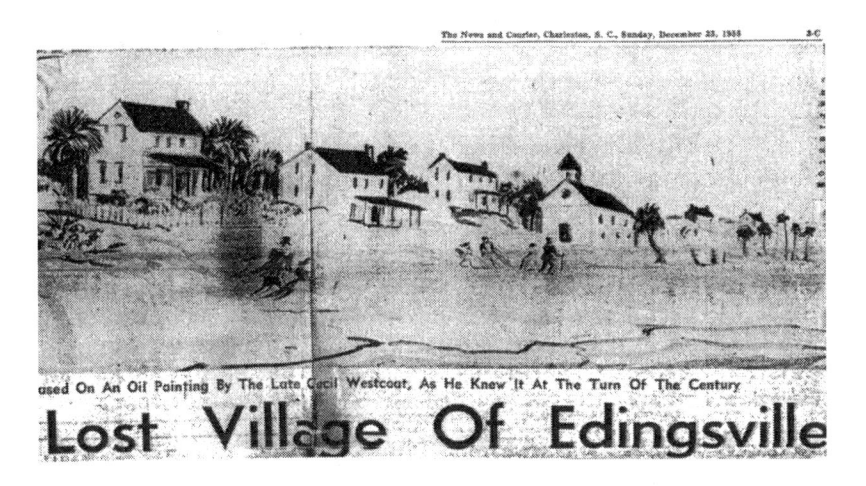

Based On An Oil Painting By The Late Cecil Westcoat, As He Knew It At The Turn Of The Century

Lost Village Of Edingsville

This picture and article with similar information that I have presented above appeared in The News and Courier on Sunday, December 23, 1955. As you can tell, it has been circulated around for quite some time. It is the best picture I could find of Edingsville and how it might have looked in its "hey day".

This picture was taken of an old picture that I believe Cecil Wescoat painted of his vision of what Edingsville must have looked like during the 1885 storm.

The following picture shows Edingsville Beach before the sand dunes were taken out by the 1911 Storm.

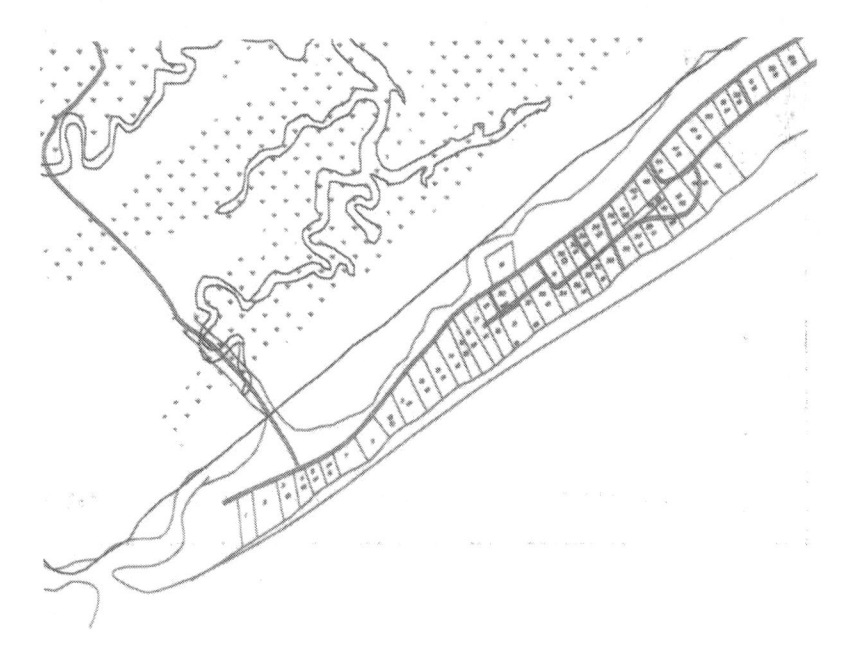

This picture shows Edingsville Beach before the sand dunes were taken out by the 1911 Storm.

These names appeared on a plat dated 1866 by White E. Gourden, CE for J.E. Edings of the Village of Edingssville.

Lot # Names
1 Geo. Owens (House Burnt) 2 Vacant
3 M. Middleton
4 Jas. Legare
5 J. Evans Edings
6 Sydney Legare
7 Vacant
8 Dr. Bailey
9 Vacant
10 J.E. Seabrook
11 Rev. Wilson
12 Jas . Hopkinson & Mrs Wm. G. Baynard 13 Miss E. M. Whaley
14 Rev. William Johnson 15 Est. William Edings 16 Theodore Becket
17 T. P. Mikell
18 Jno Wescoat
19 Mikell Seabrook
20 Billiard Saloon
21 Miss E. Seabrook
22 W.E. Seabrook
23 Col. J. Whaley
24 Maj. Jas Whaley V
25 Hamilton Jenkins
26 L. R. Clark
27 Vacant
28 Ephrain Bailey
29 Edward Baynard
30 Jno Wescoat
31 Jabez Wescoat
32 Edward Whaley
33 Vacant
34 Dr. Jas Whaley
35 Vacant
36 Ephraine Seabrook 37 E. W. Seabrook
38 T.A. Baynard

39 Dr. R. Hannahan
40 J. J. Hannahan
41 Est. Jas. Hannahan 42 Episcopal Church
43 Con Bailey (House Burnt) 44 C01. Joe Jenkins
45 Mrs. W. B. Whaley 46 Mrs. Seabrook Jenkins
47 W. Seabrook, Jr.
48 Miss Minirva Street
49 Presbyterian Church
50 Est. W. Murray (House Burnt) 51 A. J. Clark
52 John M. Jenkins.

I included all these names because when you hear a story it is just a story until you see actual names associated with the story. Many hours could be spent just finding out about all these people. Today you still find many of the descendants of these people still living on Edisto Island. My wife is a descendant of the Beckets and Seabrooks. In fact her brother is named William Seabrook Hills, Jr. I went to school with the Murray boys and Mrs. Marion Murray taught me in grammar school. In high school one of my classmates was a Bobby Jenkins of the Brick House Jenkins. When I was growing up Marion Whaley often helped me. One of my memorable trips was taken in Teddy Bailey's boat. In grammar school Mrs. Julia Mikell was in charge of our lunch room and our librarian. I dated one of the Hopkinson girls and one of the Middleton girls.

Jehossee Island: At one time Jehossee Island was part of Edisto Island until it was cut off by the digging of Watts Cut.

As you approach Edisto, look to your right just before you get to the large Dawhoo Bridge and you will see some woods off in the distance. This is Jehossee Island, the grandest of grand places up until the Civil War. Ever since I heard of this strange sounding place I have been interested in finding out all I could about it. I have personally been around the whole island in my johnboat and have actually been on the grounds and seen what appeared to be a grand boulevard lined with massive live oaks. But of course the island and field have now all grown up and if you did not know what went on in this mysterious place you would just think it was just another wooded island near Edisto.

In reading past history of the world you often come across places that were known as "City States" or small cities or areas controlled by a War Lord or King. When Joshua went into the Holy Land the Bible tells us that he had to conquer many kings. In that time the Holy Land was ruled by many small "City States" and each had a king. This king would probably be more like our current mayors but with much more power and influence over the area he ruled.

When you really think about Jehossee and all that it had going for it, Jehossee was very close to a small "City State" run by the Honorable William Aiken.

A few years ago my brother David was working on plotting all the plantations that were on Edisto around the 1850s. He came across the fact that on June 1, 1860 an agriculture inventory of Edisto Island showed that William Aiken's plantation, called J ehossee, had 1,500,000 pounds of rice on hand.

Over the years I have collected material on Edisto in hopes to one day consolidate it all in one book (this is that book) for my children and grandchildren to have as a permanent record. One of these documents that I got from somewhere is what appears to be a copy of a story published by The News and Courier in 1924. This is the best description I have ever seen about this "City State", because at the time it was written, Jehossee was a self contained rice industry that had everything it needed to perpetuate itself. Here is the article in its entirety. This is a right long description but is worth reading very slowly so you can take it all in. From what I have read about plantation life this is the best description of a large working plantation I have ever read. It also confirms some of the material I have already presented. You will see these references as you read through this account.

(This account is from an article in The News and Courier written in 1924 talking about a Letter to the Editor in July of 1844 from Edingsville.)

Jehossee Island

"At this time when the administrative and economic aspects of agriculture are receiving so much attention and it is so frequently said that the farmer is and must be essentially a business man, it is interesting to recall something of the methods employed by the great planters in the early period of the country in this section when the administration of the plantation called for business understanding of a high order. The successful planters of pre-Confederate era met and solved problems which are now frequently committed to government agencies, and a study of their operations might prove useful to farmers who are now giving so much of their time to organizing for pressure upon Congress for relief from economic burdens.

One of the greatest rice planters of this section during the nineteenth century was the honorable William Aiken whose plantation on Jehossee Island was almost a principality. It is still owned by his grandchildren and has until recent times been planted to rice. Mr. Aiken was perhaps the largest owner of slaves of his time and his plantation at Jehossee was operated by them. He owned also extensive farming land in Fairfield County and many of his slaves were kept there. He took a prominent part in public affairs, and was a member of the Legislature for several years. Governor of South Carolina in 1844, a member of Congress from 1851 to 1856 and, after the War, was elected to Congress but, because of the Reconstruction policy of the time, was denied a seat. He died at his summer residence in Flat Rock in 1887, at the age of 81 years.

In the Charleston Courier of July 19, 1844, there was published a letter signed "Visitor" written from Edingsville by a visitor to that neighborhood describing the rice plantation of Governor Aiken at Jehossee. The name of this writer is not now known but he identifies himself as a visitor from the North. Edingsville was the beach resort of the Edisto Island planters of that time. It has entirely disappeared owing to erosion of the beach at that part of the Island and relics of the cottage which then stood well back of the beach are now washed by the surf. The impression of the Aiken Plantation upon the mind of the visitor, especially in the business management of the place and the governance of the slaves who constituted a considerable community makes an interesting and illuminating record. The text of this letter, as it was published more than 80 years ago, follows.

A Great Plantation
Edingsville, July 1844

Messrs. Editors:

I have been spending a few weeks at this delightful summer retreat, employing the fresh and salubrious breeze of the ocean and partaking of the generous and kind hospitality of the inhabitants. A few days since through the politeness of a friend, I was enabled to visit Jehossee Island, the plantation and country seat of the Honorable William Aiken, of your city. It is situated at the Southern part of Edisto Island, with which it is connected by a causeway which Mr. Aiken some years since, erected as a convenience to himself and neighbors, his causeway was the work of no little labor, and few macadamized streets of your city surpass it in neatness or durability of construction.

I had heard much of the extensive improvements Mr. Aiken had made at Jehossee since his purchase of it — of his having reclaimed its land an almost valueless savnah (sic), I had heard still more of the very efficient policy he had established in the management of upwards of 700 slaves, at this plantation, of the moral, religious, and physical well-being he had been the instrument of securing to them, and leaving you all these, you may readily suppose one, curious like myself in such matters, felt no little desire to see these things with his own eyes.

That privilege I have enjoyed. This report I have to make, may be of interest to many of my Northern friends, who have been taught to believe the existence of such things, anywhere at the south, entirely utopian.

Just at the head of the causeway which connects Jehossee with Edisto Island a view of the rice land appears. The eye here glances over some 1200 acres, in one field, in state of highest cultivation. To those fond of low land scenery, the picture is one of unsurpassed beauty. Through the island passing over a course of upward of 4 miles, the main canal is to be seen, connecting the waters of the Pon Pon river, which flows around three sides of Jehossee, and with Watts Cut which separates it from Edisto Island, gives it an insular character. The canal which is upward of 4 miles in extent, 22 feet broad and 6 feet deep, was cut by Mr. Aiken at a very large expense, for the purpose of supplying his field with plentiful irrigation. This was rendered necessary from the fact that the river on one side of the Island is at times salt, while it is never found so on the other. Intersecting the canal at right angles are other canals, by which the fields are irrigated. The locks which preclude (or let in) the water of the river of which there are seventeen are of the most approved construction, the masonry indicating a simplicity and durability which would please the eye of the most fastidious architect.

On the south side of Jehossee is the overseer's summer residence, situated on a high bluff off the river, and commanding a distant view of the ocean. The spot is considered quite healthful as any one might believe, from the healthful appearance of Mr. , the overseer. This gentleman is employed by Mr. Aiken, at a liberal salary, to superintend his planting interest. After a very kind reception by him at his summer retreat which, by the by, is a perfect little bower, we were politely invited to ride with him over the plantation.

Lands Reclaimed

It is unnecessary to say more of the rice lands than that they are among the best cultivated in South Carolina. With the exception of a few acres they have all been reclaimed through Mr. Aiken's industry and enterprise. Before his purchase of the island, the lands were considered in a great degree an irreclaimable savannah. Perhaps in no portion of the southern country can a large body of rice land be seen in one field. Some idea of the extent may be formed when I tell you its area would cover all the space upon which Charleston is built. I would here attempt a description of a scene whose novel beauty so much pleased me at the time, but as most of your readers are familiar which such sights I shall not indulge the temptation. While passing over the fields we were pointed to several spots in them, upon which Mr. Aiken had experimented with various manures, on some of these we could not help remark the wonderful improvement the application of calcareous manures had produced. From acidity some of these spots had been rendered entirely unproductive. They were now yielding abundantly. In the corn field, three hundred acres of which are under culture, we were pointed to land which, a few years since, could scarcely produce seed, now yielding 30 to 40 bushels to the acre, which is an enormous yield for this part of the State. Did space permit, I am sure it would be gratifying to the planter to be informed of the many agriculture experiments Mr. Aiken had successfully tested on this plantation, but I must pass to objects of more interest — at least to those who, like myself, are anxious to look into the management and condition of the operatives of slaves upon a rice plantation.

A Complete Establishment

The entire crop of this plantation is prepared for market on the spot. To facilitate the preparation, Mr. Aiken had erected threshing, pounding and other mills, all worked by steam power, and said to be among the best planned of any in the South. When prepared for market the crop is sent there in his own vessels — this uniting a system of production, of manufacture and transportation all under one head. Upon Jehossee there are between seven and eight hundred slaves. In the management of these Mr. Aiken merits the commendation of every lover of humanity. A lesson from his book would go far to dissipate the idea which abolitionists entertain of the working of the slave system, and would prove highly profitable to many of our own planters. I know what I write will be considered a picture too highly colored; but I feel confidence in thinking anyone who will visit J ehossee will find my shades too dull.

The inhabitants of this plantation present the appearance of a neat little village. The houses are of uniform size and contain four apartments each; with double fireplaces of brick. Attached to every house is a small garden and yard in front. The slaves are required to cultivate their garden — and in every yard is a poultry house and other buildings. All the houses are kept neatly whitewashed inside and out, and the strictest and most constant cleanliness is required on the part of the occupants.

On the plantation is a commodious and well arranged hospital, to which every sick negro is carried, and attended to during his sickness. The building is supplied with numerous rooms, and comfortably furnished with clean bedding, etc., for the different patients. Nurses are always in attendance and a skillful physician is yearly employed, to minister in all cases requiring medical attention. In the same building is a large hall for invalids, and the whole arranged along the lines of the best hospital in the country. Care is taken that no negro is permitted to "play sick", While equal care is taken that every real ailment is promptly and kindly attended to. The effects of this admirable plan is not only grateful to Mr. Aiken's feeling of humanity but also repays him by a profitable return in the augmented population of his negroes, and their increased health, and ability to discharge their labor.

Slaves Well Cared For

The best kind of food and clothing is given the negroes, nor are they left, as on most plantations to grind their own corn, after a hard day's work in the field. This labor is done for them by a steam mill, erected for the purpose on the place, and their weekly allowance is measured out to them, in the best, and most wholesome grist. This with other articles of food such as meat, potatoes, etc., they cook for themselves, it having been found that the slaves infinitely prefer their mode of cookery. The food of the children, however, is cooked for them by nurses, who attend them during the absence of the parents at a building called a nursery. I never saw a finer looking set of negroes anywhere.

The great question "whether our slaves can be religiously instructed with benefit to themselves, and advantage to their owners" Mr. Aiken has most successfully solved. On his plantation he has a neat chapel at which religious services are performed semi-monthly by a minister employed for the purpose. Every slave is compelled to attend and each is orally instructed and catechized by the minister. Marriages are performed according to religious rites and a Christian code of morals is strictly enjoined upon the slaves in their intercourse with each other. More than one-half of the negroes on the place are communicants of the church; and as few cases of backsliding is said to take place as in any religious community of equal number. Felonies are almost unknown among them and those petty crimes which, on other plantations, are considered unavoidable, with these negroes are of rare occurrence.

When Mr. Aiken first proposed to introduce religious instruction among the negroes, many of his friends predicted his hopes would never be realized. They said his plan would only render the slaves greater rogues, by giving them religion as a cloak to hide their villainies. Time has proved the fallacy of these predictions. I know not whether this peculiar feature of Mr. Aiken's encouragement has produced the results, but certainly there is not to be found in all the country around, anybody of negroes more orderly, well behaved, or contented. They look well, work well, and more than all, work with a cheerfulness which no one can fail to observe who visits the place.

The Manor House

Upon our visit to Jehossee, Mr. Aiken was absent at his summer residence in Charleston. This, however, did not preclude us, his overseer inviting us to visit the mansion or homestead. This was found a neat and very hospitable building, without any pretension of show. Comfort and utility seemed chiefly consulted in the arrangement of everything around, and the visitor in glancing around, at once realized he is at the residence of one what has made republican simplicity the habit of his life.

You may readily suppose the visit I have attempted to describe advanced us pretty much on to the afternoon and as we desired to return to Edingsville before nightfall we were constrained to take leave of our polite conductor — not, however, before receiving from him a most pressing invitation to sit down with him to "pot luck", a luck, I am sure, we would have found of no mean character, judging from the savory, culinary odors which came from the kitchen to regale our olfactory nerves and tempt our eager appetites but, time and tide wait for no man and we were on our way to Edingsville.

I am conscious, Messrs Editor, the sketch I have attempted has been imperfectly performed. To have noticed with accuracy everything at this well settled and conducted rice plantation would require a year's residence at it, and an entire volume of description. What I have attempted, however, may intimate to the planter how much he may profitably and interestingly meet with by a visit to Jehossee. After passing through some of the best cultivated cotton lands anywhere to be met with in the world, he will be able to see as a contrast a rice plantation which, for extent, excellent management and productiveness, is not surpassed by any other within the State. Let him who is anxious to enjoy such a privilege feel not fear of becoming obtrusive. Mr. ----------- --, the overseer, begs us to say he will always take pleasure in presenting to every gentleman who visits Jehossee, the improvements Mr. Aiken's industry and enterprise have accomplished.

In leaving Jehossee we could not but be struck with the important lesson of political economy Mr. Aiken's example has taught us. His has been the right sort of patriotism. He has not talked of what he could do for Carolina but has done it. He has not as too many have done, boasted of his heart being in the State while all the time his efforts were out of it, but has as in the instance before us, expended hundreds of thousands, to render what was before valueless a source of wealth to himself, and a consequent augmentation of political power to his native State. Such sort of love for one's country needs no pen to emblazon it. It stands as a monument for itself, and its memorial is read in its living benefits."

Visitor

If I had researched for many years I could not have come up with a more descriptive way of describing how things were back in this part of Edisto's history. But sadly Edingsville was destroyed by hurricanes and even though it was profitable at the time Johossee came to an end when man finally came to realize that slavery was wrong. It took a great war to have this inhumanity to man come to an end.

If nothing else we can learn from Jehossee that man can do wondrous things with what is available to him if he just uses his mind and does it within the moral codes handed down to us by God. I am confident that Governor Aiken dreamed dreams and saw visions of what can be and then took things in hand and did what he could. Edisto's history and natural surroundings still amaze me every day. The irony of it all is that nothing stays the same and lasts forever. The only eternal and never ending being is God.

Therefore I believe with the proper education and work experience man can do whatever he can conceive. I say I can build almost anything I can see and understand how it works and be able to measure it. My father would go around with a measuring tape measuring things he saw along the way and then come home and build one for himself. At the present I have a shop full of tools that allow me to do or build just about anything I want to build. On one occasion I was taking my family to Disney World. At that time I wanted to see if I could build a storage shed out of river rocks and concrete. On the way there and back, to pass the time away, I figured out, in my head, how to do it and when we returned I went out in my back yard and built it. But it took a year to build it. I even put a concrete roof on it and built my children a fort on top with a concrete staircase for them to get up into the fort. It came down to, can I lift the rocks and buckets of concrete. As you will hear over and over in this book, you miss life if you do not dream dreams and see visions of how things can be.

Edisto is more than what you see now. The past and future are all wrapped up into a continuing story. Periods of calm will last for awhile and periods of storms will come. These changes have shaped and reshaped this unique island and only God knows what will happen to it in the future. So enjoy what it has to offer today and dream of the past and see visions of the things that might be. It is the dreaming and visions that bring Edisto alive for those who stop for awhile and let it all soak in.

The next time you have a chance to walk on Edisto Beach at the ocean's edge, look out into the ocean and wonder what or who walked on dry land out there when it was dry land. Then wonder how many years have gone by since a camel walked on dry land out there. I know that camels were out there at one time because I found one of their large ribs. Maybe as you read this book you will begin to think like I do about the paradise I have been privileged to experience most of my life. Remember we call it Ed - is — tow. The point of this chapter is that nothing stays the same and that many mysterious things have happened to Edisto over the past many thousands of years. We all seem to mostly think in the present but the past gives us much to think about. One thing that stands out is that man has always been smart and over the centuries he has developed more and more tools for getting things done. Christ predicted this a long time ago. Think on this verse from the Holy Bible.

"Verily, verily, I say unto you, He that believeth on me (Jesus Christ) , that works that I do shall he do also; and greater works than these shall he do; because I go unto my Father".
John 14:12 KJV

CHAPTER FOUR

"Poverty and shame shall be to him that refuseth instruction: but he that regardeth reproof shall be honoured. "
Proverbs 13:18 KJV

The evolution of Edisto Beach from obscurity to a hidden pearl.

This section is about Big Island. Remember that Edisto has three barrier islands facing the Atlantic Ocean. The northern most is Botany Bay Island, the next is Edingsville Beach and at the far southeastern corner is Big Island or what is now called Edisto Beach.

One day while sitting out on the beach writing this book, I was immediately reminded of a couple of incidents that I saw when sitting and swimming in this same spot a while back.

The first was like a dream. While sitting on the beach one day a large group of pelicans gathered off shore in front of where I was sitting and began to soar upward toward the clouds. I had seen sea gulls and buzzards do this many times near where I live but this was different. I figured they would go up a ways and then take off in a glide toward a school of fish so they would not have to fight the wind. They continued up and up until they soon seemed like little spots way up in the air to a point that you really could not tell what kind of birds they were. As I watched in disbelief they seem to funnel into brightly colored clouds and then disappear into who knows where as if they had gone into heaven. This scene still haunts me as if it were a dream of things to come. But this really happened in plain sight. This was the first time I had ever seen such a sight and I have never seen one like it again. I cannot explain why these pelicans did this. I guess they liked soaring so much that they just kept climbing as far as they could on this column of air. Incidents like this stir the mind and makes one realize that everything we see or hear may not immediately have a reason that we can explain. But when we delve into the mysteries of life it makes us realize how small and insignificant we are and that there is a greater power running things that we must learn to respect and lean on for our answers to life.

The second event happened while I was in the surf in front of the Ocean Villa with several of my grandchildren. While out there I happened to look down toward where the South Edisto River flows into the ocean and saw objects jumping out of the water. I thought they were bottlenose dolphins but was not sure because I could not see what was jumping out of the water very clearly. Therefore I kept looking at what was jumping out of the water as they came closer and closer until I could see that they were indeed dolphins. They passed me not more that about 20 feet out in the water and there must have been 50 or more. You would see large dolphins jump out of the Water and little ones would jump right beside them. These must have been mother and child. They continued jumping out of water constantly as they passed by and continued jumping until they went out of sight toward the State Park. I have never seen this many dolphins before then and have never seen this many all jumping out of the water. My only explanation of this event is that when mullet group together in the thousands to spawn, dolphins will come by the hundreds and have a field day eating the mullet. This group may have been headed for such a spawning. The question is, "How do dolphins and other sea creatures know where to go when there is a bountiful harvest to be had?"

The third event happened while I was out in the surf in front of the Ocean Villa. A large five or six foot tarpon jumped completely out of the water right next to me. If I had known it was there and knew it was going to jump this close to me I could have touched him. He was that close. I mention this because up until then I had never seen a tarpon in the Edisto waters. I had only seen them in pictures or on TV.

The last event happened in the same area when I was a teenager. On a very clear evening about 9 or 10 o'clock several kids and I were out on the beach just walking along having a good time when all of a sudden the sky began to have great waves of bright green flashing all over the sky. You would see what looked like a green cloud appearing and then over there you would see another. It did not last too long and we all stood in amazement and looked at each other saying, "Did we just see what we saw?" The next day we read in the newspaper that the northern lights had shown over Charleston for a brief time the night before.

I mention these three events because they remind me of one of the proverbs that tells us to observe what is going on around us and become wise. It tells me that the real winners in this world do what is right without someone telling them what to do. The winners just do the things that will make them a success. These events have no real lessons but I observed them and they made me think about the mysteries going on around us all the time if we just keep our eyes and ears open. If we really listen there is a small voice in us all that alerts us of things about to happen and things to avoid or take advantage of. One day man will discover that we have senses built in us that are at work that are not very obvious. This is why I tell anyone that will listen to dream dreams and see visions of the wonders of this world that many of us miss, going aimlessly to and fro with no real purpose or goal to achieve.

Proverbs 6:6-8 KJV

"Go to the ant, thou sluggard; consider her ways, and be wise; which having no guide, overseers, or ruler, provideth her meat in the summer, and gathereth her food in the harvest."

When Scenic Highway 174 comes to a point where you can only turn left onto a four lane highway after crossing the short causeway over Scott Creek, you will be on Edisto Beach. The entrance to Edisto Beach State Park will be on your left and a convenience store will be on your right. Straight ahead will be the Pavilion Restaurant. Just as you leave the causeway you will pass Jungle Road on your right, which plays a great part in the Edisto Beach experience. As you turn left on the wide four lane highway you will see beach house after beach house up off the ground on pilings. These beach houses will continue as far as you can see down the road. On the left between the houses you can see the Atlantic Ocean inviting you to take off your shoes and come on down to the beach. More than likely you will see a line of pelicans flying in formation up and down the beach. Many times they will be flying close to the tops of all these beach houses. Surprisingly, with all these beach houses, this four lane highway will have very little traffic on it and those driving on it will not be going over 35 miles per hour because that is the speed limit. As you drive down Palmetto Blvd. you will see old beach houses that have been used constantly since the 1930s and large modern beach houses that have been recently built with all the comforts of any high end houses you would find in your home town. You will immediately notice that every time a road goes off to the right a wide beach access will be on your left so that you can stop and walk out to the beach. These accesses are 50 feet wide and some of these accesses have been cleared so you can drive up in them and park while you go out on the beach. There are 34 of these beach accesses down the full length of the beach.

The lack of commercial establishments will be obvious all the way down the beach with only one that sticks out like a sore thumb with its bright red roof. This red roof building is the office of Edisto Realty. About three miles down Palmetto Blvd. the road will turn into a two lane highway and it will continue until you reach the docks and a couple of restaurants. If you continue down this two lane road it will turn into Dock Site Road. A little further down Dock Site Road you will pass the entrance to Wyndham, (Used to be Fairfield Ocean Ridge — before that Oristo) a large gated community with houses, condos and a beautiful golf course. It also has several very nice restaurants.

If you continue down Dock Site Road you are traveling parallel to Big Bay Creek on your left and its vast area of salt water marsh across the creek. On the left you will notice many two or three story narrow houses built on small lots that were supposed to be dock sites. The location and view was so great that people built these tall homes to enjoy it all. On the right past the entrance to Wyndham you will see a beautiful golf course with houses overlooking the golf course and a View of Big Bay Creek and the marsh grass that almost goes out of sight.

About the time you pass the golf course the road will turn into Lybrand Street (named after my father, Harvie S. Lybrand, for all that he contributed to the development of Edisto Beach and what it has become.) A little further up, Jungle Road will go off to the left and will take you back out to Scenic Highway 174. If you continue forward about three blocks you will end up back on Palmetto Blvd. You have just had a tour of Edisto Beach which is about four miles long and one of the favorite vacation destinations of many South Carolinians and others from all over the nation and even the world.

When you go on its beautiful beach you will notice that it is not crowded. Edisto Beach is where family groups have been coming for generations to enjoy each other and the beauty it offers. The offer of exploration, fishing, crabbing and shrimping is endless. Some come just to relax and get away from the busyness of city life. There are no stop lights on Edisto Beach or even Edisto Island. There is no commercial night life. Maybe a little night life can be found at Marion Whaley's old store, turned into a place to eat and hang out. Up where you come into Edisto Beach there is a small shopping strip, a grocery store, a liquor store and a couple of restaurants. But there is nothing to write home about in the way of shopping, etc.

If you are a full time resident or just visiting there are 14 churches on Edisto Island you can attend. There is something going on constantly at these churches. One was established about 325 years ago. There is an active art guild that puts on a Broadway type play once a year. If you want to be busy there is plenty to do. If you want to just enjoy all the natural things Edisto has to offer you can just do that and no one will bother you. The Edisto Island Lions Club puts on a Bingo Game every Tuesday and Thursday evening during the summer. It is so popular that you have to come early to get a seat.

Therefore what many have found over the years is that Edisto is a place to go and relax, meet old friends and just hang out on the beach or on your screen porch, enjoying the sea breeze, dreaming dreams and seeing visions of how this old world should be.

I hope this gives you a hint of what Edisto Beach is all about. Now let me tell you all I can remember about Edisto Beach and how it evolved from a strictly summer vacation retreat to the year round place where people come to visit and stay. Many work all their lives so they can retire on Edisto Beach. I often meet people whose families have been coming to the same beach cabin for several generations. The following is the rest of the story.

Here is how Clara Childs Puckett saw the original development of Edisto Beach in her popular book Edisto — A Sea Island Principality. I personally think she did such a good job that I could not improve on it. I have included a good bit of her description of the beginning development of Edisto Beach.

EDISTO BEACH

"Nothing has been so potent in ending the Edistonians' long-cherished seclusion as the development of Edisto Beach, one of a string of barrier islands which stretch for miles along the Carolina coast and constitute one of the state's most valuable natural assets. It was once called McConkey Beach after a former owner named John McConky, but the name is retained today only in the sign at the entrance to the four-lane boulevard which stretches from the State Park to Bay Point at the south end of the island. For historic reasons there are those who would change the name Palmetto Drive (now Palmetto Blvd.) to McConky Boulevard, but the former seems to be preferred

According to an inscription on McConkey's grave in the Episcopal churchyard, he was 'cruelly murdered,' but the criminal was never identified or caught, and McConky's murder remains one of the unsolved mysteries of the island, about which crime there is speculation even today.

The beach was first developed by a company originally from Sumter, S.C. The project was generously sponsored by Mr. Mitchie Seabrook and Mr. G. Washington Seabrook, late owners of the beach. The development had a slow beginning in the late twenties and growth was retarded by the Depression years of the thirties. Those who built cottages at the beach during these lean years were mostly close, congenial friends, many from Sumter. They all recall rather fondly these times when there was as yet no road, no electricity, no conveniences — only sand dunes, hand pumps, kerosene lamps, and the necessary 'back house.' Friendships were warm and close. Fishing, shrimping and crabbing were excellent. Surf bathing was delightful, and there was much to explore and discover.

So remote was the beach in the 1920s and so deserted its creeks that it is said a ring of rum runners, Prohibition-style, operated out of one of the back bays of the big creek that runs behind the beach. (She is referring to Scott Creek that runs off Big Bay Creek.) All over the island cedar trees were being cut down mysteriously, no one knew why. But those who inquired were told that the trees were being shipped to a 'pencil factory.' It was later learned that the cedar logs were in fact being used to camouflage the illegal liquor traffic and to cover the contraband in the trucks so it could be hauled away undetected.

Strangely enough, fifty years later in 1977 the beach was the scene of a replay of that adventure. Five young men from out of state were apprehended on the beach for smuggling marijuana in a small sailboat from Columbia, South America.

The opening of the State Park in the late thirties caused business to pick up on the island. The State Park system of South Carolina was given land for a park on an undisturbed section of the beach which contained a large stand of very ancient palmettos and live oaks amid tall sand dunes and waving sea oats. Roads, restrooms, and a park bathhouse were constructed by the Civilian Conservation Corp workers, housed in barracks nearby. The park has become a mecca not only for swimmers and fishermen, but has also become known as one of the most outstanding places in the state to bring a camper and spend a holiday week. Photographers are drawn to this semi-tropical paradise and have caught with their cameras some of the finest scenery along the Carolina coast.

The severe tropical storms of 1940 and 1954 caused heavy damage to the park property. Since then new facilities have been added, along with water and electric hook-ups for large, self-contained campers. The area has become popular year round, and there is always a waiting period for reserving space during the warmer seasons."

To fill in some of the gaps left out by Mrs. Puckett, here are some interesting facts. Edisto Beach was laid out into 75 by 150 feet camp sites or lots to build fishing cabins. Not really knowing what they had set in motion, they restricted these lots to single family homes or boarding houses. When laying out the lots on Edisto Beach, the original developers put a fifty foot access to the ocean from Palmetto Blvd. across from where future roads back into the woods would go. This opened up the beach to anyone who lived across the street from the ocean or anyone just visiting. Recently these restrictions have been increased to allow houses to be no more than 2,700 square feet and no higher that 40 feet. As previously mentioned, not long after the beach was laid out the state wanted the northern end for a State Park. Therefore in that time the political way was the "good ole boys" way of doing business. The state offered the developers a four lane highway with sidewalks for the northern end of what was now called Edisto Beach State Park. There was nothing recorded about this deal; it was just done to Edisto Beach's benefit. We now have one of the most sought after state parks and a four lane road called Palmetto Blvd.

For as far back as I can remember and find out McGowan Holmes moved to the beach as its first permanent resident and began selling lots. As time went by many beach houses were built on the beach, many with outdoor facilities. I still meet people whose grandfathers built one of the first houses on Edisto Beach in the 1930s.

In 1940 there was a storm that took away the front beach homes down to about the sixth block and destroyed most of the poorly built houses. It seems that when the surge hit the beach, it leveled out and did not destroy as many of the second row houses as you go off the beach, Where the sidewalk on the beach side of the road ends, up to where Scenic Highway

174 comes onto the beach, everything was destroyed. When we started coming to Edisto Beach to spend the summers in 1942 there was a house still standing out in ocean near where Hwy. 174 comes onto the beach. We spent the summers on the beach from 1942 until 1947 and then moved to the beach full time that fall. We were the second full time family to live on the beach full time.

Up until about the early fifties Edisto Beach was full of life from June first until September first. The other part of the year you could ride down Palmetto Blvd. and think you were in a ghost town. At night it was right scary. A place that was once full of life and people going to and fro now looked as if people had just left in a hurry and were never coming back. Then when school was out a wave of people came to the beach to reclaim it. They dropped their guard and immediately started enjoying all that God's little paradise could provide.

Edisto Beach has now gotten on the map in a big way and has become one of the most popular vacation spots on the East Coast that many can still afford.

George and Ed caused the current popularity of Edisto Beach.

Remember these names because if it were not for these two guys, Edisto would not have gotten off the ground as soon as it did. It would have stayed a forgotten family beach where a few families came to spend the summer. Here is how it happened. In the early 1940s we lived in Aiken, SC. My father, Harvie S. Lybrand, traveled, selling school books all over South Carolina. He left home on Monday mornings and came back Thursday evenings. I heard him say many times, "I just had to make one more call before I headed home." I had an older brother that from my earliest recollection caused trouble and never did anything he was supposed to do. He was a constant thorn in my family's side because he always had my parents upset, particularly my mother. While Daddy was off selling books, Mother's brothers, George and Ed, constantly came over to our house in Aiken trying to beat up on my brother to make him behave. We also had my mother's mother living with us and I cannot remember her ever having a kind word to say to me. Mother also had two small children, David and me. As a result Mother had a mental breakdown and I can still remember her crying for hours at a time. She ended up having to have shock treatment to bring her back to reality. With all this going on, my father decided to get out of Dodge. He was calling on schools down in the lower part of Charleston County and saw the sign that said "Edisto Beach" he decided to go see what it looked like. He found a beach cabin that he could buy for $4,000.00. He bought it and we spent the summers on Edisto Beach for the next six years to get Mother away from her brothers and all the trouble she was having in Aiken. I don't remember what happened to my grandmother.

One contributing factor was that I was sickly with serious sinus problems and remember not breathing through my nose until I was six years old. The move to Edisto Beach was then to accomplish two things. First, the move to Edisto Beach for the summer would get Mother away from the relatives. Secondly, Daddy had heard that the salt air would help my sinus problems.

As I remember the past, keep in mind that this is being written by a 75 year old and I am having a hard time putting things in the order that they actually occurred.

The beach cabin Daddy bought was up on pilings about eight feet off the ground. It has a small front porch which was in the center of the house and covered about one half of the front of the house. It had a living room with a fireplace and a dining room. It had one bedroom, small back porch and a small kitchen. The kitchen had a sink attached to the wall and a free standing cabinet for dishes. There was an ice box that you had to put blocks of ice in it to keep things cold. There was a smelly kerosene stove to cook on. It had one bath with a tub with feet, a commode, and a sink attached to the wall. The floor was wood flooring like the rest of the house. There was a small back porch or sort of a room. I don't remember where we all slept. But I do remember that Daddy constantly added to it to make it more livable.

To get running water in the house there was a hand pump outside that you used to pump water up to a barrel on top of the house. We all had to take a turn pumping water up to the barrel. Being five years old, I did not do much pumping. The biggest problem we seemed to have immediately was on a still night the mosquitoes just about ate us up. As long as there was a breeze, which there was most of the time, we were okay. But when it got still then all hell broke loose. I can remember Daddy getting busy screening the porch and the other windows. But it seemed that he had to try several types of screen wire as they kept falling out because of the salt air. After many tries he found that copper screen wire was the only kind of screen that would last over a couple of months. As soon as Daddy was able, he installed an electric pump for us to have running water.

Rabbit Trail: One winter after we had gone back to Aiken for the school

year, Daddy was down in the Charleston area calling on schools and decided

to spend the night in our beach house instead of staying in a hotel. When he got to the house and tried to wash-up he found that the pump had lost its prime. There was no water in the house or in the pump house to prime the pump. It was dark as it could be and there was no moonlight. Everything was still and spooky. His only choice was to take a bottle down to the ocean and get some water to prime the pump. He got up enough courage to go down to the ocean and got enough water to prime the pump. It was not as easy as he thought because when a wave came it was not deep enough to fill a bottle. He had to take his shoes off, roll his pants up and walk out in the water to get enough to fill his bottle. Then he had to come back, sit on the beach and put his shoes back on. With all this going on he forgot to be scared and was able to go back and prime the pump. This illustrates how deserted and dark

Edisto Beach was in the winters between 1942 and 1947 when we moved permanently to Edisto Beach. Back to ----- --

When I look at the way we light our houses today, I think back to my summers on Edisto and remember that all we had to light our rooms was a light bulb hanging from the ceiling by a single wire with a pull chain to cut it on and off. I was amazed when a man came and put in switches on the wall so you could cut these lights on and off. After awhile we got an electric ice box and a gas stove top for Mother to cook on. During the first summers we lived on the beach a man came up and down the beach selling blocks of ice for our ice boxes. When I think of where we keep the things that need to be kept cold I still think of it as an "Ice Box."

Recently one of my grandchildren told my wife that she did not know how we got along without cell phones and electronic games all the children now have. We had no TV and no telephone. We had a radio and I used to love to hear stories about the Lone Ranger and Roy Rogers on the radio. I loved to listen to stories on the radio and could imagine what they were doing by painting pictures in my mind of just what they were doing and how they were doing it. Today my mind can imagine things that I can do to make life a little better and I can build almost anything I can measure. Life is much fuller when we can dream dreams and see visions of what can be.

As stated, there was an ice man that came by selling ice for the ice box. There was also a man that came by selling vegetables and another selling shrimp and fish. I remember Mother getting much of what we ate from these men that came by selling things from door to door. There were three stores on the island off the beach that we often visited. The first and most important was Perry's Store. You went there and told Mr. Perry what you wanted and he went and got it. He had canned food, meat, clothing and just about anything you wanted. His store was what used to be called a general merchandise store. Up until fairly recently these kinds of stores were what people depended on for the goods they needed.

If you looked for it in Mr. Perry's store you probably could not find it but Mr. Perry knew where everything was located. It seemed that my family purchased most of our supplies from Perry's Store.

Rabbit Trail: I remember the first self-service store I was ever in. It was a Piggly Wiggly store in Charleston, SC (probably in the 1940s). I was amazed that you could go up and down the aisles and pick out what you wanted and put them in a cart and then take them to a check out station. It is interesting how things have evolved in such a short period of time. In my father's time he saw the first car, the first airplane and many other things that were unimaginable not long ago. He once told me that people believed that if you went 60 miles per hour you could not breathe. Back to ------ --

There was the ice house and the Edistonian where we bought ice and other supplies. The thing I remember about the ice house is that the ice came to the ice house in great big blocks. When you went to order ice you asked for an eighth of a block of ice, etc. People would complain to Mrs. Flowers who ran the ice house about what she considered an eighth because the blocks of ice would melt over time and if you asked for an eighth you got an eighth of what was left after the ice block had melted some. If you wanted crushed ice there was a machine that she put the ice you ordered in and it came out crushed for iced tea or whatever you wanted. Of course the block of the ice had to be just the right size for our ice box. For many years refrigerators were called ice boxes in our family.

Mr. Hunter sold gasoline. I remember going to his store and Daddy asking for ten gallons of gas. He would go to his pump and hand pump ten gallons up into this glass holding tank and then open a valve and all the gas he had pumped up to the glass tank would go down though a hose and into our car. Mr. Hunter had a few supplies but we bought most things we needed at Perry's Store.

Since Daddy still traveled selling school books he would leave Mother and us three boys on the beach and go off selling books. Our routine was to eat breakfast and then go out on the beach until about lunch time. We would then come in and eat lunch and rest. We would go back out on the beach for a while in the afternoon. This was all Mother had to do and it seemed to calm her down and things went along well. At least these times seemed to be happy and peaceful times in my life from ages five until ten years old. During this carefree time I learned to swim and began learning many things about my paradise that I still remember to this day. It is strange how I can remember what I did back then as a child but at 75 I cannot remember what I did yesterday. This is why I am hurrying to get all this down for my grandchildren before I stop even remembering what I did way back then.

Care free day on the beach

I learned to swim early by walking out into the surf on my hands until the water got to deep enough for my hands not to touch the bottom. Then I would start dog paddling and kicking my feet until I was swimming. As time went by I became a strong swimmer, using several strokes to get where I wanted to go.

During our summers on the beach the Second World War was going on. At night we had to cut off all lights. During the day there were boats constantly dragging targets up and down the ocean right off the beach and airplanes firing at them. Airplanes would fly over our house and when they got over the water they would fire at the targets being pulled by the boats. I often felt sorry for the men running the boats that were pulling the targets because I was worried if the airplanes would miss the target and hit the boat. A few times the pilots would misjudge the distances and fire too soon. The spent shell would come raining down on our house.

As I have already mentioned Botany Bay Island and Otter Island were also use as bombing ranges.

There were soldiers riding horses up and down the beach all the time, night and day. They kept the horses in a corral up in the State Park area. I went to see all these horses from time to time. Down the beach just before the road goes into two lanes there is a road on the left that goes around in a circle with a few houses. In that circle there was a tall lookout tower crudely made out of pine trees where the soldiers would climb up and survey the sound and the entrance of the South Edisto River. I remember hearing about small subs coming up in our inlets but I never actually saw any. Along the beach there was some sort of telephone system that the soldiers used. From time to time the high tides would wash up the wires they had buried to work these telephones. Many years after the war there were wires still being washed up that were used by these soldiers that patrolled Edisto Beach during the Second World War. For many years you could find spent bullets and their shell casing washed up on the beach. For some strange reason the war and all its goings on did not seem to affect the way we lived and did not cause us any hardships. I remember liking to sit on the front porch in the dark before we went to bed just listening to the ocean and all the night sounds in the woods behind us and the sounds that came from the ocean. For some strange reason the waves seem to make more noise at low tide, especially at night. Both the ocean and the woods behind our house seemed to come alive after dark.

From time to time we went walking on the beach at night and occasionally you would see what seemed to be a small light shining in the moonlight. A closer look would reveal a piece of dead shrimp or some small sea creature.

Every year on September first we packed up and headed back to Aiken to go to school. The beach was also clearing out and by the time we were set to leave the beach would be like a ghost town, with only Mr. and Mrs. Holmes left to hold the fort down.

When we got to back to Aiken and moved back into our house on Park Avenue the first thing I remember was that the water tasted funny. Each year going back and forth from Aiken to Edisto I had to get used to the water in both places. For many years individual houses on Edisto Beach had their own pump and pumped up surface water. Back then it was easy to get drinking water. All you had to do was hammer down a strainer point down about 6 feet into the soil, attach a pump and start pumping.

Things did not get better in Aiken so Daddy decided to get out of Dodge permanently. After we returned to Aiken in the fall of 1947 we packed up and moved back to Edisto. This move was the beginning of how Edisto Beach really got off the ground and became the popular beach it is now. If it were not for Mother's brothers, George and Ed, our family would probably still be in Aiken, SC.

On the weekend and when he had time, Daddy built us boys a room behind the existing bedroom and it seems that he was constantly adding to our old beach house.

Here is the main driving force that changed Edisto Beach from a sleepy summer village to the popular place it is today. Shortly after we moved to Edisto Beach permanently, the whole family was sitting on the front steps. A couple came by in their car and stopped when they saw us. They asked where they could find a place to eat on Edisto Beach. Daddy told them Jacksonboro, SC. Jacksonboro is on Highway 17 just past where it crosses the Edisto River or about 20 miles from Edisto Beach. The couple then asked where you spend the night and Daddy told them Jacksonboro. When they drove off Daddy looked at my mother and said, "Jennie, you have always wanted to open a tea room. Now is your chance." Mother jumped on the idea and the Ocean Villa was born. Daddy then extended the front porch to cover the whole front of the house and made enough tables to cover each side of the front porch so they could serve a good many people. He also enclosed the front porch with windows that would open and let the breeze in and keep the rain out during a downpour. He put a sign out front hanging from an old palmetto log that called the new business the Ocean Vfl. They started serving meals and since it was the only game in town they became busy immediately. They stayed open from June first to September first.

In the meantime Daddy hired some men to enclose the underneath part of the house. They made a small apartment on one side and about five rooms on the other side and began renting rooms. When he was doing this he put a staircase from under the house on the left facing the house to our upstairs rooms.

Rabbit Trail: The space under the house where Daddy was going to put the rooms had the bottom of the upstairs floor joists too low to get the needed height. Therefore he had to dig out under the house about a foot or so to get enough clearing to have a normal ceiling height. He then poured a concrete slab and put in the walls for each room. The commodes had to be raised about eight inches off the floor so that there was enough elevation for them to flow into the septic tank. From what I remember Daddy mixed his own concrete using cement and beach sand that was readily available. The hard part was putting boards on the wall and ceiling. The inside was made of small tongue and grove boards called headboard. I watched as the carpenters used very sharp hand saws to cut each board while a couple of others nailed them in place. The sides and ceiling of each room was made this way. This took a long time and must have been before the advent of sheet rock. Back to

This old photograph shows what our house looked like after Daddy had expanded the front porch and enclosed the area under the house to make rooms he could rent out.

Mother did most of the cooking and got her recipes from the old black families on the island. The deviled crab had crab meat in it and her shrimp creole had plenty of shrimp in it, etc. She hired a young lady who was about 18 years old to help her in the kitchen. Her name was Janie Parker. Daddy soon built her a small house behind our house where she lived with us until she got married. She also became my second mother and to this day my brother and I watch after her. She is now retired and in her eighties. I call her my mother and constantly keep in touch with her to make sure she is okay. She also calls David and me her children. The business grew and they needed more room.

Until the business was large enough to support the family, Daddy traveled the whole state selling books. Therefore he knew all the principals in the whole state by first name. He told them about the Ocean Villa and many began to come spend their vacations with us. These school officials and others who began to hear about Edisto Beach started it growing at a rapid pace.

If I have not already told you, we had no address other than Harvie S. Lybrand, Edisto Beach, SC. No ZIP, just Edisto Beach, SC. If you want to View the original Ocean Villa it is located at 1207 Palmetto Blvd. It is across the street from the current Ocean Villa apartments. When you see this old house you will recognize it by the fact that every inch under the house is enclosed. When Daddy retired he turned the Villa into apartments.

Around 1950 the Novits owned a large house across the street from us that had 12 bedrooms. It was a beautiful building. It was a two story building. The second story had six bedrooms. There were three bedrooms on each side. These bedrooms opened onto a balcony that overlooked the wide open downstairs lobby. All the walls were made of knotty pine, which gave it an elegant look. Each bedroom had a louvered half door to let in the breezes. This elegant building was one you'd expect to see in a picture book. There was a grand picture of a clipper ship on one of the walls, which is hanging in my den at the present. When Daddy sold the Villa I asked for and got this picture which was always one of my favorites. This lobby and beautiful front porch was the only place on Edisto at the time that would hold a large group and was often used for wedding receptions and other large group meetings. I have included a picture of me at about 12 years of age with a suit on, all dressed up at one of these receptions. (I am a little out of order here — keep going with me and it will all come out and make sense down the road.)

Mr. Novit owned a clothing store in Walterboro, SC and while his family and many of his relatives stayed full time at the beach during the summer, he stayed in town running his store. One time he bought 20 steaks and brought them down to Edisto for his family. He came back a few days later and asked his wife to cook him one for supper. She shyly told him that his relatives had already eaten them all.

Shortly after that Daddy approached him and asked if he would sell his place to him so he could expand the Ocean Villa. Mr. Novit jumped at the offer and struck a deal with my father. I think I am right in that Daddy paid $25,000.00 for this large house on the front beach. Daddy used the larger house for a few years, renting the rooms out. A few years later during the winter Daddy got one of his nephews, Kenny, a skilled carpenter who lived in the Aiken area, to come down and help him build a dining room off the back of the Novit house. When he went to the lumber yard to get the lumber the owner of the lumber yard had just cut a lumber yard full cypress trees and offered to cut all the lumber he needed out of cypress. That was great for the coastal air, which rots anything that is not protected in a hurry. Of course Daddy jumped at the idea and got all the lumber he needed out of cypress.

He and Kenny built a large dining room and began using it the next season. Therefore instead of having five rooms to rent, now he had 17 rooms to rent and his business grew.

I can remember that Daddy would rent you a room on the beach and Mother would feed you three very good meals for $7.00 a day or $45.00 if you stayed all week. Over the years the same people would come back year after year to spend their vacations at the Villa. People would dress when they came into the dining room to eat. One day this family checked in during the evening and the next morning after breakfast they put on their bathing suits and went out on the beach. When they came back in for lunch one of the little boys was heard to say where everyone could hear him, "People surely look better with clothes on!"

Afterwards many of those who came back over and over again bought or built houses of their own on Edisto Beach. Therefore if it had not been for George and Ed giving Daddy such a hard time, all this would not have happened. Maybe someone else would have done it but Harvie Lybrand is the one who took a chance and got Edisto off the ground and running. I can clearly remember that I heard him say, "This place is going to go one of these days." Therefore after this he began buying everything he could get his hands on.

The next few pictures are of the Ocean Villa. Of course I had to include one of me because this book is about me and what I remember about Edisto.

This is the road side view of the Ocean Villa before the dining room was added.

In the meantime, there were two houses next to the Villa that came on the market for $4,000.00. He purchased them. They were on one lot and built out of salvaged lumber from the old Morris Island Lighthouse caretaker's house. It was torn down when the sea started washing Morris

The ocean side of the Ocean Villa

Island. When you looked up under the houses you could see the places where holes were chiseled out to fit and peg the old beams together. He turned the one nearest the Villa into five more rooms to rent, now giving him now 22 rooms to rent. The other house he turned into a rental.

Rabbit Trail: One afternoon Daddy rented two of these rooms in the house next to the Villa to five college kids. During the night Daddy was awakened by the noise these kids were making. They were fighting and it seemed like they were tearing the house apart. He went over and asked them to go to bed. He noticed that there were holes in the sheetrock and

Lobby looking out toward the ocean. Note the balcony and heart pine paneling.

blood on several mattresses and that all five rooms were damaged. The guys threatened to beat him up. I heard him tell someone later that he thought he could take them but decided not to hurt them and just try to get them to settle down and go to sleep. The next morning real early before they got up Daddy called the local police and had him come over and hold these five guys until he could call a contractor. The contractor came over and estimated it would take $5,000.00 to repair the damage they had done. The police found out that they had two late model cars and were from prominent upstate textile families. Therefore they held one car and sent these guys home to get $5,000.00 to repair the damage before they would release the car back to them. During this time there were two CEOs in charge of large textile factories in the upstate staying at the Villa. They asked for these five guys' names and addresses and told Daddy that none of them would ever work in one of their mills. Back to

Lobby facing the street with steps going up to upstairs balcony rooms.

In the fifties Daddy also bought the house on the left side of the Villa facing the ocean and bought the house to the left of the house we lived in. He rented out these houses also. He would buy anything anyone wanted to sell at a price he thought was fair or a little less than market value. As far as I know, he never took advantage of anyone. He just looked for good deals and bought them.

Up the street from us was a tavern that he bought for $13,000.00 and turned into apartments. By this time the Villa and his rentals were bring in enough that he quit selling books and concentrated on all the property he had acquired. In the winter during this time he built two houses to rent and bought another up the beach from us. He also bought several, if not many, vacant lots. By this time it is estimated that he owned more property than anyone else on the beach.

Front porch overlooking the ocean.

Inside of the dining room. Daddy built the dining room and all the tables.

The original Ocean Villa

(Above) Ocean Villa with dining room.
(Right) Janie Parker – head cook.

Me at a wedding reception. Ocean Villa was the only available place on Edisto at the time that was large enough for a formal event.

The following are some pictures of houses or properties he owned.

This building below was originally a tavern. I personally went into it as a teenager. As you first entered into it there was an open dance floor. Further back was a counter where they served drinks and food items and a few other items. Daddy bought it for around $12,000.00 and turned it into apartments.

As I have mentioned before, every lot on Edisto Beach is restricted to a private home or a boarding house. Riding down Palmetto Blvd. you will notice that this is the only business on it. When they developed the beach they left this lot unrestricted — thus it has been a tavern, an apartment building, and now a real estate office.

When Daddy retired my brother David bought it from him and turned it into the Edisto Realty place of business. This is how it looks today.

These are the two houses Daddy bought next to the Ocean Villa on the right facing the ocean. This is a roadside view. These two houses have been removed from the lot. One was made into Kapp Lyons Real Estate office building and the other was taken over to Big Island off Sand Creek.

This is the house he bought next to» the house we lived in on the left facing the road. It was called the red house. He also bought the house across the street on the left side of the Ocean Villa. Both of these houses have been torn down and new ones built in their place. Daddy also owned another house down Palmetto Blvd. and built two others. If I am not mistaken, Daddy owned 10 buildings and many lots on Edisto Beach when he retired. He sold them all except the house he lived in and traveled the world.

Here are a few points of interest that may seem a bit unique. Early each summer Daddy would go up on the Island and get two or three runt pigs from J.G. Murray. He put them in a pen behind our house, fed them on kitchen scraps, and at the end of the summer they would weigh about 400 pounds. That fall he would take them to auction and sell them. Many times, when a sow has piglets, one or two will be runts because they are too small to get a fair share of sow's milk. Most farmers would just do away with these runts. Therefore Daddy could get these runts free. What a deal, free piglets and free scraps turned into cash in a few months.

Mother had a garden in the winter that came about by turning beach sand into black dirt. She would grind up palmetto fronds and put the mulch into her garden so the sand would hold moisture. She also had a compost heap and put kitchen scraps in it and put this back into her garden. The young yard boy who helped her called her process, "Slopping the garden." She grew beautiful flowers in the off season and rooted oleanders in gallon cans that came from the Ocean Villa. Many of the oleanders now growing on Edisto Beach were originally rooted by her. Mother became so famous with her gardening ability that she and the gardener at the William Seabrook Plantation became good friends and swapped plants and ideas.

The first telephones on Edisto were crank type with the boxes on the wall. When you wanted to make a call you turned the crank on the side of the phone to get the operator. Originally there were only four phones on the Island and we had the only one on the beach. I am not sure who had the others. When you got a call you knew it by so many rings. Often you could hear people listening in on your calls. If someone wanted to get in touch with someone on the beach they had to call us and we would deliver the message that someone was to call operator so and so and then that operator would put them in touch with whoever was calling. I got a dollar for delivering a message.

Shortly after we moved to Edisto my mother's mother died. The local policeman was called and given the message to deliver to us. He was also a farmer and was busy with his crops and did not deliver the message until two days later. Mother just about missed the funeral because of the delay in getting the message and never really forgave that policeman for not promptly delivering the message.

One time during the winter Daddy kept hearing big trucks coming on the beach late at night and leaving before first light. After hearing the trucks for several nights he called the local police and they found that a large liquor still was being operated near the big sand dunes and the trucks were picking up the liquor (moonshine as the locals called it) each night. Of course this was stopped and the people running it were arrested. The point of this is that Edisto Beach was so deserted in the winter that the people operating the liquor still thought no one would notice the trucks coming and going at night.

During the summer Mother fed the lifeguards that worked at the State Park. They came to the Villa for their meals. Mother had worked out some kind of deal with the state to feed them. During the early fifties there were several full time lifeguards at the State Park. Besides doing lifeguard duty they would show movies out in front of the old bath house that the CCC (Civilian Conservation Corp) built during the depression. I attended several of these showings. People would sit on the ground and watch a movie screen set up out on the grass in front of the bath house. There must have been 50 to 100 people that came to these movies. Back then you took advantage of any entertainment that came along. In the State Park there were large sand dunes with picnic sheds made of massive beams that were also built by the CCC where we often had church outings. I am not sure how many are left but the CCC built many useful structures during the depression and many were still standing in the fifties.

During the summer the gathering place for all the teenagers and young adults was the bowling alley. It was the only place that young people could meet. It was located on the first lot where Scenic Highway 174 met and turned into Palmetto Blvd. It was across the street from the ocean. It had two kinds of bowling alleys, a dance floor with juke box, a soda fountain and a short order cook. What it was primarily used for was for young people to meet. I spent many hours at the bowling alley as a teenager. Many times I would walk from our house to the bowling alley which was a distance of a mile and seven tenths.

The above photo is the only old picture I had of the Bowling Alley. This picture was taken from an old fishing pier that used to be across the road from it. I watched as a northeaster tore this fishing pier down one stormy day.

At age 13 Mother had me waiting on tables at the Villa. The Villa served three meals. Breakfast was served from 7AM to 9AM. Lunch was served from 12 Noon to two PM. Dinner was served from 6PM until 8PM. After I had cleaned up I was free to do whatever I wanted to do, just so I was back to set up for the next meal. I can remember at a very early age waiting on 65 people one Sunday at lunch. The average tip was a quarter. During the whole summer I would make about $300.00. Once Senator Strom Thurmond (he may have been governor at the time) ate with us with his first very pretty wife. I waited on him and his wife and he did not tip me. I never really forgave him for that. The Senator and my father were friends and grew up together in Aiken and Edgefield County which are next to each other. Thurmond later would play a great part in helping the Town of Edisto Beach get their first volunteer fire department started.

When we moved to Edisto in 1947 we joined the Presbyterian Church which I will talk about in great length later. Before we came to Edisto Daddy was Methodist and Mother was Baptist. Since there was neither a

Baptist nor Methodist church on Edisto at the time, Daddy told everyone that we strayed into the Presbyterian Church. During the summers Daddy started having church services on our front porch so he would not have to get formally dressed to go to church.

When we moved to Edisto Beach there was no Lions Club. Therefore around 1951 Daddy organized a new Lions Club on Edisto Beach. In Aiken he was District Governor and he wanted to continue in the Lions Club organization and all it does for the local community it serves. Currently this same club has Bingo each summer to a full house. I am a currently a member of this club.

Rabbit Trail: When I got out of the service my first job was in Orangeburg, SC. Soon after I settled down, Daddy came to Orangeburg and signed me up in the local Lions Club. Not long after that, Orangeburg needed a polio drive and no one would step up. Therefore the Orangeburg Lions Club bought enough vaccine to vaccinate the whole county and offered it free to everyone.

They did ask for donations but did not require anyone to pay a fee to receive the polio vaccination. After we had finished vaccinating everyone and paid all the bills, we were surprised that we had $5,000.00 left. This club did not keep any significant money and met in a local restaurant. Therefore the club looked around town to see what they could do with this $5,000.00. The club found that Orangeburg County Hospital had old baby incubators and bought two of the best on the market which were placed in the hospital.

Guess whose baby used it first? My third child was born prematurely and was put in one of these incubators for about two weeks because of his small size. He is now 6' 2" and the purchasing agent for a large saltwater boat manufacturing company in Summerville, SC. Therefore the Edisto Lions

Club indirectly saved my son's life. Or at least Harvie Lybrand had his hand in it by signing me up in the Lions Club. Back to ---- --

For what it is worth Daddy became a Ruling Elder in the Presbyterian Church on Edisto and served for approximately 30 years. One Sunday, after Daddy had been an elder for about 30 years, a preacher from Johns Island came over to preach while our preacher was gone. He was introduced to Daddy. The Johns Island preacher commented that it was nice for newcomers, referring to Daddy, to help out. Since we lived on the beach the island people considered us "Beach People" and never really considered us locals, even after 30 years and the fact that Daddy had doubled the value of their land by helping to develop Edisto Beach and thus brought along the Island values.

Besides buying everything he could get his hands on, he owned one tenth of the second Beach Company which he and several other men bought from the first Beach Company that originally developed the beach.

Not long after we moved to Edisto, Marion Whaley built and started South Point Services, a general merchandise store, back off Palmetto Blvd. where the road makes a sharp turn to the right. Over the years he played a significant part in my Edisto experience.

You sometimes ask what makes one man successful and another fail. Daddy was successful because people began to find out that any time of night or day they arrived on Edisto Beach he would rent them a room. Many times I heard people knocking on Daddy's door at 2AM. Daddy would get up and give them a key and tell them he'd settle up with them in the morning.

As time went by other people began to live on Edisto Beach full time. Not long after we moved to Edisto the Fontaines moved their shrimping business from Bennetts Point to Big Bay Creek on Edisto Beach. Others began to come along.

Up until 1954 I had the 500 acres behind our house to myself. I will talk about the wonderful experiences I had in these woods later. One day in 1954 I heard some hunters coming through the woods with dogs. At this time I had about 12 steel traps set. I said to myself that I was going to catch a dog. Sure enough I did. I knew then that civilization had come to my paradise. About this same time the Beach Company sold Sam Fox all the undeveloped land from where Scenic Highway 174 comes into Palmetto Blvd. down to what is now Lybrand Street. He developed what is now called Jungle Shores and started selling lots. From what I remember, Sam Fox paid the Beach Company $35,000.00 for all this land. I understand that the main reason the Beach Company sold this land to Sam Fox was because they wanted another road off the beach in case a bad storm cut Palmetto Blvd. in half and they could not get off the beach.

Here is how Jungle Road got its name. Before the land was developed, there was an old sandy logging road that went from the corner I just talked about down to about where Lybrand Street is. The teenage boys would take their girl friends down this road and get stuck in the sand. They would then show off by getting their cars out of the sand. The teenagers called this old logging road Jungle Road. Therefore Sam Fox heard about this and kept the name. It might have been because he had two teenage daughters at this time and they probably told him the name this old road was called. I knew his daughters and remember them because they used to ride around in a Cadillac convertible.

When Sam Fox bought and developed the large tract that took in all the land from behind the row of houses on the left side of Palmetto Blvd. back to the marsh and from Scenic Highway 174 to Lybrand Street, this gave Edisto Beach many more places to build beach houses. Providing affordable lots not far from the beach is the second reason Edisto got off the ground. In most cases there is only a block from Jungle Road to the beach because this part of the beach island is narrow.

As you have already come to understand, we had two beach seasons. One ran between when school let out and ended when school started up again. The second season was when 99% of the people that were on Edisto Beach during the summer left and did not return until school was out. During the winter when things were not so hectic, my father often talked to me about how things were. There are three things that he told me over and over again and I still apply them in my current daily life. The first thing that Daddy told me many times was that there was a power available to us and if we did not use it we would miss about a third of our lives. He was talking about the Holy Spirit that God sent to be our Comforter and to guide us in our daily lives. He told me to be constantly in tune with this gift from God. I actually never heard him curse; he took us to church every Sunday and he was always nice to other people. The second thing he told me over and over again when he told me to do anything was to do a good job. We heated the house with oak logs we cut out of the woods. We used the chips to start the fires. When he said pick up the chips he meant all of them even if there were three baskets full. On every job he assigned me he wanted the best and most complete job I could do. The third thing he told me over and over again was about how to use your mental abilities. He told me that if I wanted to do anything just tell your brain what you wanted to do and it would start helping you and showing you ways of doing what you wanted to do. Today it still surprises me how much I know how to do and how I can figure out anything I want to do. When I look back at all he accomplished during his lifetime I now understand how he went about accomplishing all these things.

Because of the Ocean Villa and all the school officials he had told about Edisto, it began to take off and began the climb to where it is today. When I look back at all that happened on Edisto Beach and the way it is the popular place it is now, I think of four reasons. The first is the Ocean Villa and how Daddy had told all the school people about it and how many came. The second reason is selling Sam Fox Jungle Shores and all the building lots it added to the beach. The third reason is organizing Edisto Beach as a town and the fourth is the building of Oristo which is now called Wyndham. I'll tell you a little about these last two now.

Daddy closed the Villa in the late nineteen sixties and turned it into six or seven apartments and began just renting the houses he owned. During the nineteen seventies, Daddy saw the need for some sort of organized government on Edisto Beach. He therefore got a group together and incorporated Edisto Beach into a town. He became the first mayor and served for two terms. I heard him say that after a while people started fussing at him about the garbage pick up. He thought to himself that there was something wrong with this because they were not paying him anything for being mayor and they were fussing at him. Therefore he served his two terms and told them that he had organized it and now they could run it.

During this time Charleston County, which Edisto Beach was a part of, was taxing them and providing Edisto Beach with very little service for the tax money they were providing to the county. At that time there were no Charleston politicians that owned property on Edisto Beach. But there were several Walterboro or Colleton County politicians that owned property on Edisto Beach. Therefore it seemed to Daddy that they would be better off being in Colleton County. Therefore Daddy read up on how you move a county line and called an election to move the county line for Edisto Beach from Charleston County to Colleton County. Charleston County Council got wind of what was going on and asked Daddy to come see them. Daddy told them that they should come see him. Believe it or not, the state's most powerful county's County Council came to his front porch. Nothing came of this meeting as far as I can find out. I understand that all the property owners were contacted and asked how they would vote if they could vote. The majority said they agreed that it would be to Edisto Beach's advantage to be in Colleton County. The election was held and what I understand is that there were approximately 75 registered voters. Fifty voted for and 12 against and approximately 12 were challenged as not permanent voters. Therefore the vote to move the county line was for the move. Now the Colleton County line goes down the Edisto River and when it gets to Edisto Beach it jumps across the river and takes in Edisto Beach. Therefore Edisto Beach and a small part of Edisto Island are in Colleton County and the rest of Edisto Island is still in Charleston County.

As the town got started a couple of houses burned and there was no fire department to help put out these fires. Daddy then contacted Senator Strom Thurmond and Senator Ernest Hollings, our state senators at the time, and the representative for Edisto Beach and told them that he knew that the state kept used fire fighting equipment in reserve and what was the possibility of getting enough equipment to start a volunteer fire department for the new Town of Edisto Beach. He did not hear from the representative. Hollings told him that he could not help him. In about 10 days he got a call from Strom Thurmond's office asking what the problem was. He told the man from Thurmond's office his situation and within six weeks of his letters he had enough equipment to start a volunteer fire department. I am told that Daddy went to Columbia, SC and drove the fire engine back to Edisto Beach. Strom Thurmond got the town of Edisto Beach a large used tanker fire truck and enough hose to start a volunteer fire department. I understand that all this equipment was given free to the Town of Edisto Beach.

About the time the new town of Edisto Beach was being formed my brother David bought out the remaining property owned by the second beach company and began developing the remaining part of the woods into Oristo, a gated community with a very nice golf course. We both graduated from The Citadel in Charleston, SC. I graduated in 1955 and he four year later. I received ad degree in Business Administration and he received a degree in Civil Engineering. Therefore there was no opportunity for me to make a living on Edisto after I got out of the service but David used his engineering to develop the Edisto property. When the project was finished it received raving reviews for the excellent golf course. By this time I was in real estate full time and began helping him sell lots for people to build on. We could sell the lots easily but we could not finance them because it was during the Carter Administration and the interest rates were 18%. Because of this David lost Oristo but did not lose all the property he bought from the Beach Company. Oristo changed hands several times and was finally purchased by a sound company that has made the present golf course into a show place.

Of course this gated community has played an important part in the development and popularity of Edisto Beach.

David learned much from developing Oristo and then developed the Neck and Middleton Subdivisions up on the main part of Edisto Island which was successful ventures.

Other than the first group that bought and developed Big Island the four things that I think put Edisto Beach on the map were the Ocean Villa, Sam Fox's development of Jungle Shores, the Incorporation of Edisto Beach into a town and finally the building or Oristo, the original name of the current gated community. Of course Marion Whaley, Paul Atwood, the Fontaines, the Collins and many others played a part also. But this book is about the Lybrands. Someone else needs to fill in their part.

When Daddy traveled he used to take some of the school people he was doing business with to play Golf. But when we moved to Edisto and he stopped selling books because the Ocean Villa grew large enough to support the family there was no golf course close by. When David developed Oristo Daddy was in hog heaven. Sometimes I'd come home from Columbia, SC where I settled in 1970 and began selling real estate and find him in the back yard practicing golf. Mr. Unger, a few lots down, complained that Daddy kept hitting balls into his yard.

One of the high lights of Oristo to Daddy was that David bought a red golf cart for him to use anytime he wanted. The rest of the golf carts were green. Therefore Daddy was Mr. Lybrand and his cart stood out like a sour thumb.

As time went by Daddy finally sold all the property he owned and put the money in tax free bonds and began traveling all over the world. When I think about all the property Daddy owned I used to think about how he was going to pay for all the property he had bought. A streak of luck came when the family owned company Daddy worked for wanted to sell out to a national company. To do this they had to sell them all the stock. Sometimes back this company sold, at a very low price, ten shares in the company to several of it top salesman so that they would have a real interest in the company and stay. Daddy was one of them. Not long after Daddy had acquired all this property the company he worked for contacted him and told him that they wanted to sell the company and needed his stock and offered him $25,000.00 for his ten shares. Of course he took the offer and paid off most of what he owed on all the property he had bought. Keep in mind that he only paid $200.00 for some lots and only $4,000.00 for a lot with two houses on it. Therefore this money went a long way back then.

David purchased some of the property Daddy sold and began Edisto Realty where he began to rent houses and also sold property. Mr. Paul Atwood also started a rental agency about the same time. Mr. Atwood started the Atwood Agency a little before or after David began Edisto Realty. I am not sure of the exact dated. Mr. Atwood and his wife became close friends of the family. When I got married between OCS and my first U.S. Coast Guard assignment Mr. Atwood took the wedding pictures which I have to this day. If it were not for him we would not have had any pictures of our wedding to remember.

Over the years Edisto Beach has had trouble with beach erosion like Edingville Beach. First in the 1950s the state got involved and began installing breakwaters in front of the old bath house in the State Park made out of palmetto logs which did not last very long. Then to protect the road the State began installing breakwater down the beach away from the State Park. There is a current the runs down the beach toward the sound and when you get a northeaster it speeds this current up and causes beach erosion. When they put one breakwater in it washed on the other side of the breakwater. It would build on the north side of the breakwater and tear down on the south side. It took a While before the state and town to realize that they had put the breakwater in backwards. They also realized that wooden breakwaters would shortly be torn up by the wave action and when it got holes in them it would not stop the current.

The picture on the following page is what the second attempt to stop the erosion looked like. If you will look closely you will see that it was building on the left side and had washed out on the right side. Oh, here in another picture of me during this time.

Therefore they began using large stones which have last until now. They should have started where the ocean beach turned into the river beach and worked northward. Breakwaters are now installed all along the beach and the erosion is now somewhat under control. Several times the town has paid to have sand pump on the beach to keep ahead of any problems caused by erosion. This is an advantage of having a town that watches out for the beach. The town tax money now helps keep the beach up.

Edisto Beach is now a year round small town where people come year round to enjoy my paradise.

Let me wrap this all up. In the 1930s a group of men bought Big Island and cut it up into fishing cabin lots and restricted it to single family homes or boarding houses. They also made provision so that the beach would not be cut off from the public who did not own front beach property by including many public accesses to the beach. They included two unrestricted lots for a tavern which was turned into an apartment house and then into Edisto Realty. The developers gave the upper end for a State Park for a four lane road with sidewalks. Harvie Lybrand came to town to get away from my mother's brothers, George and Ed. He and Mother started the Ocean Villa which brought many school people to Edisto Beach and many built their own homes. The original beach company was sold to another group which included my father. They sold Jungle Shores to Sam Fox because they wanted another road off the beach. Sam Fox developed it into lots. The Beach was incorporated into the Town of Edisto Beach. The county line was moved. The fire department was begun. David Lybrand bought out the second beach company and developed Oristo. While all this was happening Edisto Beach evolved from a summer retreat and ghost town in the winter to slowly having more and more people calling it home year round. While all this was going on Harvie Lybrand faded out from being in the forefront of everything and David Lybrand stepped in and continued what Harvie had started. I had the best of all situations. I lived in Columbia, SC from 1970 until I moved back home in 2000. Every couple of weeks and sometime more often I came back to Edisto to visit my parents and to keep enjoying the paradise I knew as a young boy. Today we have a beautiful well kept safe beach for families to enjoy.

Sometimes during all this they named the longest street off Palmetto Blvd, Lybrand Street after my father. He led a great life and accomplished much. He went to his reward in 1997 at the ripe old age of 93 after traveling the world. Mother, which was affectionately known as "Ms. Jennie" went to her reward in 1987 and was probably the best known lady on Edisto Beach and Edisto Island. Her passion was growing flowers and loved to have parties at her house so she could show off her flowers. The old place looked like a palace after she decorated it with her flowers for a party. Daddy's passion was golf and he shot his age until he was about 90 years old. As of this writing David is still alive doing what his wife Doris tells him to do. I retired from real estate early in 2011. As I am writing this my wife Joyce just told me for the fifth or sixth time, "Sam come take a bath, you did not take one yesterday and you worked in your garden all day."

If you want to come and see what Edisto Beach is all about you can call Edisto Realty which is now owned by Matthew Kizer a long time employee of Edisto Realty. A couple of years ago he purchased Edisto Realty from my brother who retired. Edisto Realty's number as of the publishing of this book is 843-869-2527 or 800-868-5398. They have around 400 rentals and many properties on the Beach and on the Island for sale. There are other real estate companies on the Beach but I mention Edisto Realty because they are a continuation of what I helped start back in 1947.

Like I have said many times before this book is for my grandchildren and what I did or know. If you want to know more about Marion Whaley and the others that have contributed to the evolution of Edisto you will have to look up their children and see what they say about them. They all were part of my coming up but they are not a part of what I want my grandchildren to remember. Therefore since I want to leave as much as I can remember about my past I have decided to leave these other out for some else to write about.

I have probably left out much of what also happened on Edisto between 1942 and the present but there are many books also written about Edisto. I hope this gives you all a good idea of how Edisto went from a ghost town in the winter to a year round community. My favorite seasons on Edisto are still the spring and fall.

1 Peter 2:9 NAS

"But ye are a chosen generation, a royal priesthood, an holy nation, a peculiar people; that ye should shew forth the praise of Him who hath called you out of darkness into His marvelous light."

In the winter when everyone went back upstate to school I could walk for hours on the beach and not see anyone. After a northeaster I found many fossils and beautiful sea shells on the beach because there was no one to pick them up but me.

CHAPTER FIVE

"A wise son makes a father glad, but a foolish son is a grief to his mother."
Proverbs 10:1 KJV Chapter 5

Here is what I know about The Presbyterian Church on Edisto Island. If it had not been for a ship sinking off the Charleston harbor entrance, this church may not have come into being. In the late 1600s it seems that a preacher name Archibald Stobo was traveling from a failed church in Panama to Scotland when the ship stopped off the harbor of Charleston for him and his wife to go ashore to take care of some business. While they were in Charleston a storm came up and sank the ship. Therefore they were marooned. Not being able to get back to Scotland immediately he got busy and planted Presbyterian churches on Edisto Island, Johns Island, James Island and in Willtown Bluff. He then became the preacher for the Edisto Church 20 or so years. It is believed that the church was started in 1695 or there about

The present church is the third building for this congregation and was built in 1830. I can find no pictures or anything about these first two churches. The current church is designed after the original reformed churches in Holland and Germany. It has a high pulpit and slave balconies on both sides of the sanctuary. The family pews, as they are called, have doors and until recently the pews were narrow and had straight backs. You had to sit erect and it was hard to go to sleep sitting in these pews.

The slave balconies could only be reached from the outside on both sides of the church. There were double doors to the entrances to the staircases that led up to the balconies. The risers on these circular staircases were about eleven inches and had to be literally climbed up. You could not walk up these staircases like you would walk up a normal staircase. I understand that many of the slaves that were captured and brought over to America were already Christians and felt at home worshiping in this old church. I also understand that during the period of slavery this old church had more slave members than plantation owners and their families. They were considered part of the congregation.

Communion is served on four long tables up near the pulpit where everyone is seated to be served bread and wine. For those that don't care for wine or cannot drink wine there is grape juice. Each person is served individually and as the Elders pass the bread they say, "Sam, this is the body of Christ broken for you." When the wine is served the Elder says, 'Sam, this is the blood of Christ shed for you." If there are more people in the congregation than can be seated all at one time around these four long tables then there is a second seating and maybe even a third or fourth seating until all can come forth and be individually served. Then after all have been served the elders and preacher sit at one of the long tables and serve each other.

When I first joined this church they served only strong homemade Muscatine wine. When you drank this very strong wine out of the small individual glass communion cups, you knew you had been served communion.

The collection is taken up by two elders with a foot deep cloth bags at the end of long poles that can reach down each pew for each member of the congregation to place their offerings or tithes. The elder reached down the first pew with the bag on the end of a long pole, allows people to put in their offering and then he pulls back the pole and carefully reaches down the next pew being careful not to hit anyone in the head or touch them in any way. Being able to take up the collection this way takes a little practice.

Everything in the church is white except a little stained wood because all your attention should be toward the pulpit where the word of God is preached. That is why communion and baptism are all done down by the pulpit.

The current choir is up between the old slave balconies so they can be heard and not seen in order that all attention focuses on the glory of God and not the choir members. I am not sure where the choir performed in years gone by or even if they had a choir.

The following is a good description of what went on in the Presbyterian Church in times gone by that came from Turn Backward 0 Time In Your Flight by Chalmers S. Murray.

A Story by Chalmers S. Murray

"We attended the Presbyterian Church, a handsome structure built over a century ago. Some of the white people attended the Episcopal

Church, which was nearer our house, but it was not until later that I attended services there. My father said it was too much like a Roman Catholic Church to suit his taste. Strangely enough, almost all the Episcopalians lived on the southern end. They would pass each other on the Sunday drive to church. There was some crossing over. If a Presbyterian got in a row with the preacher or didn't like the way things were run, he would change over to the other church. It was the same with the Episcopalians.

There were numerous Negro churches—Baptist, Methodist, one Presbyterian and one reformed Episcopal. On Sunday the road was full of Negro worshipers on their way to church. Most of them went by cart, some of them by buggy; some were on horseback and some on foot. They were very polite. The men lifted their hats as the white churchgoers passed, and the whites exchanged greetings with them. The white men, however, did not go so far as to lift their hats.

We always arrived half an hour before services began. If the weather was good the members stood in front of the church and gossiped, but the women and children soon withdrew to the church porch, while the men gathered in little knots across the road near the pump and talked crops.

The young men would come up on their spirited mounts, making a show for the ladies. Mr. Willie Edings, an old bachelor, rode up sometimes on his fiery stallion, and the people scattered. Legend had it that the stallion could make a mile in a minute.

As soon as the Doxolog was sung, the men drifted slowly into the church. But some would wait until after the long prayer to enter.

The sermon usually lasted an hour and, when I was a very small boy, I was allowed to sleep in the pew, my head resting against my mother's knee. Even after I was a big boy I would doze sitting up and my father would punch me to wake me up. Just across the aisle I would see my cousin, Girardeau Murray (then a middle- aged man) dozing in his seat.

Everything was stiff and formal at the Presbyterian Church. The pulpit stood on a raised platform at one end of the church. It was made of mahogany, but it had been painted a deep brown and was covered with a piece of red cloth between the slats. Years after, the cloth was ripped off and the brown paint removed. It was then a handsome piece of furniture. Above the pulpit was a beautiful window of plain glass. Three deacons' chairs stood on the pulpit platform — one for the minister and the other two for visiting ministers.

When Holy Communion was held, three long tables with benches were placed on the floor in front of the pulpit, and there the members who were entitled to take communion sat. Only a few men did not come up and they were regarded with scorn. The children sat in the pews but were not admitted to communion until they confessed their sins and joined the church. I think I was fourteen before I joined the church. Then I took communion in fear and trembling for the minister said that any who committed any known sin and drank of the cup and ate of the bread brought down the wrath of God.

My father was then one of the deacons who took up the collection in a little bag attached to a long pole. The bag was rather deep and I suspected that sometimes a child took out more money that he put in! After the collection was taken the two deacons would march to the pulpit with the offering.

Outstanding members of the choir were my Cousin Lilla Mitchell, my cousin Jim Murray and Mr. Edings. Lilla sang soprano, Mr. Edings bass, and Jim a squeaky baritone. It was not a harmonious group and even as a child the singing grated on my ears. I don't believe there was a good voice on the entire Island."

My first experience with this old church was going to a wedding not long after we started coming to Edisto for the summers. When I went into the church as a child it seemed like it was cut up into little cubicles and was drab and dark. Over the years when money was tight there was not enough money to keep the church up in the condition it should have been kept. Therefore it was drab and needed much repair. As the years went on it was gradually updated and taken better care of. When we moved to Edisto permanently we joined the church and I made a confession of faith at about age 13.

Back when I joined the church in the late forties or early fifties you were taken over to the Session House and a group of old men, as it seemed to me at the time, gathered over me, laid hands on me and prayed for me. It is believed that the Session House may have been moved to the current location from where the previous church building was located. Therefore the current Session House is older than the current building. When I joined the church the only other building that the church had was the Session

House. It gets its name because this small building is where the Session met. In the Presbyterian Church the group of current Ruling Elders are called the Session.

For those that are not Presbyterian the church is run by Ruling Elders, a Teaching Elder and Deacons. The Deacons handle the church, grounds and the money. The Ruling Elders nurture the people, serve communion and other duties. The Teaching Elder is the preacher. Once you elect an Elder or Deacon you have no further say. They make all the decisions. The only way you can get rid of an Elder or Deacon is to vote them out at the end of their three year term. Plus an Elder or Deacon can only serve two terms. He has to lay off at least a year before he can be reelected.

Each Elder is assigned a committee chairmanship to handle part of the churches activities and reports back to the full Session when a group decision needs to be made. Deacons cannot make major decisions without the Session's approval. Many do not know that our US government was formed using the Presbytery form of government patterned after the Presbyterian Church government except our US government does not always have term limits across the board.

Since the church had no other building until recently, all the Sunday school classes and any other meetings had to be held in the sanctuary. Therefore sometimes it could get noisy in the church before time to worship with so much going on at one time.

Coming up most of my outside activities were around the church. We had parties at each others' houses, sang Christmas carols and many other activities. I don't know why I remember this incident. On one of our Christmas caroling outings one of our teenagers had just gotten his own used car. At one stop while we were going from house to house one of the cars we were riding in bumped the back of the car that the teenager has just gotten and the gas tank dropped to the ground. Of course this was a happening and it ended our caroling for the evening. During this time it was very unusual for any teenager to have his own car. I guess this is why I remember this incident. I guess I felt sorry for the boy and wished I had my own car.

The first preacher I remember was a Rev. Goodman. He was a kindly old gentleman and if Daddy was under the house fixing something when he came to visit he would get under the house with Daddy. For some strange reason he always came to visit at meal time. Of course mother would invite him to eat and he always did. A life time memory of him and his little wife was that he called her his bride. Keep in mind that I am sure they had been married over 50 years and he still called her his bride. She in turn fixed fancy breads and treated him like a king with her cooking. This was my first lesson on how couples should treat each other.

Since we lived on the beach we were known as "Beach People" and not really natives since many of the member's families went back to the 1700s. After Daddy had been a Ruling Elder for 30 years one of the Johns Island preachers came over to preach one Sunday. After the service he told my Daddy that it was nice for us newcomers to help out at the church.

Up until recently the church was a corporation and the male members were the members of the corporation. I have seen a list where each male had signed a document making them a full member of the corporation. Harvie S. Lybrand had signed that document as a member of The Presbyterian Church on Edisto Island even though he was one of the "Beach People." "How about dem apples."

While I was away raising my own family the church grew and need a meeting building for Sunday school classes, an office for the preacher, etc. Daddy told the story that they had a right well off gentlemen living on Edisto at the time and he and his wife were members of our church. On one occasion Daddy was talking to him telling him about the church's need. He told Daddy and several other Elders to have a money drive and when they had raised all the money they could for the Elders to tell the congregation that they had raised enough money to build the current building. In reality the church raised about 5 to 10% of what was needed and he provided the rest. For many years he did not want anyone to know that he provided the majority of the money to build this large building. It is now the only large building on Edisto that can handle over 500 people. This gymnasium was built when the current building was built with money provided by one of the members. Recently we had an island wide revival of all 14 churches in the gymnasium and over 600 people of all denominations attended.

In 2001 the church was in bad need of repair. The congregation took it upon itself to restore it back to its original glory when in the 1800s it was one of the richest churches in the world, as I am told. In the late 1800s the church had had the same preacher for around 50 years and he could no longer climb to the high pulpit it once had. Thus the elders lowered the pulpit to about three to four feet off the floor of the sanctuary so he could get up to the pulpit to give his sermons. (Note that the section I included by Chalmers Murray told of the pulpit being on a platform. Therefore his story was after the pulpit was lowered.) When the restoration committee started making plans to restore this old church they had no picture or drawing of what the original pulpit looked like. Someone remembered or read that William Seabrook, one of the plantation owners at that time with considerable wealth had a son that was friends with the famous architect Robert Mills. Robert Mills designed several of the U.S. Capitol buildings and several churches in Charleston, SC. Therefore the restoration committee started looking at the churches Robert Mills had designed and ran across a pulpit designed by him that had not been built. They brought the plan back to Edisto, tore down the lowered pulpit and there were scribes on the floor that matched the pulpit drawing they had found. Therefore the restoration carpenter used these plans to rebuild the pulpit to its original design. It took the restoration carpenter four months to rebuild the current pulpit out of mahogany and heart pine. It is now one of the most impressive pulpits I have ever seen. From the new pulpit the preacher can see the congregation below and those in the balcony.

When the restoration began they wanted to connect the balconies with the main body of the congregation by cutting an opening from the main body of the congregation to the stairs going up to the balcony. But the architect said there was not enough room and you could not have a staircase you entered from the main body of the congregation and ending going on to the balconies. But my brother David, who worked for a time in a steel fabrication plant, and the restoration carpenter got together and designed a new staircase using metal supports attached to the walls of the old staircase and covering these metal supports with heart pine. Now there is an opening from where the main body of the congregation sits on both sides where the old circular staircases were to a beautiful staircase that goes up to the balcony and opens into the balcony. The architect said, "Oh." In addition, the two slave balconies were connected in the back and now the choir sits there. A generous church member donated a large forty to fifty thousand dollar organ that can blast you out of the church if the organist sees fit. Now the old slave balconies are used all the time because some of the congregation and especially visitors prefer to sit up there where they can see everything that is going on and even who is sleeping during the preacher's sermon.

The pews have been extended where you sit and the backs have been slanted back a little bit so the seats are now more comfortable for those who want to sleep during the service.

Several noteworthy things happened during the restoration. When some of the structure was being checked out it was discovered that the main beam that held up the back of the church was about to fall in due to termite damage. The back right hand corner of the church was about to fall off due to this very badly damaged beam. Therefore they had to bring in a house mover to jack up the church, ever so slightly so the old beam could be replaced by a treated wood beam. This was a sight to see. It seems like a dozen hydraulic jacks had to be placed under the church so it could be lifted evenly so as not to crack the existing plaster, window and door frames. It seemed like a hundred hydraulic rubber pipes were going under the church from a truck where the hydraulic pumps where located. I guess where there is a will there is a way.

Another interesting thing that I noticed during the restoration was that the heart pine flooring in the church sanctuary was made of very long boards extending almost the length of the inside of the church. The siding on the outside of the church was also made of these very long boards. This kind of lumber is nonexistent in today's lumber yards.

This old church has weathered every storm since it was built. I believe the reason is that it is built of very large framing material and highly braced. During the restoration I saw some of the framing. It was made of bigger than normal wall studs with braces chiseled and pegged together. It must have taken a month of Sundays to frame such a building. But it was built to stand for ages and it has.

The Session house is now used as a prayer chapel and is left open all the time. People often stop and use this prayer chapel to let their requests be known to God. Cards are left for visiting people to leave prayer requests. These are picked up and read at every service after they are found. These prayer requests are then prayed for during the services.

I can truly say that this old church is the prettiest church I have ever seen now that it is back to its original glory. It is in high demand for weddings and other special occasions. Come visit us and feel the love of

God overflowing in this beautiful old sanctuary whose congregation goes back about 325 years as of the writing of this book.

The following are a few pictures I took of this old church. Just think of the souls that this old church has introduced to Christ's saving grace. Praise the good Lord for such a congregation and this old church that has stood the test of time.

The Session House was originally used for the session to meet and conduct church business. When I joined the church the Elders took me out to this old small building, prayed and laid hands on me. After this I knew something special had happened to me. It is now used as a prayer chapel and is kept open for anyone to come pray and leave prayer requests to be prayed for at our next Sunday's service. Many now just stop and use it to pray their hearts out for some kind of relief or answer from God for something that is going on in their lives. This old church just keeps on giving.

This beautiful high pulpit makes this church seem very special when you worship God where the children of God have come to worship for many generations. It is believed that Robert Mills designed this lovely pulpit carefully built by a restoration carpenter. It took four months to build using mahogany and heart pine. Most of it was built with hand tools, paying close attention to each detail. The plan called for rope molding to be used on the corners under the staircase to keep the wood from flaking off where the boards meet over time. The architect said that rope molding was no longer available. My brother, David, worked out a way to make rope molding and purchased mahogany dowels and personally made the rope molding needed. The architect said, "Oh."

The top picture on the next page shows the individual family pews. The bottom picture shows the old slave balconies.

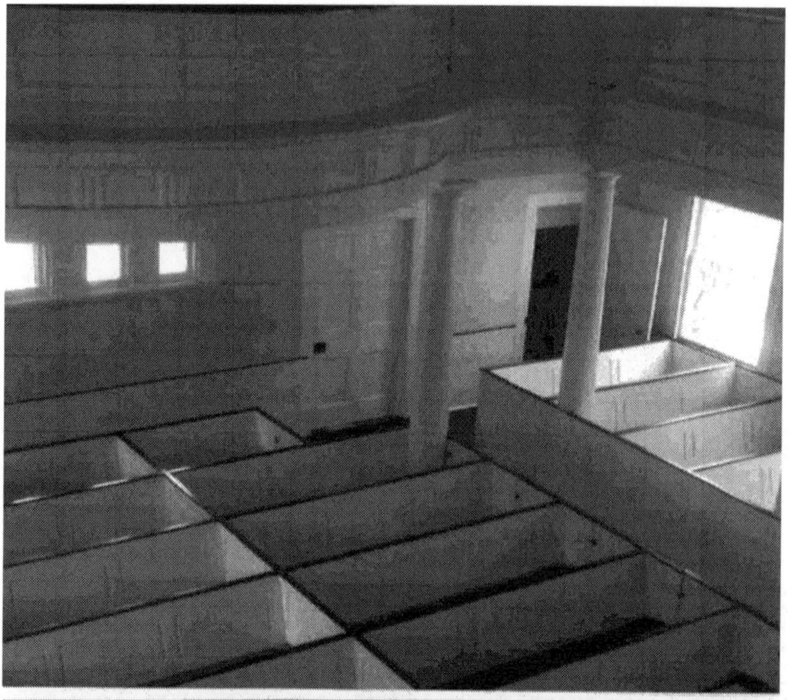

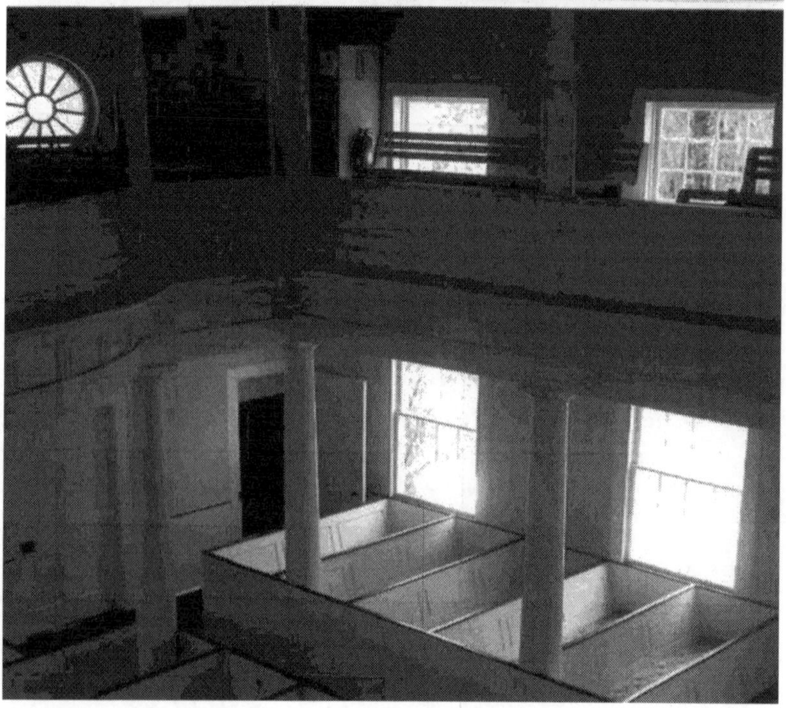

This picture shows the communion tables and benches used during Holy Communion. Each person is served individually by a Ruling Elder during communion. The section I used by Chalmers S. Murray stated that there were three of these table used. During the 2001 restoration an additional communion table was built by the restoration carpenter so that more people could be seated at one time. Thanks to the restoration carpenter it is hard to tell the new table from the old communion tables. There are now four communion tables.

The Presbyterian Manse, the preacher's house, was built about the same time as the present church was built. It is situated on a high bluff overlooking Store Creek. Joyce and I live directly across the creek from it and it is clearly seen as a stately place among large live oaks with their 40 foot limbs. During the 1800s this was a working small plantation where the preacher had some slaves and raised the food needed to support his family. Recently it was also renovated and a modern kitchen was added to make it more comfortable for the preacher and his family. The house has large rooms and a grand porch to comfortably handle a large church gathering. The Manse is on 40 acres that the church owns. The church property used to run from Store Creek all the way across Highway 174 and a ways back behind the church. During the 1800s, when times were tight, the church sold off a small section to an adjacent farm. But it still owns a large track of land that it plans on developing in the future for church and local activities.

CHAPTER SIX

"Righteousness exalteth a nation: but sin is a reproach to any people."
Proverbs 14: 34 KJV

The Spanish came to Edisto in the 1500s looking for gold. The English found it in the 1 700s by exporting indigo, rice and Sea Island cotton.

There is so much written about the old plantation houses on Edisto that all I am going to do in this book is to include some of my personal pictures of these houses. Then I am going to tell a little bit about how a few of these old houses fit into my story about Edisto.

The first fall after we moved to Edisto to live full time a hurricane hit Edisto. By this time we had met the Hopkinsons and they invited us to ride out the hurricane at their plantation house on the corner of Store Creek and School House Creek called Governors Bluff. It is also situated on a high bluff where most of the old plantation houses are built. Shortly after we got settled in the house the wind started blowing and as time went by it got stronger and stronger. There is nothing that can adequately describe the sound of hurricane winds when you are in the middle of one listening from the inside of a house. All along you are thinking, "Will this building hold together during all this awful wind?" Daddy was especially worried about the tide that was getting higher and higher in Store Creek. He was afraid that we would not only have to worry about the wind, but also the tide as it kept getting higher and higher. There is not much that can stand up to hurricane winds and high water. The two of them usually mean disaster. I am not sure how long the wind blew but the sound was out of this world and something I had never heard before. Then suddenly the wind stopped, the sky got blue with white clouds and the birds came out of hiding and started singing again. The eye of the hurricane actually went straight across us. I am not sure how long this lasted but all of a sudden the wind started coming from the other direction from where it came a short time ago. To Daddy's surprise the wind from this direction sucked the water out of Store Creek.

The next picture is of the Hopkinson's plantation home in which I rode out the 1947 hurricane. As you go through this book you will notice that many of the pictures I have taken for this book were taken from the water. This is because Joyce and I do a lot of shrimping and fishing and I take my camera with me. I stop many times when I think I can get a good shot of some of the things I will be talking about in this book. I believe, as many do, that a picture is worth a thousand words and tells a better story than I can tell or describe.

Governors Bluff

As I got older I realized that these old plantation houses were built like the Presbyterian Church I just talked about and most of them could stand most hurricanes. At least the Governors Bluff house stood this hurricane. This was before they started naming hurricanes. Since then I have seen what hurricanes can do. I would not suggest anyone try to ride out a hurricane on the beach or anywhere else in a low lying place. But have heart. The chances of a hurricane hitting where you live is not very likely. It can happen but the odds are on your side. But playing the odds is not a thing you want to do on the coast, especially on a barrier island.

When Mother and Daddy went out of town on business we usually stayed with the Murrays at Cypress Trees plantation. They had two sons and one was my age. We spent time together when we became teenagers. What I remember most is that we got up very early and the Murray boys had to go out to feed the livestock and take care of whatever else you do on a farm early in the morning. When they came back in for breakfast, Mrs. Murray would fill your plate until it was overflowing with grits. I am not sure what else we had. I just remember the large plate of grits. My mother also fixed grits for breakfast but I don't remember her serving the amount Mrs. Murray served. As I go through the motion of writing my point of view it amazes me what I remember and how I remember it from where I stood at the time.

Here is a picture of Cypress Trees, the Murray's house. The house is situated on a sort of Island and sticks out into the marsh on Store Creek. One thing that I remember about this house is that you had to pass through a gate to get to their house and at this gate was a cattle guard. A cattle guard is a series of metal bars placed side by side with about six inches between each bar. When cattle see this they will not cross because they fear that their legs will fall through and get broken. It seems to never occur to them to jump over it. They will just not cross a cattle guard. You see these kind of guards all over the local farms.

Cypress Trees

One more place I'd like to mention is Peters Point Plantation. Coming up I spent some time with Mr. and Mrs. Mikell. I remember visiting this old run down plantation house with guinea fowl running around the yard making constant strange noises and seeing them fly up in the live oak trees when they thought danger was around. Inside the house were large high ceiling rooms that needed painting.

Mrs. Mikell was always gracious and kind. She was also the lunch room cook and librarian at the two room school house where I went to school. This grand old house has had its large front porches rot off because no one really had title to the property and no one would spend money to keep the place up because they did not have a clear title to the property. I do not have a picture of this old house to share with you.

The following came from a newspaper article written back on February 26, 1971. It was published in the Charleston Evening Post. (Now The Post and Courier.) It was written by Beth Brown Dickey, a Staff Reporter. I came across this old newspaper article I had cut out some time ago. It had turned brown and was falling to pieces. I taped it together and hope I have it right. When I read it I thought it gave a good insight to the thinking of those cotton farmers in the 1800s.

"Edisto Changes, But Somehow Remain the Same."

"What a place Edisto Island must have been in the 1800s. Cotton was king then — 'The center of the kingdom.'

The plantation owners planted Sea Island cotton and became almost unbelievably wealthy. They carefully guarded their seed, and it was illegal to take any off the island.

Their cotton was prized throughout the world. It is said that the cotton from the Edisto Island plantations was never put on the market. Buyers from France made purchasing arrangements before each crop was put in the ground. Even the Pope's fine garments were said to have been made from Sea Island cotton.

The planters built handsome mansions, set out formal gardens filled with imported shrubs and entertained lavishly beneath crystal chandeliers in their dining rooms and ballrooms. They sent their sons to Europe for schooling.

In her book, 'Tales of Edisto', Neil Graydon relates the following story, 'When William Seabrook's son by his first marriage returned home after studying a year in France, he talked enthusiastically and endlessly about the wonders of Paris. Finally, becoming a little bored, his father looked indulgently at the young man and lapsing into the gullah of the Island said, 'Yah like'um son, I buy 'um fur yuh.' With so much money available, the planter's idea of his wealth became a little much. Finally, becoming a little confused, the buying of a glamorous French city seemed a minor matter.'

The courtship of Edward Whaley and Abigail Baynard resulted in what has been called 'The most glamorous the Island had even known.' Neil Graydon tells the story this way: 'Steamboats loaded with guests docked at the private wharves. A week before the wedding the plantation houses on Edisto were filled. Dining and dances that lasted until the early morning were daily occurrences. The bride's trousseau came from France — gowns, chemises and pantalets, exquisitely sewn and embroidered by the nuns. The heavy satin wedding gown, bearing the label of a famous Parisian designer, would stand alone; and the gossamer veil, fragile as cobwebs, had taken ten women six months to make. It is said that the thread they used came from the famous Sea Island cotton grown on Edisto. It was all like a fairy tale come true.'

Peter's Point, derived from Point Saint Pierre, is pictured here. The house looked toward St. Helena Sound on a point between two tidal creeks. It is built on a high foundation of brick and tabby. Isaac Jenkins Mikell built the lovely house which had 12 'Great rooms with white and colored marble for inside adornment, a spiral stairway, broad brown stone steps and double piazzas.'

The first owner of Peter's Point married four times. As he was nearing the end of his life, a grandchild once said to him, 'Grandfather, please tell me about all your wives.' The old man replied. "My dear, it has been so long ago I don't remember the first one, the second one was your grandmother, and she brought me wealth and success; the third was the love of my life; and the fourth is the comfort of my old age."

For many years, the Island was shut off from the outside world. Now, there is a modern paved highway and the beach is lined with summer cottages.

Nevertheless, Island residents are in agreement that 'Edisto changes, but somehow remains the same.'"

In the first part of this book I have included recent pictures I have taken especially for this book. I'll leave the telling of the other plantation information to others.

(If you know anything about me you will understand I do some things just because. One evening about dusk the sky all of a sudden turned a strange pink color. I ran and got my camera and took this picture right in front of our house. The color only lasted a few minutes and then it all of a sudden went away as fast as it came. --- Oh, the mysteries seen on Edisto --- What a fascinating place to live!)

CHAPTER SEVEN

"For the word of God is quick, and powerful, and sharper than any two edge sword, piercing even to the dividing asunder of soul and spirit, and of the joint and marrow, and is a discerner of the thoughts and intent of the heart."
Hebrews 4:12 KJV

Over the years I have enjoyed being around all kinds of people and hearing their life stories. When I got my driver's license I used to pick up hitch hikers just to hear their views of life. The following are observations of some of my favorite characters or groups of people I knew or observed coming up on Edisto. These are my impressions and are not intended to insult anyone.

When I think back over my life, I have come to realize that I learned more from things and my natural surroundings than I learned from individuals. Like the proverb I quoted back a ways in this book, God tells us to observe nature and learn. Animals, fish and birds in nature adapt more than you think they do. Since I have been living on Store Creek I have observed that mud snails quietly go about doing their snail thing day after day. But let a piece of dead fish or any organic thing fall on their mud bank and all thousand of them head for it. Terns use to nest behind the high water mark above the State Park by the thousands. When the people activity picked up in the State Park the whole flock moved out to Deveaux Bank to nest. Raccoons usually get their food out in the marsh but let me have an unprotected cantaloupe in my garden and before I realize that it is ready to eat, the raccoons have already eaten it. Many of the American Indians were hunter gatherers. When the game ran out in one place they moved on.

The point is that if you want to survive in this world you have to learn to adapt and go where you can survive or just lie down and die. The fool is the one that does not observe what is going on around him and does not get out before the walls fall in on him. Nothing stays the same and the wise man feels when a change is about to happen and reacts. Now let me give you my observation of several people I was exposed to coming up on Edisto.

Boy Rat: Or Bo Rat - His real name was Johnny Reed. Boy Rat, as I came to know him, must have been the smartest man I ever knew and he lived into his 80s. On first impression you would think he was a bum. You could find him around the docks most of the time when he was not working on odd jobs. He is what I would call a real hunter gatherer in modern times. You often saw him on the docks and say, "Boy Rat, where did you get those fish?" He would say, "I caught them." I would say, "Boy Rat I know you did not catch those fish and someone gave them to you." He would say, "I got them, don't I!" Now who is the smartest? The guy that spent several hundred dollars on gas in an expensive boat to go catch a few fish or Boy Rat who now has the fish and did nothing but hang around the dock and take what was given to him?

On one occasion a man I knew wanted Boy Rat to do some work around his place on Edisto that required Boy Rat to drive his car and go a few places on Edisto to get supplies, etc. When he called or got in touch with him Boy Rat told him that his old car needed tires and he could not do the job. The man knew Boy Rat would do a good job if he ever got him started so he sent him a credit card to get new tires for his old car. When the man got the bill he noticed that Boy Rat had charged two sets of tires on his credit card. When he later asked Boy Rat about the bill Boy Rat told him his wife needed tires also.

I often heard people ask Boy Rat how he kept a wife. He would tell them that he just kept promising her. Every time you saw Boy Rat he was smiling like he did not have a care in the world. Now who is the smartest, the one that has millions and is constantly worrying about what is going to happen to his property or investment or Boy Rat that just lived one day at a time and even one meal at a time? He lived to a ripe old age and had children surrounding him when he died. Maybe we should work when we need to and play when we can. My Daddy liked Boy Rat so much that when he had gotten older and could not get around as well as he used to, Daddy had a large fruit basket made up especially for Boy Rat and personally took it to him.

One story that I heard Boy Rat tell was that when he was young he was taking an ox cart out from the Neck full of corn liquor covered with fire wood. Not too far from Highway 174, a couple of revenuers came by and asked him if he knew anything about a liquor still back in the Neck. He told them that he did not know anything about any liquor still. Therefore the revenuers went on by. Boy Rat said, "Any fool would know that fire wood would not make the cart wheels go down in the dirt three or four inches."

Seaph: I am not really sure how you spell his name. He too used to hang around the dock and was known as an accomplished sea captain or at least good around boats. Therefore he made his living doing whatever needed to be done around the dock. He might take someone's boat here or there or meet them somewhere and bring a boat back to Edisto. I remember him well because when Daddy bought David and me our first sailboat and helped us bring it home and put it the in the water. He then gave us a book on sailing which I soon memorized. Since we had never actually sailed a sailboat, we asked Seaph to show us how to sail the boat on our first outing. Seaph agreed and took David and me out the first time to show us how to sail. I later found out that he had the jib set wrong but how he set the sail made it sail and go where he wanted the sailboat to go. I am not sure who we would have gotten to help us begin to learn how to sail.

On another occasion he took David and me over to the marsh area behind Pine Island to hunt marsh hens on a spring tide. The fog was so thick that you could barely see from one end of the old homemade boat to the other. We ask Seaph how in the world he thought he could get over there in this fog. He told us to leave it to him. Since the tide was very high we did not have to worry about sandbars. Seaph made a straight line over to the Pine Island area and we ended up exactly where he wanted to go. We killed a few marsh hens and he headed straight back. On the way back I asked Seaph how in the world he was doing this. He pointed to a bright spot in the fog and told me that the fog always had a bright spot in it caused by the sun. He said he just put that spot on his right shoulder and followed that spot until he got where he wanted to go. Of course to be able to do this you would have to have memorized the surroundings you were navigating so you always had a mental visual picture of where you wanted to go. What I guess you can learn from Seaph is that you need to be very good at what you do. There is a proverb that loosely says that if you highly cultivate your God given gifts and talents kings will seek you out to help them or the world will be at your feet. In a small way Seaph knew his stuff and people on Edisto sought him out for his help. Of course Seaph played the part by always having a captain's hat on and dressed for the part. If you are going to be a sea captain, look like one.

Captain John Flowers: He was my story teller. He was an old man when I got to talk to him. At an early age anyone over 40 years old was old to me. I guess Captain John was in his late 70s or older. He told me that when he was younger he used to dive off clipper ships' spars docked on Big Bay Creek and loved to be around these large beautiful sailing ships and to see then under full sail off Edisto. I guess my later love of sailing might have begun talking to Captain John.

One day when there was talk of a possible storm approaching Edisto he told me that I did not have to worry about a storm catching us by surprise because God gave us a three day notice. He told me the first thing to look out for was that there would not be a bird in sight, especially the sea birds. I guess God gives His birds plenty of time to get out of the way of storms and tell them to go inshore as far as needed to keep out of the way of storms. The second thing you would see when a big storm was approaching is large swells hitting the beach a long ways apart. There would be one large wave and then a few minutes later another would hit. The normal waves come ashore much closer together. A storm has a large wave built up in front of it that causes wave to go off it. If you watch a barge going down the river it will also have a wave built up in front of it. He said that when you see these waves you had better be on the alert and know what you are going to do if a storm does hit. The third thing he told me was that you would see all the clouds racing toward one direction. They would be racing toward the center of the storm. He said when you see this you had better already be on your way to a safe place. The last thing you would see is all the palmetto fronds blowing in one direction. When you saw this you had better be looking out a window in a secure place away from where the water and wind could get to you. I guess I liked him because I have always been a story teller in my own right.

Mac Holmes: When you looked at Mac Holmes with his captain hat he usually wore he looked like the perfect sea going man. Most people did not like him because he was very plain and rough spoken. I liked him as a kid, and especially after I became a teenager, because he took me places that I would have never been able to go by myself and he brought me things for use in the woods for no particular reason, He would just come by and give me things. On one occasion he dropped by and gave me a Japanese field glass with mortar cross hairs on one of the lenses. Another time he brought me a pair of snake leggings.

From time to time Mac Holmes would rent a shrimp boat and its captain and take a good many people over to the Rockville Sailboat races. Luckily, he always invited me. I am not sure if he charged the other people or not but he never charged me. Teddy Bailey of Brookland Plantation had a large river boat yacht or tug boat that was very wide and with a shallow draft. Later in his years Mac Holmes bought it from Teddy Bailey and let me and several of my friends take it over to Rockville by ourselves. While we were over there it broke down. We called Mac Holmes and told him that it had broken down. He told us that we got it over there so for us to get it back. At the time we had a whale boat which I have talked about before. Therefore we got it over to Rockville and lashed it to the back of Mac Holmes' boat and pushed it home. It was a calm day so we took it home via the ocean instead of going on the Intracoastal Waterway because it was shorter and we wanted to get it home soon and return it to Mac Holmes. Believe it or not a ten horse outboard motor in the whale boat pushed the whale boat and a right large river boat from Rockville to Big Bay Creek. What a trip for a bunch of teenagers. I don't remember who went to Rockville with me. It must have been some of my summer friends that I only saw three months out of the year.

To show my relationship with Mac Holmes, he one time asked me to follow him to Columbia in a friend's car that was left at his house on Edisto Beach. Many people did not know that at one time Mac Holmes was an alcoholic and he took in alcoholics to help them get off the wagon. When we got to the friend's house it was about supper time and his friend had two daughters about my age. Mac Holmes gave me several dollars and told me to take them to the movies. When we got back home they realized that I had not had anything to eat so they made me a dill pickle and pimento cheese sandwich and a glass of milk. I almost was not able to eat such a combination but got it down and we returned to Edisto the next morning.

I am not sure of the dates but a while back the beach people built a yacht club on Bay Point well before Fairfield was built. It was an immediate hit. Mac Holmes was made Commodore. There is a famous picture of him somewhere with his Commodore hat on that really shows that they picked the right man at the right time for their leader. Later the yacht club burnt down and condos are now built on this sight.

One thing that stands out about Mac Holmes is that he often sat on one of the docks on Big Bay Creek and watched me sail up and down the creek. He would tell me not to drop my sails until I had a line on the dock. He told me that I was smarter than the tide and wind and not to give in to it. Therefore I became an excellent sailor because I learned how to bring my sailboat to the dock and make it stop dead, put a line on the dock and then drop my sails.

Over the years I have found out that Mac Holmes was in the midst of almost everything that went on, on Edisto. His name and what he did pops up every now and then when I least expect it. I guess he was my first hero.

Teddy and George Fountaine came to Edisto to set up their shrimping business shortly after we moved to Edisto. The thing that I most remember about them was that they were always building something and I learned much just by watching them. On one occasion they were working on one of their shrimp boats when I had taken my Lightning sailboat out by myself. Things went very smoothly until I rounded Bay Point and the wind off St. Helena Sound blew so hard it just about turned me over. I knew I could not get back home with all my sails up. I remembered that the main sheet had reefing holes in it. I therefore shortened the sail by pulling the sail down one reefing section and then tried to sail but there was still too much sail for the strength of the wind. I kept on reefing the main sail until I only had about six feet of sail going up the mast. Then I was finally able to control the boat in the heavy wind. I tell this story because I later learned that Teddy and George were watching me and were about to get in a motor boat and come get me. They were pleased to see me take control of the situation and get myself back home by myself. But it was comforting to know that someone was watching out for me.

Marion Whaley came to live on Edisto as a young man right out of school. I am not sure if he graduated from college or not. He was able to buy a small piece of property off to the right where the four lane highway goes into two lanes and built a small store. It was called South Point Services. Over the years he developed it into a store that had whatever you needed to fish with or have a good time on the beach. He was always around and became one of the full time residents on Edisto Beach. From time to time I depended on him for his help.

Mrs. Holmes, Mrs. Mikell and Mrs. Stouby: Over the years I have come to make these three ladies as my heroes. They all were happy and cheerful every time I saw them. In later life Mac Holmes became very hard to live with and sick and they had to move to Columbia to be near children. As time went by he became bedridden and Mrs. Holmes kept him alive by feeding him nourishing food. He lived to be around 90 years old. When he died she moved to a church retirement home in West Columbia. My first wife and I went to see her in the home on Christmas one year shortly before she died. We found her in high spirits but with a very large aneurysm in her stomach. We asked about it and she told me that she had lived a long life and knew that it would soon pop off and that would be the end of it. She told us this smiling. She had done her duty and was ready to go on to her reward. When we went to see her the retirement home was about to have a Christmas party. We ask if we could come back later because of the party. She told us that she would rather be with someone she loved instead of going to the party. We therefore stayed a long time with her talking about old times. One summer my mother got very sick and Mrs. Holmes took her into her own home for about two to three months and nursed her back to health. From my point of view she spent her life helping her husband and others with very little worldly reward. But I am sure she now has a mansion in heaven with many angels watching after her.

Mrs. Mikell, who I have already talked about was always smiling even though she lived in a rundown plantation house she could not afford to take care of. In the fifth grade I came down with low blood sugar and she got me out of class and fed me every so often until I grew out of it. Note that the article I put in about plantation life on Edisto tells of the grandeur of the Peter's Point house. When I visited it in the 1940s it showed that the current generation could not afford to keep it up. It sort of reminded me of the old houses you saw in the movie, Gone With the Wind, when it showed the once beautiful house and how it had gone down during the Civil War. But despite this Mrs. Mikell made the best of it and never complained. From my view point Mrs. Mikell was love in its truest form.

As an Elder in Columbia I went to see a Mrs. Stouby who had just broken her hip. I went there to see what the church could do for her and to console her. When I got to her apartment near her daughter I asked her about her fall. She told me she fell outside her apartment on some concrete and could not move because she had broken her hip. She stayed there four hours before someone found her. She told me the concrete was cool and she knew someone would find her. She also told me that she had lived a right simple life because her husband had had an accident shortly after they got married and was not able to work much of the time they were married. All the time she was talking to me she was smiling. I went away feeling uplifted by Mrs. Stouby. Over my life I have had a serious heart by-pass; my first wife died of lupus after being sick for seven years; I ended up financially bankrupt; and I was told that I was going to die of pancreatic cancer in 2004. I believe the way I got through all this is by the examples set by these three ladies. You just take life as it is handed to you and make the best of it, smiling as you go along.

What I learned from these three ladies that had nothing to be thankful for from a worldly standpoint is that you can be content in any situation you find yourself in. Every time I am feeling down I think about the little ladies no bigger than a minute smiling as if they owned the world. What a life lesson.

Cliff Bunton: Edisto had its colorful people. One of these was Cliff Bunton who lived close to the Edisto Grammar School where I attended as a child. It was well know that he made his living making corn liquor but as far as I know he never was caught. One story that I think is worth telling is that one time he and his workers had a still out on one of the marsh islands I have already talked about. One cold winter day the revenuers found out about his still and came and took his boats and went away to get help. Cliff always had a man up in a tree to watch out for who might be coming and who might find out about his still. This man saw the revenuers take their boat and figured that they had gone for help. Cliff and his workers then drank as much corn liquor as they could to make them numb and then swam the creek even though it was freezing cold. When the revenuers came back, Cliff and his workers were nowhere to be found. The moral of this story is that even if you support yourself illegally you need to be good at it. I guess Cliff was good at what he did. In days gone by many locals preferred good smooth corn liquor to store bought liquor because if it was made right and it went down smoothly and just was superior drinking liquor.

Stray Dog Story: Have you ever seen a trunk load of dead rabbits just killed by a group of hunters? Well, I have a couple of times. The local men would take in stray dogs, feed them a little bit, pet them a little and make them feel needed and wanted. They would then take this mixture of every kind of dog imaginable and let them run up every rabbit for miles around for the local men to shoot. In these car trunks there would be enough meat to feed several families for months. The moral of the story is that you can take any old stray dog, feed them a little, pay them a little attention and make the best rabbit dogs you have ever seen. I have seen smart ladies take a not so well educated men and feed them a little bit and pet them a little bit and make a wonderful husband and dad for their children. We can all learn from these local men and how they got thrown away dogs to work for them in a great way.

Janie Parker: If I could provide for only one person in my life I would be hard pressed not to choose Janie Parker. I call Janie my mother and she calls my brother and me her children. Janie came to work for our family in 1947 to help cook in the Ocean Villa kitchen and help my parents run the Villa. She was always there and took up for me every chance she could. Even when I was not so good she was there for me and never turned me in. When I got married and had children she cooked special pancakes for my children and paid special attention to them. When my daughter got married she came to Columbia, SC and spent a week helping my wife get ready for the wedding. When I got married she was there and was the most dressed up lady there. Not long after she came to work for my parents, Daddy built her a small one bedroom house behind our house and she actually lived with us until she got married. When Daddy closed down the Villa she went to work for my brother at Oristo and then later she went to work for Fairfield when they bought Oristo. Later in life I asked her why she stayed with us and she told me it was the cost of having to go get her in the morning and having to take her home in the evening and the time lost doing this. She is now in her 80s and when she really needs something she calls my brother or me and we go running to her aid. From time to time I just stop by her house to speak and stay a few minutes and sometimes stay four hours remembering with her. When I get home my wife will say, "You have been at Janie's house, have you not?" It is this kind of relationship born of love and trust that makes life worth living.

Judge Seabrook: Briefly, Judge Seabrook was the magistrate on Edisto when I was coming up and he knew everyone on Edisto. One time shortly after I graduated from high School I got caught speeding and had to go before Judge Seabrook. He charged me twenty dollars and then gave me a ten dollar graduation present and told me he would not tell my parents. Of course this was the best present of all.

Nick Lindsay: Once in a life time you have the privilege of knowing a truly smart and talented person. Nick is a truly talented man. He can build anything no matter how complicated it is. He is a prolific writer and has recorded much of Edisto's history. He can speak Russian and there is no telling what else he can do. Daddy bought a salvaged 28 foot long Navy whale boat lifeboat that had a rotten keel. Nick came over and took out the old keel which he took to a salvage yard. He found a long piece of heart pine, made a new keel, came back and replaced the old keel. He also put an outboard motor well in the whale boat in order to power it with a ten horse power motor. If you used anything bigger than a ten horse motor it would cause the boat to dig in and not make much headway. This was because it was designed to be rowed by six to eight oarsmen and thus it did not take much to power its hull design. The well was next to the keel and one rib back from the center. Therefore you could not steer the boat by the motor so Nick put a huge rudder on the back to steer it with. Later he put a "Dog House" on it large enough to sleep two people or just get out of the weather when you needed to. This cabin was also designed to shed any water that came over the bow in rough weather. This small cabin was a work of art. As of the writing of this book Nick is still alive and even sings in our church choir. I am not surprised what all he can do.

David Ladson Lybrand (June 23, 1941 to Present): Of course when I talk about David I am talking about my brother. He is four years younger than me and until I got about to the end of my high school years we had very little to do with each other because of our age difference. But as time went by we did more and more together. He became a high school football star halfback and was so good that The Citadel gave him a full scholarship. He took Civil Engineering and came back to develop Oristo. I took Business Administration and thus there was no way for me to make a living on Edisto so I ended up in Columbia, SC selling real estate.

Over the years David has been a driving force that helped Edisto become the sought after place it now is. He developed Oristo, the Neck and Middleton subdivisions on Edisto which are the largest subdivisions now on Edisto. He also started Edisto Realty which was sort of an extension of Daddy's Ocean Villa adventure. He is now retired and doing what his wife Doris tells him to do. Good wives have a tendency to do this so that their men stay on track for the good of us all.

Thomas Harvie Lybrand (April 5, 1933 — January 18, 1972) Tommy was my older brother who was four years older than me. I hesitated to put much in this book about him. But as I think about his unfulfilled life, I realized that I learned what not to do from him. From my earliest recollection he was causing trouble and in a way was partly the reason we ended up on Edisto. Until his death he was a thorn in my side that was ever present because he was constantly upsetting my parents. I don't mention him very much in this book because he was not around a lot when I was coming up. But I will tell you a couple of stories that are worth telling.

Tommy became a very good shrimper and moved around following the shrimp. To his credit he went where the shrimp were and did not just depend on the shrimp off Edisto to make a living. One time when he was shrimping off Key West, Florida, David and I caught a bus and went down to spend a few days with him while he was shrimping. We left port and soon hit 20 foot swells. The water was so deep that several shrimp boats would tie up together using one boat's anchor instead of all anchoring during the day. While tied up to these other shrimp boats one minute you would be looking up at the boat in front of you and thinking it was going to fall on you. When the wave went by and the next wave came by you would be looking down at the boat in front of you. This was one of the strangest feelings I have ever had. They shrimped at night because the water was so clear that the shrimp could see the nets and get out of the way. At night the boats would break apart and began pulling their nets. It was so deep that it took a long time to get the nets to the bottom. As the night went on the wind began to blow very hard and waves began breaking over the bow. Flying fish began hitting the deck as they flew out of the water trying to get away from bigger fish. And yet we kept pulling the net. In the morning the net would be pulled up and the shrimp, along with other fish and sea creatures, would be dumped on the deck for sorting and put under ice so they could be sold at the dock. Dolphin and large mackerel would follow the boat all night and be ready to catch any waste fish we threw overboard. Believe it or not, a huge dolphin could beat a mackerel to any fish he wanted by just one push down on his tail. We were told that a dolphin would not take a hook. So we put a large hook on a heavy line with a waste fish on it and threw it in the water. The mackerel would take it immediately. If a dolphin came up to a fish with a hook on it he would stop a few inches from it and not take the fish. When we had separated all the good shrimp from waste fish and thrown all the bad stuff overboard Tommy would begin figuring out where he was going to shrimp that night. All the while the dolphin would just stay with the boat swimming effortless as the day went on. We stayed out three nights and headed back in to Key West for David and me to catch a bus home. Early in the evening of the third night Tommy was getting sleepy and told me to take the wheel and run south for three hours and wake him up. It was rough so I got a wooden box and sat on it and put one foot on a part of the wheel and my hand on another just to keep it on course. It was so rough I could not stand behind the wheel and steer it. After three hours of fighting the wheel I woke him up and he took a depth reading and told me to run east for one hour and wake him up. I ran another hour and woke him up. He then took the wheel and in about a half an hour we were in port. The only way I could figure out how he did this was by reading the water depths and knowing what depth it is everywhere off Key West. After going out on this trip in 20 foot seas I decided to come home and study because I surely did not want to become a shrimper.

  The summer after graduation from college I decided that I had done everything that society had expected of me. I had my degree, I was going in the service to serve my time for our country and I was engaged to get married. Therefore I was going to do something for me before I got married and went into the service. I was engaged but we had not set a date. Tommy's wife Josephine and their two children were in town and Tommy was then shrimping out of Texas. I decided to go to Texas and spend a year or so exploring Texas and Mexico before I had to settle down. I drove Josephine and her two small children to Texas with the children screaming all the way. When I got to Texas there was telegram from Daddy stating I had four days to report to OCS. I ate one meal in Texas and got on a bus and rode night and day and got to OCS one hour before I would have been AWOL. The reason I thought I had time to spend a year in Texas was because I was told that it might be two years before they called me into the U.S. Coast Guard. I guess my buddy did too good a job with my interview and they called me sooner than I expected. Maybe the reason for me for being so crazy is because I have never had a whole summer off. My mother had me waiting on tables at the Villa every summer since I was 13 years old and I had to go into the service in August after I graduated from The Citadel in June.

In my opinion Tommy was the smartest of the three of us because he learned and mastered things very easily. But he would never settle down and did not take care of himself physically. Because of this he died at an early age. I guess the lesson learned is to become good at what you do but also learn, "How then shall I live."

Harvie Samuel Lybrand: (August 2, 1904 — November 25, 1997) My Father. There is a proverb that I have already mentioned that says if you train up a child in the way he should go, even when he is old he will not depart from it. I know better than anyone else that I am not perfect and am very far from being good most of the time. When asked how I am doing, most of the time I respond by saying that I am better than I deserve. But the way my Father raised me, it is hard for me to be mean or inconsiderate to anyone. I often think that he would come out of his grave if I deliberately did something I should not do. At The Citadel only nine of the fifty that started with me in my company graduated. If I had come home Daddy would have said, "What are you doing here, boy?" If I had responded, "It is hard", he would have said, "Life is hard, get back in the car." He would have taken me back to The Citadel and they would have made me walk tours. Therefore it never occurred to me that I could quit. My mother told me that if it took me 14 years I was going to graduate. I graduated in 1959 in four years including most of the summer schools.

When I was a teenager we heated the house with oak wood that my brother and I had to cut with a large cross-cut saw every day. If Daddy told me to pick up the chips that he started the fire with, he meant all the chips, even if there were three baskets full. I was alright if I was hunting, building a tree house, looking for fossils or anything constructive but not sitting down. I dared not tell him I was bored. If I did he would give me a job that would have lasted all day. When I got elected to go to Boys State (only two out of each high school in the state are elected) I came home all excited and told him about my being appointed out of the whole high school to go to Boys State. He then asked who was going to pay for it. I told him a civic club. He asked how I was going to get there because it was going to be held in Columbia at the old Second World War airport facilities. I told him I did not know. I hitch hiked there and when it was over I hitch hiked back. When I got to Hollywood, SC near Edisto it was storming and he did come get me.

In looking back I had everything I needed and a great role model. He put as much responsibility on me as early as he could. His goal was to get me to be responsible for my own self as early as possible so if something happened to him I could take care of myself. He was always there for me but he expected me to carry my share of the load. When my children were coming up they told me that my fun was hard work. Since I learned how to work and build things early, my enjoyment still comes from creating and planting things. Because I was told over and over to do a good job, it is hard for me not to put my best foot forward in everything I do and not stop until it is finished. My wife constantly tells me that I go at things too hard and should stop to rest. I tell her I will stop when I get finished and everything works like it should.

One of my lasting memories of Daddy was often when we came home from church and he realized one of the water pumps on one of his houses needed some attention he would go get a wrench and start working on it immediately. I can still hear Mother hollowing out the window, "Harvie, come in the house immediately and take off your good suit." He would say, "Oh, Jennie I'll just be a minute." She'd hollow back, "Come in this house right now because that is your best suit." He would say, "Oh well, I'm coming in" while muttering to himself, "It would only take a minute, why do I have to come in". I guess I am a feather off the old hat because I often go to fix something in my good clothes and end up messing them up.

Oh, have you noticed that my Daddy spells his name Harvie instead of Harvey? When he was in grammar school he had a friend named Barnie.

Therefore he thought his name should be spelled with an "ie" instead of a "y" and changed it. It stayed Harvie the rest of his life. His first son was named Thomas Harvie Lybrand and his grandson was named Thomas Harvie Lybrand, Jr. Therefore this misspelling of Harvie has gone three generations.

Jennie Owens Lybrand: (March 4, 1910 — January 6, 1987) My Mother. Ms. Jennie, as she was fondly called, was a pretty lady. In her later life I heard someone say that she was the prettiest old lady they ever knew. She was a great cook and people came from far and near to eat her food at the Villa. To many she was affectionately known as "Ms. Jennie." I was sickly when I was young but she nursed me into my teenage years with a lot of love and attention. I can remember to this day that every time she called me she would end up the call by telling me that she loved me. While in Columbia, SC I did a lot of fancy rock work. Many times she and Harvie, as she called him, would be riding down the road and she would tell him to stop. She would get out of the car and pick up a large, pretty rock and Harvie would say, "What are you going to do with that rock?" She would tell him that she was going to take it to me because I probably could use it on one of my projects. The last one I remember her bringing me was a large rounded river rock which I shortly used on a rock building I was building. But boy she could fuss. She wanted things done her way and done now! One day I called home and got Daddy on the phone and asked him how Mother was doing. He told me that she was not fussing as much lately. As I have mentioned before her passion was growing flowers. Coming up I carried leaf mold, top soil and compost until I would drop helping her with her gardens. I told myself when I had my own home I was going to concrete everything and paint it green so I would not have to do all that gardening she did. But guess what? I now do more than she ever did and now growing camellias is my passion. I now have around 100 different varieties of camellias.

When Mother died I felt like I had lost my best friend and that she was the only person that really loved me unconditionally besides God. She had her faults but she was my mother.

I could go on for many more pages because when I was growing up on Edisto there were many colorful and interesting people you could learn from. I learned you could learn what not to do from the not so successful people and what to do from the more successful people. In general no one had much money in the 1940s and 1950s so you had to depend on each other. Everyone I knew went to church and everyone worked. It was a very pleasant time in our history in which to grow up.

Proverbs 17:22 KJV
"A merry heart doeth good like a medicine: but a broken spirit drieth the bones."

Sometimes you do something for no good reason. This picture has no good reason for being here. I just like the picture.

CHAPTER EIGHT

"The fear of the Lord is the beginning of knowledge: but fools despise wisdom and instruction."
Proverbs 1:7 KJV

What kind of education do you think you could get from two teachers in two rooms with seven grades to cover and only 37 students? Let me tell you about my experience going to the Edisto Island Grammar School, the rest of my formal education and how I ended up serving my country as an officer in the U.S. Coast Guard.

When we moved to Edisto in the fall of 1947 my parents enrolled me in the Edisto Island Grammar School. The school house had five rooms. Two rooms were for teaching students. One had the first through the fourth grade. The other room had the fifth through the seventh grade. There was one teacher for each. Mrs. Jenkins taught the first through the fourth and Mrs. Murray was principal and taught the fifth through the seventh.

Another room or auditorium was where we had the assemblies for all the students and where plays were held each year using all the students in the school. It was also the gathering place of most of the Island's activities such as concerts put on by local bands, womanless weddings and whatever was going on at the time. As most would think, not that much goes on in rural areas such as Edisto in the 1940s. But there seemed to be something going on all the time.

There was a lunch room where we all ate lunch prepared by Mrs. Mikell. Many times Bible School was held in this lunch room because it had tables for arts and crafts. The 4H club meetings were also held in the lunch room. And from time to time local artists would come and teach art to the students. In these art classes I remember learning about how to put depth in a picture, how to make an apple shine and how to put the center of attention in a picture. Then there was a small room for the school library.

When I was evaluated when I first came to this school it was found that this small rural school was ahead of the large grammar school I attended in Aiken, SC. Therefore they had to tutor me to catch me up with the rest of the class. I remember Mrs. Jenkins going around the room and getting this group started on a project and then moving to the next and etc. Every now and then she would stop the whole class and take out the Readers Digest or a similar magazine and pick out a word and then sound it out and have the whole class repeat it. I don't know why I remember it but I remember her picking out accommodation and saying, "Ac — com —mo — da — tion" or something like that. Even with all her hard work teaching us to read and sound out words, I am still not a good speller. Many times the lower classes learned what the upper classes were doing and learned more than just what they were studying.

Shortly after I arrived I noticed two little girls in the second grade that could spell all the books of the Bible and could write them on the black board in order. They were Ruthie Harrison and Joyce Hills. They impressed me greatly. One time one little rough looking little boy used a curse word and Mrs. Jenkins washed his mouth out with soap in a sink that was in the room. You soon learned to say, "Yes ma'm" and do what Mrs. Jenkins told you to do with no back talk. She was a nice old lady but she meant business and you learned it fast.

At recess we all went out in the yard in front of the school and played games. My favorite was marbles. I had a friend one year behind me named Buck Fisk. He had a thumb like a twenty-two rifle. We would draw a circle in the dirt and each player, usually four or maybe five, would put in three to four marbles. Then we would draw a line and roll a marble to it and the one closest to it started first and so on down the line. Someone would take his two hands and push all the marbles together. The first player would go to just outside of the circle and take his best marble and put it between his thumb and index finger and use his thumb to shoot at the bunch. From the line any marbles he knocked out by his shooter could be kept by him. If the shooter got a marble out of the ring he could keep shooting until he missed knocking a marble out of the ring. If we were not careful Buck would clean house and the game was over and he had all the marbles. I never was a good player because I did not have a strong enough thumb to knock many marbles out of the ring. Buck is still around and I recently was talking to him about our school experiences and he said he still had all those marbles he won from all of us.

Recess was over when Mrs. Murray came to the school porch and rang a school bell.

I don't remember exactly what grade I was in when I began to black out while playing hard or running. I was taken to the hospital and it seems that they tested me for hundreds of things. There seemed to be an endless procession coming into my room taking blood out of my arm and then testing it. I remember crying every time the nurse took blood. After a day or so they determined that I had low blood sugar and began feeding me very often. This seemed to solve the problem. When I went back to school Mrs. Mikell would come get me from time to time and make me eat some crackers, etc. To this day I still have to eat often to keep my blood sugar up.

I was the only one in the seventh grade. Therefore I had to answer all the questions and do all the home work. One time I did not do all my home work and Mrs. Murray made me stay behind after the school bus left and walk home, which was about eight miles. After I did my home work I got out on Scenic Highway 174 and walked down to the New First Baptist Church. Marion Whaley picked me up in his jeep and took me home. I stayed out of sight until the school bus came by so my parents would not know I had to stay after school. I don't know if Mrs. Murray ever told them. I really never forgave her for trying to make me walk all this way. I often wondered if she knew that I would most likely catch a ride home. Teenagers hitchhiked a lot back then because very few of us had cars of our own.

Once or twice a month a man came to our school to check on those students that had joined the 4H club. I don't remember what the 4H stood for. It was a club where you took on a yearly project such as raising a farm animal, planting a garden or even raising bees. I took on the project of raising honey bees. If you want to know the life cycle of a honey bee I can tell you. Daddy helped me buy a hive of bees that came in a wire cage with a queen bee in a smaller wire cage with a hole filled with wax. By the time the bees in the wire cage dug through to the queen she had absorbed the smell of the other bees and they accepted her as their queen. Daddy also helped me buy beehives. When the live bees came we put the wire cage filled with bees in it. The cage also had a hole filled with wax and by the time the bees dug their way out they had accepted the hive and it became a working hive. The hive had two sections. The lower half had large narrow racks with wax indents that was the design bees used to make little wax cylinders in which to raise young or to store honey. The bottom half was used by the bees to start raising new little bees. The queen, who was bigger and longer than the workers constantly went around depositing eggs in the wax cylinders the workers had made. When the eggs hatched the workers would feed the young bees until they were able to start helping gather nectar and pollen that honey was made off. A group of bees would constantly be around the queen feeding her and grooming her or doing whatever she needed.

To work a hive I usually put on a netting hat that covered my face and neck. Of course I wore a long sleeve shirt, long pants and gloves. I had a smoker, which is a quart size can with a funnel top. It had a bellow in which you put dead leaves, set them on fire and pumped. When you pumped air into the smoker, smoke came out. When you put smoke into a hive the bees would eat as much honey as they could so they could be ready to leave the hive and start another one if need be. When they were full of honey they could not sting you. Therefore there was a fine line on how much smoke to put in the hive.

After you smoked the hive, you could open the hive and begin to work it by cleaning out old wax and generally keeping it clean. When you smoked a hive you could also remove the honey racks and replace them with empty ones.

The upper part of the hive was used by the bees to store honey for the winter. It is from these smaller racks that we harvested honey. Of course we only took what the bees could do without. You had to check the smaller areas very often because if the bees filled up all the upper part they would start building their own storage places to store their honey. One time I did not work the hives for several weeks and when I did open the hive I broke a new section the bees had made and the whole hive got after me. I headed for the ocean. It is reported that I hollowed to Daddy or anyone nearby that they could have those bees. This ended my 4H project raising bees. My next project was helping Daddy raise pigs on food scraps from the Villa.

At the end of each year the whole school put on a play for the community. Since there were only thirty or so students in the whole school every student had a part. Some had big parts and some just sang in a group but everyone was involved every year. When I was in the seventh grade I had to sing a solo. All I remember is that the name of the song was I Will Make a Song of Sunshine. I remember that I was not a very good singer and I did not sing out very loud. That year they debated whether they would have graduation because they only had one student to graduate. That one student was me. But they went ahead and had a graduation for me. I was the best and last that year. The next year I went inland to St. Paul's High in Yonges Island, SC between Adams Run and Hollywood, SC.

The following is the best picture I could find in my stack of pictures of Edisto Island Grammar School which I attended from the fourth grade through the seventh grade. It is now the community center across from the New First Baptist Church located on scenic Highway 174. It is now in a rundown condition. Every time I see it I want to buy it and turn it into a nice, neat little school for children and to able to see them playing in front of the school like I did years ago.

The section on the right housed the two classrooms, the lunchroom and the library. The section on the left was the auditorium where we met for assemblies and where the yearly plays were held. There was a covered breezeway connecting the two sections. The creek called School House Creek coming off Store Creek runs all the way up behind this school house, thus the name.

Edisto Island Grammar School

St. Paul's High was also a rural school with only 200 students and included the eighth grade through the twelfth. The round trip from our home on the beach to St. Paul's was about 82 miles. We left for school at sunrise in the winter and got back about sunset.

In high school we had a small band and I played the snare drum. In my senior year about six or seven of us formed a small combo. We called it the Hollywood Ramblers. Our theme song was The Muskrat Ramblers. We were what you'd call a twelve piece band. We had twelve pieces of music. We played for local dances and here and there and mostly just had fun.

As I have mentioned before I took Agriculture in the eleventh and twelfth grades or FFA (Future Farmers of America) instead of Latin. I still use much of what I learned in FFA today growing things. Our teacher, Mr. Shealy, was the FFA teacher, the principal, the algebra teacher, and the football coach. He ruled with an iron fist and if you were sent to him for misbehaving you probably ended up writing something 10,000 times. After a few times doing this you decided it was better to behave than spend weeks writing something 10,000 times. I learned to write with four pencils.

Mr. Shealy took my FFA class to Washington, DC one year and this was great for someone who had really never gone very far off. I still remember riding up to Washington, DC in an old school bus driven by Mr. Shealy.

In this small high school I took a full load, including such things as chemistry and physics and when I got to The Citadel I was as well prepared as anyone.

As mentioned before I was elected to represent St. Paul's at Boys State and enjoyed the experience. When I got to The Citadel there were 12 young men enrolled in the freshmen class with me that also went to Boys State with me.

One thing that stands out is that when Mr. Shealy found out that I was accepted at The Citadel he called me into his office and told me that I was going to waste Harvie's money by going to The Citadel because I'd never make it. He told me just go get a paint brush or hammer and go to work. Every time I was feeling down at The Citadel I thought of what he said and studied a little harder. Over the years I have met several people that Mr. Shealy told the same thing and all graduated. When I got my diploma I took it by and showed it to him and he just grinned.

My senior year I drove the Edisto school bus and was paid $35.00 a month. As stated my route was 82 miles round trip. I had to go down every country dirt road between Edisto and St. Paul's to pick up students. The bus was the longest they made. Sometimes I'd get stuck in sand and had to use double low. When you put the bus in double low it would begin to turn the back wheels over slowly and sort of lunged forward. The bus seemed to be coming apart until it got moving enough to use low gear and then up the gear line until it was back moving normally. It was like driving heavy equipment. The bus would only go 35 miles per hour. To get it to go a mile or two over 35, I would remove the vacuum tube that ran the windshield wipers. It was slow going but we got there.

Here are some pictures of my high school days.

St. Paul's High

From St. Paul's I went to The Citadel, the Military College of SC. I will not go into all this except to tell you I was in the first performing Bagpipe Corp at The Citadel, playing the Scott Drum. The Bagpipe Corp was established by General Mark Clark who was the president of The Citadel at this time. The General had a bagpipe corp in North Africa and wanted one at The Citadel.

Outstanding Seniors

ANN JONES
Teen Time Representative

SAMUEL LYBRAND
Boys State

LOIS CHAPLIN
D.A.R. Award

DELL HENDERSON
Girls State

EDDIE MACK GOODMAN
Boys State

PATRICIA MUCKENFUSS
Miss-Hi-Miss

Picture speaks for itself

Because of him we marched in Eisenhower's inaugural parade. Clark told us that there would be a lot of his friends in Washington and he wanted us to look as big as we could and make as much noise as we could. I remember very clearly in my mind that when we were coming up on the reviewing stands the announcer said, "Here comes General Clark's private army." At that we broke into playing Dixie. We made him proud.

This is a picture of the group I went to Boys State with. I am the fellow in the third row up and the third from the right. Boys State was to train how government works. It lasted two weeks and was held in Columbia, SC. About 12 of these guys went to The Citadel with me.

(left) School Bus Drivers (Pm in the dark shirt — top middle) BETTY LOU CAISON SAMMY LYBRAND (right) Biggest Flirts

Another highlight was because of General Clark, the band and Bagpipe Corp were invited to play before the New York Yankees' game for a week. This was the last time the Braves played the Yankees before they

273

moved to Atlanta, GA. I remember that some of us in the Bagpipe Corp were standing outside of the stadium when this big man came right toward me and grabbed my kilt by the edge and ask what we wore under it. Of course he did this in jest. Most of us only wore the least we could and that was jock shorts just to be macho. The Yankees gave us each $7.50 to spend and I still have a picture of me and several other cadets in Greenwich Village at 2 o'clock in the morning drinking beer.

I have kept the following picture over the years to remind me to have a little fun as I go through life. Here I am with several of my friend having the time of my life.

While at The Citadel I took my sailboat and docked it at The Citadel Yacht Club and spent a great deal of my time out in the Charleston Harbor. Three of us started the first Citadel sailing team at the time and even had our own regatta.

The following are several old pictures of us having fun on my sailboat. The sailboat picture in the top left hand corner is not my sailboat, but it is the same class and shows what my sailboat looked under full sail. The class of sailboat was lighting and you can see the lighting patch on the sail of this boat. The other pictures are of us having fun. The bottom right hand picture is my sailboat tied up to the dock at Fort Sumter out in the Charleston Harbor.

While at The Citadel many hours were spent practicing with the Bagpipe Corp getting ready for some dignitary to visit The Citadel. I played the Scott drum and it was my job to keep the Bag Pipe Corp at 120 paces per minute. I had to cut the seconds in half. The following are some pictures of me in different uniforms. The following after these individual pictures is a picture of the Bag Pipe Corp during a parade. I am in the back beating out the cadence.

(above top right) Before Graduation the seniors formed "The Long Gray Line" while the Corp held "Pass and Review" for the Seniors. (above lower right) This is General Clark giving me my diploma at my graduation in 1959.

In general The Citadel was hard but I found ways to have fun with the Bagpipe Corp, sailing and with all the girls downtown. I met my first wife dating Charleston nurses and married her between U.S. Coast Guard, Office Candidate School and my first assignment in Puerto Rico.

Here a few pictures of me while attending OCS in York Town, VA. I reported for duty in August of 1959 and graduated as an Ensign in December of 1959. I can honestly say that while I was at OCS I studied harder than I ever have in my life. But the struggle was worth it. It set me on the course for success the rest of my life by all the responsibility that was heaped on me at an early age. I have also added a picture of me after I graduated from OCS in my blue officer's uniform going on my honeymoon. I got married between OCS and my first assignment in Puerto Rico.

When I first arrived at OCS we wore regular sailor's uniforms because if we did not complete OCS we had to go in the Coast Guard as a seaman -- thus the first photo.

If they thought we were going to graduate they gave us a uniform similar to a chief's uniform with an OCS emblem on the uniform hat.

I graduated from The Citadel in 1959 and have already had my 50th reunion. The Citadel has been the best network I could have ever wished for during my business career. To show the competitiveness of The Citadel, 50 started out in my company and only nine graduated on time. I studied the hardest while I was attending OCS. When I became an officer after The Citadel experience and OCS's intense training, I was ready to take on the world at age 22.

I guess I must include these two pictures to show how handsome I was in 1959.

After we were commissioned we worn an officer's uniform like the one I wore leaving on my honeymoon.

Therefore in a few years I went from being a small boy attending a small country school to being an officer in the U.S. Coast Guard with many great experiences along the way. This totally prepared me to meet the many challenges I have met along the way.

With this varied an educational opportunity, I have met the world head on and never looked back. Big is not always the best. All the schools I attended were relatively small by today's standards but I believe I got as good an education as I could have been gotten at the time. The one thing that flowed through it all my education was the awareness of God and how His teaching and our behavior determined our real success in life. Today we have lost much since we have tried to remove God from all our educational institutions. As a nation we are paying dearly for this foolish decision based on trying to be "Politically Correct" and not offending anyone. If anyone or nation denies God they will not live a very contented life and nations will soon die of their own doing,

James 1:17 KJV

"Every good gift and every perfect gift is from above, and cometh down from the Father of lights, with whom is not variableness, neither shadow of turning."

(From time to time you just have to do something out of the ordinary. Here are a few pictures I wanted to include so I put them here.)

CHAPTER NINE

"Wherefore gird up the loins of your mind, be sober, and hope to the end for the grace that is to be brought unto you at the revelation of Jesus Christ."
1 Peter 1:13 KJV

Many people live in or close to a large city and have much to entertain them. Can you imagine what a boy can do with the ocean in front of his house, 500 acres behind his house and more creeks than he can count to explore. Many tell me that my youth must have been like living in a paradise and something many could only dream about. Therefore this section is about what I found to do coming up on Edisto Beach with no one or no organization to entertain me and only a few teenagers my age with which to hang out with.

Since the place I spent my youth is called a beach, I will start with the beach and try to explain how I took advantage of it. When I first experienced the beach it was with my mother and other two brothers making sand castles and swimming in the ocean, especially at low tide when the waves were not so big. When it was high tide the larger waves frightened me as a young child. As the years went by I began to discover live sand-dollars with their green fur-like covering that you could feel with your feet as you walked in the shallow water at low tide. If you picked them up they would turn your hand green. But you could take them home, put them out in the sun and they would turn a brilliant white.

Seaweed that you found floating in the surf or washed up on the beach sometimes had sea anemones attached to them. You could put them in a large glass jar in sea water and they would open like a flower with all their little arms sticking out, trying to catch a meal floating in the water. If you really looked you could find live sea shells and hermit crabs running all about. At high tide when the large waves came in and then went out there would be large groups of periwinkles (some people called them coquina but most locals called the periwinkles) digging back in the wet sand. You could easily dig them out and see all the different colors. A periwinkle is a small clam like sea shell that is only about a half inch long with sharp ends so that it could easily dig back in the sand with its soft looking foot. Sometimes I would take them home and save the pretty, small shells. I got the live part out of them by putting them in hot water, which would open them. You could take the soft part out and be left with a pretty sea shell.

Another thing that I often noticed at high tide is that when the waves went out there were sand shrimp digging back into the sand like the periwinkles did. But the sand shrimp were much larger. They were about the shape and size of a large pecan with a bunch of little legs used to dig back into the sand. I later learned that there are very little creatures that are very hard to see. They hung on a grain of sand in order to keep from being washed out into the ocean and helped clean up the beaches of organic material. I have only seen pictures of them and they look like little monsters of many types and shapes. I understand that this is why beaches clean themselves up sooner than we expect them to do after a fish kill or when other things come ashore and mess up our beaches. When digging little ponds near the ocean edge I saw little red worms. I guess what I am telling you is that if you really look and pay attention to the ocean there is something going on all the time.

Many people that fish in the surf find out that their best bet is to fish in the breakers because when the waves come in they stir up all these little sea creatures and the fish are more easily able to make a meal of them.

I often wondered how and what all the sea shells ate. The couch and snail- like shells are holy terrors. The knobbed conch has a sharp edge on its shell where its snail-like body comes out, which is as sharp as the open end of an oyster. This conch finds a shell like a clam that has two shells that attach to each other which protect the body of the clam. It then puts this sharp part of its shell between where the clam opens and presses down until the clam opens with this constant pressure. Then the conch eats the inside as clean as a freshly washed dish in our own kitchen. Have you noticed that you never find a shell on the beach with a half eaten animal in it? Nothing is wasted in the ocean. The clam and other two shelled sea shells make their living by filtering out organic material in the sea water. They just sit there and pump water through their bodies and get fatter until a conch comes along and eats them. The moon shell or buckeye has a unique way of eating. It come across any kind of sea shell, even their own kind, and grabs it with its strong foot and then with a rough tongue it drills a small hole in it and sucks the soft part of the shell out. You will often see a shell with a small hole in it. This was done by a moon shell.

The starfish just wraps its five legs around a clam or oyster and puts pressure on the clam. When it opens it puts its stomach down on it and eats it. In the past, oystermen saw starfish eating oysters and tore them up and threw them back into the water. What many did not understand is that starfish can regenerate themselves and each part of the starfish formed another full size starfish. When I was coming up I found starfish with a fork at the end of one of the starfish's legs. I guess one of the legs was eaten or broken off and instead of repairing the end, the starfish got confused and made a fork.

When you find pieces of conchs on the beach that look like they recently came from a live conch, they were probably broken by a sea turtle. A large sea turtle can break a large conch open and eat the soft part. I understand that Scotch Bonnets eat sand dollars. I am not sure how they do it. I have just read this somewhere. Therefore there is warfare going on in the ocean all the time. The small fish eat even smaller sea life and then they are eaten by larger fish, etc. The snail like sea shells are hunters and the clam like shells just sit there and pump sea water through themselves and take out the good stuff. Nothing is wasted. What some leave behind after eating their fill, another comes by and eats. Of course the sea gulls come along and pick up what floats to the surface. How can you be bored sitting on the beach and knowing all this is going on?

After a storm when the ocean would wash live clam like shells up on the beach you would see sea gulls pick them up in their beaks, fly up about 50 feet or so and drop them on hard sand to break them open. They would then come down and eat them. They would do this until all of these live shells were eaten.

Have you ever thought much about how a pelican gets its food? A pelican has a large membrane that stretches out like a peck bucket when it hits the water. This membrane turns into a bucket and surrounds the fish. He flies up and down the coast or creek and when he sees a fish near the surface he dives down to try to catch the fish. Sometimes this is from a great distance in the air and sometimes the pelican is close to the water. When he gets a fish in its beak, he closes the membrane, flushes the water out and then swallows the fish. When he catches a fish he lifts his head and swallows the fish. If you see one come up after a dive and not bring his head up, he did not catch a fish. They are not successful all the time. The tragedy of the pelicans is that they put so much stress on the membrane by diving from so much height that the membrane finally tears loose and the pelican is no longer able to catch fish. I guess that, like humans, some have flaws in their makeup. Thus pelicans are born with a flaw. But I still like to sit on my screened porch overlooking Store Creek and watch the pelicans work the creek. Maybe we can learn something from the pelicans and the ants in that they persist in what they do until they get the job done. I have never seen an ant or pelican sitting back and waiting on the welfare check. They get out and go at what they were born to do. We have screwed up our society by giving help to those that can work.

The terns are the ones that puzzle me. They can be flying down the beach with several small fish in their beaks and then dive down and get another until their beaks are totally full and cannot hold another fish. I've seen them fly past our dock with five or more small fish in their beaks.

Again, when you look at the ocean, know that there is total warfare taking place on the ocean floor. The sea snail sea shells are constantly looking for another clam-like shell to eat. The clams are sucking in the plankton and other organic material to eat and who knows what is going on. Little fish eat plankton, bigger fish eat them and even bigger fish eat them. Nothing is wasted in the ocean. I guess only the strongest or fastest make it to large sea shells or large fish. I guess fish have to spawn thousands of eggs to get one fish that makes it to adulthood and oysters have to spawn even more to get one new oyster. Therefore the salt water has literally millions of fish eggs and other sea creatures' eggs and thus can support an untold variety of sea life. Yet each creature seems to survive by putting out enough new life to keep his kind creating the next generation.

As I got older I began to get interested in the sea weed that washed up on the beach that was a sort of red color with little air bubbles on the branches that you could pop. These bubbles make the weed float. When I read up on these strange looking sea weeds I learned that they were Saragossa weeds that came from the keys below Florida. Over the eons of time the Gulf Stream has taken these weeds out into the middle of the Atlantic Ocean and they have formed a very large sea of weeds. This sea of weeds covers that area below Bermuda down close to the Bahamas and is called the Saragossa Sea. This is like a desert in the ocean and old sailing ships used to get caught in it. I guess this is caused by sea currents on both sides of the Atlantic Ocean directing the wind up and down the coast and not across the ocean in this area. This is my estimate of why there is little or no wind in this area. It is also a place where young sea turtles and eels spend some of their time. As you begin to observe the beaches and ocean life you will find that it is all interconnected in many different ways. For example, what in the world would make sea weed from the Florida Keys have anything to do with sea turtles? The following are two Rabbit Trails worth talking about on sea turtles and eels that I learned as a youth because I was interested in such. These tales may not be exact but they will give you a good idea of the life cycle of these two Edisto creatures.

Rabbit Trail: In the summer, as a teenager, one my favorite things to do was walk on the beach at night with my girlfriend, looking for sea turtles that have come up to lay their eggs. These huge sea turtles would come out of the water at low tide, go above the high water mark, dig a hole about a foot or so deep and lay about 100 or so eggs. They would then cover up the eggs and return to the sea, usually at high tide by then. I guess they become so tired after dragging themselves up on shore after swimming so freely in the ocean. It was nice to have the ocean nearby when they were ready to return to it.

We would walk down the beach with a flashlight and look for what looked like bulldozer tracks that went from the low water mark to above the high water mark. Sometimes you would see where the turtle had come up, turned around and goes back into the sea. I guess something scared it and it returned to the sea. When we saw these tracks we would follow them up and usually find a turtle digging a hole, laying eggs or covering up the hole. I have seen a turtle laying her eggs. They looked about the size of a ping pong ball and about the same color or maybe a little grayer. When the turtle got finished she would return to the sea. I guess hauling around two or three hundred pounds on the shore would be quite tiring if you were used to paddling around in the ocean.

In about 60 to 90 days (I am not sure how long) the baby sea turtles hatch out. They dig their way out of the nest and begin crawling toward the ocean. Some do not make it because sand crabs, birds and no telling what else catches and eats them. Those that make it to the water will swim for about two days, living on the egg yolk still in them. They look for some floating marsh grass that I have talked about earlier. They will float with this marsh grass, eating whatever small creatures that also caught a ride on this marsh grass. They will float around in the ocean currents for a while until they end up in the Saragossa Sea. It is my understanding that these small sea turtles may even come close to the other side of the Atlantic before they end up in the Saragossa Sea. When they get a little bigger they return to the American side of the ocean. The same turtles that hatched out on Edisto Beach will return when they get mature and lay their own eggs on the beach where they were born.

Rabbit Trail: Anyone that has ever fished in one of Edisto's creeks has caught an eel. These snake like fish are hard as they can be to get off your fishing line because they wrap themselves around the rig trying to get off. These eels that you find around Edisto may go as far as they can up the Edisto River, even into fresh water swamps and anywhere they can. When they mature they return to the ocean and swim out to the Saragossa Sea, mate and lay their eggs. When they get big enough they return to the creeks and rivers around Edisto or from wherever they came. Therefore I hope you will see that everything is connected. The marsh grass provides sea floats for young turtles to hide, the Saragossa weed makes a place for sea turtles and eels to grow up in, and the beach is kept clean by little sea creatures many never notice. What a wonderful world God created and it all works. We really don't have to worry about man messing up nature because nature has so many safeguards built in that, if we don't heed the warnings given to us, nature will just get rid of us. It may take hundreds of years for nature to clean up what man messed up but the systems are in place to do just that. Therefore like Proverbs tells us, "Observe the ant" or periwinkles or all the other sea creatures.

Genesis 1:20-23 KJV

"And God said, Let the waters bring forth abundantly the moving creatures that hath life, and fowl that may fly above the earth in the open firmament of heaven."

And God created great whales, and every living creature that moveth, which the water brought forth abundantly, after their kind, and every winged fowl after his kind: and God saw that it was good.

And God blessed them, saying, Be fruitful, and multiply, and fill the waters in the sea, and let fowl multiply in the earth.

And the evening and the morning were the fifth day.

A couple of other things I'd like to mention about what I did and the impressions I gained living on the beach are fossil hunting and weather watching. I have already talked about the fossils that I found on the beach.

This took a great deal of my time and I regret not keeping most of them to show my grandchildren. But when you are growing up you are not very smart and things have different values as you get older.

When you live on the ocean you become aware of the weather more than when you live inland in a city. The northeasters were always a time when you had to stay off the beach because of the sand that was picked up by the wind which made it hard to walk on the beach. I soon began to recognize that a northeaster blew one day, two days or three days. Most of the time the northeaster blew for three days. When you saw a big black cloud, you knew that wind was in those clouds and if you were in a small boat, you knew to get your feet on dry land. One day while sitting on our front porch I saw six water spouts come down out of one black cloud and when they hit the water it looked like a bomb had hit the water. These spouts were a ways offshore and did no damage to anyone. One day I saw several small fish on the road near our house. The only way they could have gotten there was that a water spout had sucked them out of the water and when the cloud released its rain, the fish came down with it.

Because I spent a lot of time on the beach as a youngster, one thing that haunted me for some time was that when the moon cleared the horizon, the next wave that came in came in a little less than the previous wave. I checked it over and over until I realized it was true. When the moon clears the horizon, the tide starts out at that moment.

Here is another story I just stuck in from one of my newsletters called Edisto's "Old Man of the Sea" that I wrote while I was selling real estate on Edisto.

Edisto's Coral Reef

"When I was growing up on Edisto Beach back in the fifties, I got a six- passenger license to take people fishing. For four dollars apiece, I took fishermen out to the reef off Edisto where you could catch fish on any tide and in any weather. I could carry up to six people and I stayed four hours. My family had a 28-foot long navy lifeboat, called a whaleboat, because both bow and stern were pointed and would take anything the sea could throw at it. Of course I came home before the sea got too rough. But some old fishermen wanted to stay no matter the weather.

The whaleboat was powered by a ten-horse outboard motor that was placed in a well that was one rib back from the center and next to the keel.

This way when the boat pitched and rolled it always had power and the motor never left the water. Since the motor was in the center of the boat, you could not steer with it, therefore we had a very large rudder installed on the stern to steer the boat. People often asked why we did not use a larger motor. The answer was that an open whale boat was designed to be powered by 6 to 12 men using oars and a larger motor would just make the boat want to dig into the water and actually slow it down. This kind of boat is easy to power and the ten-horse motor did just fine.

We had a doghouse installed on the front quarter of the boat so that any water that came across the bow would be shed and not fill up the boat. When it got rough I used to wish that my passengers would get sick so I could come home sooner than the four hours they bargained for. Many of my passengers got sick but I never got sick. In fact, I have been out in 20-foot seas in a shrimp boat and never got sick. I guess I am just lucky that way.

Therefore at one stage of my life I could officially be called "Captain Lybrand" due to my license to carry passengers. Oh, I did not marry anyone while they were offshore with me!

You can still catch fish at this old dead coral reef that is about a mile off Edisto Beach. If you look at a nautical chart of St. Helena Sound you will see a knoll off Edisto Beach that comes up to 10 feet. It is approximately at latitude 32 degrees 28.6 seconds and longitude 80 degrees 18.1 seconds. I used to line up the Ocean Villa with a radio tower to tell me how far to go down the beach and put the Edisto Beach State Park's water tower (no longer there) in a saddle in the trees which told me how far to go out. When I thought I was over the reef I lowered my anchor and if it felt like it hit rock I knew I was in the right spot.

Evidence of this old reef can be seen on the beach. The ocean currents keep breaking off pieces of the reef and washing them up on the beach. The pieces that wash up on the beach look rounded because they have been rolled over and over in the sand until they reach the beach. It is hard to go walking on the beach without finding a small piece of this old reef.

Nowadays you hear a lot about global warning. Well, at some time in our past the ocean off Edisto had to be much warmer because the water was warm enough to support a coral reef. How long ago this was will depend on if you believe the evolutionist or the creationist. I personally believe it may have been thousands rather than millions of years because of all the changes I have seen to the South Carolina coast in my short lifetime.

So if you bring a boat to Edisto that is large enough to go out in the ocean, find this old reef and catch a few fish for the pot. Spot tail bass seem to really like this old reef. If you have a question about where it is, come into my office and I will show you where it is on the chart hanging on my wall. Charts are made to hang on the wall and look at and then we can dream about our collective fish tales. The one that got away is always the biggest one. The Edisto "rock" is just another of life's little extras that Edisto has to offer

One last tale — I once took a group out to the reef (or rock as it is now often referred to) and an old man, using a large ocean rig, baited his line with shrimp. Before I could cut off the motor and get the anchor out he threw his line out and, bang, something big hit his line as soon as it hit the water and kept on going. Even his big ocean rig could not turn whatever he had hooked. Pointless to say, he was hooked on fishing on the reef. He either hooked a large stingray or large shark, but only a good fish tale will ever know what hit his line. He was sitting sideways when he threw his line out and the fish pulled so hard that it actually turned him around facing the side of the boat. This event was so exciting that I still remember it 50 years later. I was 17 or 18 when I was "Captain Sam." Oh, I still have the original copy (since expired) of my six-passenger license hanging on my office wall. Part of living a full life is remembering our pleasant memories. Edisto leaves most people with lasting pleasant memories. To experience Edisto's little extras you have to get out and seek out all that Edisto Island has to offer."

One more thing about the wind and what a boy can do with a little imagination is sailing a bicycle. From time to time when there was a good wind I would tie a pole to my handlebars with a cross piece on top of the pole and attach about a fourth of a bed sheet to it. I would then tie a string to each bottom corner and bring it down to the end of the handlebars where I steered the bike from. I'd then turn the bike in the direction the wind was going catch the wind in my square sail and off I would go. I'd use the two strings to adjust the sail so it would catch the wind the best. Away I'd go and I would sail all the way down to the pavilion. I'd have about a two mile run. Cars that went by looked at me in amazement. But the off side was that I could not sail against the wind. I had to take the sail down and pedal back home against the wind.

I could spend another year just talking about all that goes on in the ocean near the beach. With all this to learn and observe how could anyone be lonely or bored living on the beach?

Behind my house on Edisto Beach there were approximately 500 acres of undeveloped marine forest that I spent a great deal of my time in when everyone went home for the winter.

At about thirteen years of age I began exploring the woods behind the house. My first encounter was walking a short distance into the Woods and hearing what sounded like a huge panther jumping from one palmetto tree to another and come running out of the woods. Shortly thereafter I found that it was a squirrel jumping from one palmetto frond to another, which made a loud noise. Just shaking a palmetto frond will make a loud noise.

After that we started building tree houses near the house up in the large live oak trees. Daddy was always building something and had lots of lumber thrown in the back yard and plenty of nails lying around. Instead of cutting boards the size we wanted we would look for a board the size we needed and use that. We used the nails that were available. To this day I don't understand how just any nail would hold things together.

As time went by I got up each Saturday morning real early and go out in my jungle to hunt for squirrels and occasionally raccoons and maybe an opossum. One Saturday morning I was out hunting squirrels with a 12 gauge bolt action shot gun I had bought with my school bus money. I had killed two squirrels with bird shot which is all I had at the moment. As I was looking around I saw four raccoons off in the distance up in the top of a live oak tree picking acorns. I kept my eye on the tree and quietly walked over to the tree. When I got there the raccoons were nowhere to be seen. I knew they had not come down because I had kept my eye on the tree. I then looked a little closer and saw that the four raccoons had balled up like squirrel nests hoping I would not see them. I then pointed my shot gun at the largest of the four and shot at him with the bird shot I had. He came alive and started down the tree. When he got to a fork right above me he jumped down right at me. I guess he figured that a good defense is a good offense. If he had landed on me he could have torn me to pieces. On the way down I fired at him and missed him. Thanks goodness I had the state of mind to step back and have him land on the ground instead of me. I was so excited that when I fired my bolt action shot gun and tried to reload I pulled the bolt back so hard that I shared the pin that held the bolt in place. Therefore I had a bolt in one hand and a gun stock in the other hand and a raccoon coming down after me. When the raccoon hit the ground I stepped back a little further and drew back and hit him in the head with the stock of the gun.

After that I figured I had had enough excitement for the day and put the large raccoon in my hunting vest and headed home. In the meantime I had put the bolt back into my shot gun and reloaded just in case. When I got within sight of our house the raccoon came alive and started making such a fuss that I then thought he really was going to tear me apart. But he jumped out of the vest and started running away. I fired again and missed. This time I ran him down and really killed him with the stock. Now, where can you find excitement like that on an electronic game board?

Over the years I set steel traps and made box traps and caught many raccoons and opossums. I took them up to Perry's store and sold them for a dollar or two. Selling raccoons and opossums is where much of my spending money came from. I became an excellent trapper and very seldom missed what I went after.

Not far behind our house were fresh water lagoons that extended from near Scenic Highway 174 all the way down to what is now Lybrand Street. One year we built a little house on a very large dead cedar tree log that had fallen over into one of the lagoons. We got the material from one of the houses Daddy was repairing. I say we because as I got a little older, David, who had also gotten a little older, could then participate in some of my explorations.

We built a bridge over the lagoon where our lagoon house was built so we could get to the main part of the jungle without going way out of our way. It was built out of small trees we cut down. The walk area was built out of boards we got out of Daddy's wood pile. It would hold us but wouldn't hold a very heavy man. One day we heard a hunter come through the woods and try to cross our bridge. He fell in and we could hear him scream in disgust

From time to time whole flocks of ducks would land on these lagoons and seemed to cover the entire lagoon. One day I was out on my trap line and came across one of the lagoons full of ducks making a lot of noise and seeming to be having a good old time splashing around and quacking up a storm. I only had a single shot 22 caliber rifle with me and just shot into the flock and did not kill one duck. The whole flock took off, which sounded like a large airplane was taking off the lagoon.

When I first started exploring my jungle I often heard what I thought were bull frogs sounding off real loud. Many times I would hear splashing in the lagoons in front of where I was walking and thought it was a raccoon getting out of my way or a bull frog jumping in the water. One day I was walking in a right muddy area and saw a track about as big as my hand with a four finger like footprints pressed down in the mud about an inch. I got a little uneasy because I had never seen such a print. I took out some of the wire I used to wire my steel traps to trees so caught raccoons would not carry off my traps and made an impression of it. When I got home I looked at all my books on animals and could not find a track that looked like it. I then looked at a reptile book and realized it was the front foot of an alligator track. Later David and I caught a four foot alligator in a culvert and his front feet were only about four inches long. What I had seen was the track of a very large and heavy alligator maybe 12 or more feet long. From then on I carried a good size wooden staff with me and made noise with it when I walked near any of the lagoons. To this day I do not like to take a walk anywhere without a walking stick. I could take the head off a man with my current walking stick. I guess old fears never leave us. I also don't like to go anywhere without a weapon. I very seldom leave home without a large folding pocket knife in my pocket. I guess spending so much time in the woods coming up has left me with the need to be prepared to defend myself at all times.

One late afternoon I was sitting under a large pine tree waiting on some squirrels to come near me. I had heard them off a ways eating palmetto berries and dropping the hard part of the berries on the forest floor. I had often heard this and knew they would be coming my way when they had eaten all the berries in that tree. As chance would have it, I fell asleep leaning up against that pine tree and dark caught me. When it gets dark the whole woods come alive and you begin to hear all kinds of noises. I began walking down the old logging road in the woods toward home when I scared up a great horned owl that flew down toward the ground right in front of me and I about wet my pants. I hurried home as fast as I could and never allowed myself to be caught in the woods again in the dark.

One day we caught several baby raccoons and took them home. We put them in a chicken coop and made a small water tight wooden container to put small mullet in to see what would happen. As soon as we put the mullet in the water the raccoons jumped in the water and caught them with both front and back feet, bit them to kill them and then threw them out on the chicken pen floor. When they had caught and killed all the small mullets they jumped out and ate them. A raccoon will tear you up if you are not careful but as I got older I could catch a raccoon behind its neck with one hand and just before his tail with the other hand and control any raccoon I caught. By then I had strong enough hands to control a raccoon. I don't suggest anyone trying this unless they are fast enough and strong enough to hold a raccoon.

My jungle had large sand dunes. One of them was called Mount Hope and I understand that it was 65 feet above sea level. We used to go back and play on them by cutting grape vines and swinging out like Tarzan and Jane. We also made sleds out of two-by-fours and slid down the sand dunes on the pine straw. Some of these sand dunes were so steep that you could not climb up them. You could see where trees had been surrounded by these sand dunes in the past where the wind had moved the sand dunes and caused the sand to almost cover up trees and palmettos. At sixty-five feet you could go up on the highest of these and see all around the beach area.

By the time I got ready to go to college I was walking all the way down to the docks through the woods and back. It would take most of the day to do this and I enjoyed every minute because of the things I saw along the way.

One day while I was out squirrel hunting in the woods near the Sound area I noticed a bright peace of metal sticking out of the ground. At the time I was looking for an old motor block to anchor a buoy down to tie my sailboat to. Back then we did not have floating docks and had to be careful not to tie our boat up against oyster shells that attached to our dock. I took out my machete and cut a small tree down and started wedging around the piece of metal. It was much larger than I first figured. As I was probing it I notice a knob at the end and knew what I had found. David was with me and we got Marion Whaley to try to pull it out of the woods with his jeep, but his jeep would not even move it at all. We hid it and went home and told Daddy what I had found. He hired a man with a tractor with a lift to come lift it out of the ground and take it to the Ocean Villa lawn. When the word got out, the News and Courier came and took a picture of it. It was later found that it and another cannon were placed there during the Civil War to guard the entrance to the South Edisto River and Big Bay Creek. Another larger cannon was found in the same area when David developed Oristo. The cannon was about six feet or longer and was made of cast iron. It had a four inch bore and was probably an old ship's cannon. It is now on display in the State Museum in Columbia, SC, located on Harden Street. I still have the original newspaper picture that was published. My daughter recently took a picture of this old cannon with two of her children standing behind it and gave me a framed copy of it. I still have fond memories each time I look at this picture of my cannon that I found at around 16 years of age. How many teenagers do your know that found a real cannon?

After the newspaper article came out a bunch of teenagers came one night to steal my cannon but all of them together could not move the cannon one inch because it was so heavy.

This is one of the pictures my daughter Amy took of my cannon as it is displayed in the State Museum.

On the following page is a picture that I have saved all these years of the newspaper article and picture of my cannon. It has been hanging in my house all these years and I often tell this story to anyone that will listen. The pictures show me and David. I am not sure who the lady is. She was just a guest at the Ocean Villa at the time. When Daddy sold the Ocean Villa I took my cannon to Columbia, SC where I then lived and it ended up in the State Museum.

Having my own 500 acres to explore was a great way to come up. I now feel sorry for children that don't have vast open and wooded areas to explore and learn about how nature works and all there is to learn about nature. I am thankful every day for these wonderful memories. Oh, I became a deadly shot. Most of the time I carried a 22 caliber single shot rifle that you had to cock every time you wanted to fire it. This meant that I only got one shot at what I was shooting at. If I missed what I was shooting at, it was gone before I could reload.

Along with my jungle I had so many opportunities to explore the creeks and rivers on Edisto my choices were unlimited. Who could complain when I had a 19 foot sailboat, a 28 foot whaleboat, and several small boats to row and play around with? Many people would die to have this many opportunities to enjoy the rivers, the creeks, a big sound and a large track of land with giant sand dunes found in and around Edisto.

Let me start with one of my early passions, sailing. It used to send chills down my spine when I was lying alongside the dock with the sails flapping in the wind and the lines knocking about. As I slowly tightened the lines, I heard the water begin slapping on the bow as the boat began to move with no sound of a motor or oars hitting the water. Man has been using the forces of nature for eons of time. The glorious thing about this is that the sailboat will not move an inch unless the one at the rudder holding the sheet lines understands and uses these forces of nature. But in order for a man to capture these awesome forces he must put aside all his worries and concentrate on what is going on. Thus for a few hours one is able to enjoy nature at its best while leaving his worldly life behind. If the one running the sailboat loses his concentration, the sailboat will just stop and the sails will flap around in pure chaos. I guess this is where I learned to be contented in whatever situation I was in. If you just accept life for what it is and deal with what you can control and don't worry about what you cannot control, life is just more pleasant and you may live a little longer.

At about the age of 13 I began to be interested in sailing and asked Daddy to buy me a sailboat. He considered having Mr. Boineau, a cabinet maker in Adams Run, build me one, but somehow Daddy found out about an old wooden Lighting Class sailboat in the old village of Mt. Pleasant, SC under someone's house. We took an old boat trailer over to look at the boat in case it was in good enough shape to buy. When we found the old run down house in Mt. Pleasant overlooking Charleston Harbor the owner came out and showed us the boat. It was dusty and run down but seemed in a sound condition. Daddy offered to buy it and the man accepted his offer. Two sets of sails and even a large spinnaker came with the boat. A spinnaker is a large balloon sail that goes out in front of the boat when running before the wind. One of the sets of sails that included a mainsail and jib was made of Egyptian cotton and lasted as long as we owned the boat. The other was made of nylon and never really was much good. The spinnaker was made of silk and thus was very light.

After we got the sailboat on the trailer Daddy told me to get behind the wheel of the car and drive it home, pulling the large heavy 19 foot sailboat because I had just gotten my drivers license. It was okay at first but then we had to cross the old two lane Cooper River Bridge with only two lanes, one going each way. That would have been okay but I got behind a logging truck and had to follow it all the way across. Daddy did not say anything but I made it across and then all the way home. David and I cleaned it up and got all the rigging to fit and work and then put it in the water. In the meantime Daddy bought a book on sailing and I literally memorized it. As I wrote about sailing, Seaph took David and me out for the first time. The next time we went out to the sound from our dock and on the way back we only ran aground three times before we got back to the dock. From then on I learned more each time I went sailing. It was a nice boat because it would easily carry three couples and I took many young ladies out sailing even at a young age.

After two years of sailing I entered the boat, named "Jennie O" after my mother, in the Rockville Races and learned more in one race than I had learned the previous two years of sailing on my own. It all boiled down to surface and drag against the water and the foil of the sail so they would pull like an airplane wing. If you had as little of the boat in the water as possible and the best foil or setting of your sail you won. The race all boiled down to who best understood the forces of nature and knew how to use them best.

My second year at The Citadel I took this sailboat to college with me. I did not have a car but I had a sailboat. One year I sailed it home from The Citadel through the Intracoastal Waterway. Somehow while I was in the service and off raising my family it disappeared. But I still have an old oar I used on "Jennie O." Later in life Mother found this oar and had a local artist paint low country scenes on it and gave it to me for my birthday. It is now hanging in our computer room. When I see it, it brings back pleasant moments and the hours upon hours I spent sailing this old wooden sailboat.

I have already mentioned the small rowboat we had and how I learned to row it and a few tales about using it. Therefore I will not repeat them.

One day an airplane dropped a large eight to ten foot long wing fuel tank in the ocean near our house. I was able to retrieve it and took it home. I found that it had two sides. One side had an indent in it where it attached to the wing and the other side looked like a small boat. Both sides were bolted together with small easy to get off bolts with a gasket in between. I took the wing tank apart because I thought I could make a small sailboat out of it. I took the side that did not have a indent in it and bolted a piece of quarter inch plywood to it with the same bolt and used the same gasket to make it water tight. I then cut a hole in it about three quarters back from the front and made a seat for me to sit in. I next took a small shrimpboat outrigger stabilizer and bolted it to the bottom for a keel or centerboard. I then placed a 6 to 8 foot mast on it, made some sails, put a rudder on it and an outrigger and put it in the water. Behold, it sailed and was easy to handle. I used it most of one summer until the stabilizer, moving back and forth, tore the bolts loose from the bottom of the boat so that I could no longer use it. One time I went fishing in it in Mud Creek and caught a croaker and he pulled the boat along.

I have already mentioned the old Navy lifeboat Daddy bought. And I have already mentioned how Nick Lindsay altered it so we could use it. Therefore all I want to mention is a two week trip two cousins and I took down the Intracoastal Waterway in this open whaleboat before the cabin was built on it.

One summer, between my first and second year at The Citadel, my first cousin Ralph and I were waiting on tables in the Ocean Villa and wanted to take a trip down the Intracoastal Waterway about to the Florida line. At the same time Ralph's brother Owens and another young man had built a homemade canoe and wanted to paddle it down the Altamaha River from Athens, Georgia all the way to the coast. But the kicker was that Ralph and I did not have any money to speak of. At least we did not have enough money to pay for such a trip. Therefore we put the charts we were going to use on the trip on one of the serving tables in hopes that the Villa guests would get interested in our trip and help with the trip. We went ahead and made our plans. We put 2 by 4s up in the whaleboat and borrowed a canvas to go over it if it rained. We borrowed another small motor in case our outboard motor gave out and we borrowed another five gallon gas can.

We set a date and told Ralph's brother Owens when we planned on leaving and for him to plan on how long he thought it would take him to paddle to the coast. I sent Owens a chart of the Altamaha River where it meet Highway 17 and told him not to go beyond that point and we would pick him up. When the Altamaha gets close to the coast it splits into three rivers and Highway 17 crossed all three of the forks in the river. We talked to Owens and he left Athens and headed to the coast with his friend. In the meantime we had not gotten any significant tips from the guests at the Villa. The night before we were going to have to leave in time to meet Owens all of the families that were guests at the Villa gave us five dollars each for a total of $85.00 which we figured was enough. Therefore the next morning we fueled up and headed out in our 28 foot open whaleboat powered by a 10 horse power outboard motor and headed for the Altamaha River to pick up Owens.

The first day went fine and we passed by Beaufort headed for Thunderbolt. I am not sure if it is in Georgia or South Carolina. When we got to the Marine Base at Paris Island the Intracoastal Waterway took us around Paris Island. I looked at the chart and there was a creek large enough to go behind Paris Island and cut off a considerable distance. Therefore I took this creek and a ways into it I noticed on the chart that this was a firing range for the Marines being trained at Paris Island. You had bet your bottom dollar I turned around and got out of there fast and continued on down the Intracoastal Waterway. Behind Hilton Head Ralph and I stopped on an oyster bank and caught fish. We cooked them there and had a meal. When we got back underway I began to notice that we did not have enough gas to get to Thunderbolt and not enough gas to get back to Beaufort. We notice that a large dredge was not far ahead and headed for it in hopes of getting some gas but they had none. I took out some navigation instruments I had and made an arc of how far I thought we could go on the amount of gas we had and the only life was Tybee Beach off Savannah, Ga. So we headed to Tybee Beach and ran out of gas in the breakers. Ralph, who was a big man, at least much bigger and stronger than me, held the boat into the breakers while I went up on the beach to try to get someone to help me go get some gas. A nice lady had been watching it all and came running down to see if she could help. She took me to a gas station where I filled up our gas cans. We went back to the boat, filled up our gas tank and went back through the surf which the whaleboat had no trouble doing because that is what it was designed for. We looked on the chart and went down a ways south and went through an ocean inlet to a marina behind Tybee Beach. We spent the night after we found two old lard cans that we could carry more gas in. That night the mosquitoes about ate us alive. The next morning we almost got lost trying to find our way back to the inland waterway.

I had been told that mosquitoes would not fly over one hundred feet from the marsh out into a creek. Therefore from then on we found the largest river or creek we could find away from the tug channel on the Intracoastal Waterway where we anchored and slept from then on. It turned out to be right because we were no longer bothered by mosquitoes. Even during the summer I got cold in the early morning before dawn. I had heard that if you keep your feet warm the rest of you would be warm. After the first night sleeping on the boat I put a laundry bag over my feet and stayed warm and comfortable the rest of the trip.

The next morning on our way I turned pale when I realized we had crossed the Savannah River. If we had run out of gas in it on an outgoing tide, we may have been taken out to the Gulf Stream and would never have been seen again. Back then we did not have small radios like those available now so we could not call for help. We were just on our own. From then on I read the charts in detail. The next day was uneventful and we took our time taking in all that we saw along the way, stopping when we saw something we wanted to look at closer. The following day we came to the first branch of the Altamaha River and Owens was not there. We found a small creek that took us to the next fork and Owens was not there. We had to go out toward the ocean to be able to get to the last fork and asked ourselves what we were going to do if he was not there. We had made no plans for such an occurrence and had no cell phones. But we had been talking to Owens as he came down the river every time he came to a settlement and knew about when he should get to the point where we were to meet. When we got to the last point where that fork went under Highway 17 he and his friend had been there about half an hour. We had traveled two and a half days and it had taken Owens a week and a half to travel by canoe. When he saw us he said we looked like a hotel compared to the small canoe he had been in for the last week and a half. We tied his canoe onto the whaleboat and continued on down the Intracoastal Waterway. Owens' friend had to go back to Athens because it had taken them longer than he expected. Then my two first cousins and I took the rest of the trip together.

On our way Owens told us about his trip down the Altamaha. He told us that the first day out the wooden slats that he had built the canoe out of began to swell and break the canoe apart. It was a pretty frugally built canoe out of slats and covered with painted canvas. He had to take out his pocket knife and start cutting away at the slats to give them room to expand being careful not to cut the canvas. He told us that it was scary because they were already down the river, quite a ways from civilization. Every now and then they would come to where the river widened and went through a swamp with no clear channel to follow. They had to just stop paddling and let the current take them to the other side of the swamp not knowing where they would come out and hoping they would not be taken off in some side creek that went nowhere. But every time the current took them back into the main river channel.

One night they were sleeping on this sand bank high enough up on the bank so if the river rose during the night they would not be swept off in their sleep. They were awakened by a bull that was between them and their canoe. They became very still because they were afraid if the bull felt threatened he may destroy their canoe and no telling what he would do to them. But after awhile the bull went on about his business and they were able to get to their canoe and drift down a ways in the dark, far enough away from the bull to feel safe. They did not get much sleep that night. They finally realized that they had camped in a cow pasture.

He told us many such stories and often started to find a highway and go back home because of the long hours of paddling and other hardships that come with an adventure like this. He did not quit because he did not want to start a trip and not finish it. Besides, what would we think if he did not show up as there was no way to contact us.

What this trip involved was two adventures tied into one big adventure.

Once we picked up Owens and tied his canoe behind our whaleboat we slowed down and began taking in all that we saw as we went along. If we saw an interesting looking creek off the Intracoastal Waterway, we would go down it to see what we could see. We passed small and large settlements on our way. We just passed some, but stopped and walked around those that seemed interesting. We navigated in small waterways and crossed large bodies of water but our old whaleboat took all of them in stride and we felt safe because she could take whatever was thrown at her.

We often stopped and fished and sometimes we hunted for our next meal. We ate whatever we killed. Along the way were many old looking docks that seemed to have not been used for some time. These were our favorite ones to tie up to and go ashore to explore or hunt.

Along the way we were impressed at the wide expanse of marsh grass and small creeks that separated the mainland from the sea islands and barrier islands we passed and explored. From where we left to where we turned around and headed home there was an island then a sea island, island and then a sea island. It seems that between each sea island there was a large body of water that we had to cross and sometimes is was not obvious where we should go after we crossed these large bodies of water. But I had purchased navigation charts from Edisto all the way to Florida and they were easy to read. But we had to pay attention to where we had been and where we were going to keep from hitting a dead end creek. Therefore we had to stay alert all the time. As stated before, we were careful to anchor off the tug channel at night when we stopped to sleep to avoid being run down by a large tug pushing several barges. Of course we passed all kinds of boats and yachts on our way. Many kept looking at these kids with straw hats in a whaleboat, wondering what they were doing out in never, never land just cruising along, seeming to be having fun.

If you have never taken the trip down the Intracoastal Waterway from Charleston to the Florida line you have missed the experience of a lifetime. The scenery is breathtaking and there is something new around each bend in the rivers and creeks. We were in an open whaleboat and were able to take it all in.

Since my two cousins did not know much about the coastal waters I took over as captain, sometimes to their objections. This proved to be the right decision when one night we were anchored in a large river. It was raining cats and dogs and the canvas sides we were under kept blowing open. Owens tied his boots to the canvas bottom to keep it from allowing rain to blow in on us. But one of them came untied and fell into the water. Owens wanted to go in after it and I would not let him because it was very dark and the current was moving very fast. I explained to him that if he went over under these conditions and could not swim against the current by the time we got the anchor up we may never find him again. After he understood what I was telling him was for his own safety, he thanked me and I had no trouble being captain the rest of the trip.

As we went along the inland waterway it often would bring us right by marinas where we would stop and buy gas to run the boat. We also bought sardines, saltines and other easy to eat food and we never seemed to get hungry. As stated above we also stopped at old pulpwood landings and fished. I would also take the 22 caliber single shot rifle I had brought along on the trip up on shore and go hunting. We ate anything we could kill and any fish we could catch. We ate rabbits, squirrels and even raccoons. We found out that you could eat almost anything if you cut it up in small pieces, put it in water with some kind of vegetable, let the fire go out under it overnight and then lightly fry it the next morning. One evening we stopped at this dock and I went ashore to see what I could find and there were squirrels, raccoons and even deer everywhere. I killed two squirrels and a raccoon very shortly and could have easily killed a deer but wondered what I would do with it. My two cousin's fished off the boat and caught 13 saltwater catfish. That night for supper we had a raccoon, two squirrels and 13 catfish. The raccoon was a little wild tasting but when you are hungry you can eat almost anything. The next day on our way I was looking closely at our chart and found that the reason there were so many tame animals on that island was because it was a game preserve. But by the time I saw this we were long gone past the island.

As we went along we stopped to look at anything that interested us. One afternoon we saw a very large marsh island out in the middle of nowhere, far away from any land that a bridge could have connected it to. It had a large dock with a large modern looking house and farm animals everywhere. It was a working farm out in the marsh. We saw someone on the dock and stopped and asked if we could look around and we were given permission. It turns out that the owner invented the current coupling the railroads use to automatically connect their boxcars and engines. We were amazed at what we came across and there was never a dull moment.

One thing that we found sort of strange was that when we got drinking water from a town or some settlement we passed it went stale in a short time. But when we were able to get artesian well water it would last until we drank it all. After we found this out we tried to get artesian well water every time we could. We discovered this quite by accident when someone along the way suggested we get artesian well water for our drinking water and offered us some. What a difference the artesian well water made. Sometimes we'd get hot and it was nice to have fresh water to drink.

I am often asked how we slept on the whaleboat since it had no cabin or any flat place wide enough to sleep on. We carried some boards with us and at night we laid the boards down across a few seats that were used in the whaleboat to row it from and slept on them covered up by sheets or thin blankets. Of course we had the makeshift canvas over us. In the morning we just stacked the boards up for use the next evening. When we had to go to the bathroom we just hung it overboard and let it go since there were no ladies with us.

We stopped at one old Spanish fort park that fronted on the waterway we were on, tied up to a cannon and went exploring. We were eventually asked to untie our boat from the cannon, but we were finished looking it over by then.

After we had been out about a week and a half we began to figure out how long it would take us to get back because all of us had to get ready to go to college. After figuring awhile we allowed four days and when the time had come we headed back home, only stopping to get gas and food. One day we were crossing one of the big rivers or sounds and the waves got so big that our ten horse motor would not easily push the boat over the swells. Because of this, it took us four hours to cross this body of water. We'd go up the wave and then stall out as the wave passed us by. But there were enough smaller waves that we were able to cross the body of water. Most of the time it was easy going in the Intracoastal Waterway and we made good time. We figured we made about ten miles per hour.

We got back safely and used just about all of the $85.00 Ralph and I gotten from the guests at the Ocean Villa. What a trip! We stayed out two weeks and traveled just about to the Florida line from Edisto in a 28 foot open whaleboat pushed by a ten horse power outboard motor. We mostly slept under the stars and no telling what we ate. We learned how to keep out of the mosquitoes and how to stay warm in the early morning hours of summer. None of us shaved during the whole trip and must have looked like river bums but no one we met along the way seem to mind what we looked like. In fact my belt broke shortly after we got going and I used a piece of rope to keep up my pants. I don't remember if we even washed any clothes along the way. What a trip to remember!

Now in this day and age would you let a bunch of cousins go off on such a trip not knowing where they were for two weeks? Our parents did. But guess what? When you take such a trip you quickly learn that there is no one looking over your shoulder. You had better know what you are doing and what your equipment is capable of doing. I can't remember if we called home during this trip but we told my parents when we would get back and we arrived back the afternoon we told them we would be back.

Now do you know what a boy can do when he lives on the coast with very few kids to play with?

Now find a quiet place and turn on some soothing music. Sit back and let everything go. Imagine sitting on the back of this old whaleboat holding on to a large tiller, steering it wherever you decide to go without a care in the world for two whole weeks. You can do what you want to do and go where you want to go and no one is telling you what you can do and what you cannot do. The sky is blue, the temperature is warm and there is a constant breeze because of the forward motion of the boat. You need a shave, but who cares? Sit there and dream of what it would be like to be a teenager and just slowly exploring the world because your boat will not go fast in the first place. You are just cruising along, singing a song, side by side in the best of one of God's creations. Do this for an hour or so and you'll feel better about the world we live in.

Now come back to reality. Go into another trance and imagine you are holding the tiller of Sam's sailboat with your best girl beside you sailing up Big Bay Creek on the way to the sound. Imagine your sailboat leaning way over and sailing as fast as it will possibly go using every ounce of energy the sails will produce. Imagine how all this is happening Where the only sound is coming from the strain of the mainsheet line and the slapping of the water against your bow.

Then quietly imagine you have an oar in each of your hands. You are rowing down Scott Creek and with every strong deep dip in the water with your oars you lunge forward a little bit more. When you get into the swing of it you effortlessly row down the creek for hours without a care in the world. After a while you dip your oars and glide along and then dip them again and glide some more, stopping every now and then to listen to the marsh hens and to watch the osprey dive into the water and come up with a fish.

While you are daydreaming, know that a skinny boy named Sammy actually did these things and though they were commonplace for a boy at his age living in the midst of God's special paradise. Dream this often enough and you will be drawn to "Ed-is-tow" where you can still experience these kinds of pleasures God created for us to enjoy. The only difference is that a motorboat may pass you by and cause an occasional bothersome wake. But with all of Edisto's small creeks there are still plenty of places where you can row or sail along without being bothered by those motoring along, not stopping long enough to enjoy all that God created for us to enjoy.

The next set of photos two are some old pictures I have been able to save over the years of this trip my cousins and I took and a few pictures of our old whaleboat and my sailboat. Be careful to notice Owens' homemade canoe that we are pulling behind the whaleboat and how small it is compared to our whaleboat. Also note how un-nautically dressed we all were on this trip. I still often dream I am on this trip getting ready to stop and explore another place that seemed interesting.

The three boats I had at my disposal, the small rowboat, the whaleboat and our sailboat.

Our sailboat getting ready to set sail.

Me and the tiller.

Off on our adventure

Cousin Owen. Note how small the canoe is.

On large river –Note the canoe.

Cousin Ralf

Fooling around

Stopped at unknown dock

Rabbit for supper.

More fooling around

"But, beloved, be not ignorant of this one thing, that one day is with the Lord as a thousand years, and a thousand years as one day".
2 Peter 3:8 KJV

CHAPTER TEN

"And above all things have fervent charity (love) among yourselves: for charity (love) shall cover the multitude of sins."
1 Peter 4:8 KJV

    This chapter is about hurricanes, what I know about them and how I have personally experienced them. Hurricanes should be tracked but are nothing to be constantly worried about. The odds of being hit by a hurricane are about the same as being bitten by a rattlesnake. Snakes and hurricanes are a fact of life but you just know about them and act accordingly. The odds are that you will never be hit by a hurricane. But from what I know and have actually experienced, I respect what hurricanes can do because I have been in the eye of a hurricane. When it was forecasted that one would hit Edisto, I would take my wife and any grandchildren I had staying with me and head for higher ground. From what I have seen and read in the past, I will not try to ride out a hurricane of any size. I have mentioned hurricanes further back in this book, but in this section I am going to try to tell you what I know and have actually experienced about hurricanes.
    Up until fairly recently, houses were not built on barrier islands except for Edingsville, which was wiped out by the 1885 storm. Therefore hurricanes can be very bad when they hit the barrier islands. There is not much except high land that can stand against the surge that builds up in front of a hurricane.
    But now we have billions of dollars worth of homes built right in the path of any hurricane that may hit our coast. Edingsville found that out when the 1885 storm destroyed that quaint village. It is my opinion that if someone builds a house on the front beach they should be able to stand the loss and consider the house as expendable and to be used for their pleasure until the next hurricane.
    The worst one that hit Edisto that I have a record of was the 1893 storm that was called the "Sea Island" storm. It came ashore below Edisto around Savannah and seemed to have gone up the Highway 17 corridor. It did severe damage all the way up to Georgetown, SC. At this time the communications were still very limited and very few people in America

realized that our area had been hit so hard. Therefore help was long time coming. I understand that Little Edisto was covered by water and many people on Edisto were killed by this storm. As I have mentioned before, the storm waters were so high that a two-masted schooner was taken off the North Edisto and floated up Sand Creek almost to Scenic Highway 174 where it eventually rotted. I remember seeing it when we moved to Edisto in the 1940s. I understand that two tides were held in by the wind and the tidal water was extremely high all over Edisto.

It is said that those who stayed in their houses during the 1893 storm lived and a few that ventured out of their houses died in the raging wind and sea water that came ashore.

By now you probably realize that I like Chalmers Murray's account of things that happened in the first half of the 1900s. The following is a short account of how one family survived the 1893 storm.

A story by Chalmers S. Murray

"When the storm was at it worst and the breakers were rolling in, Maulsey's mother opened the doors of their house and let the breakers roll right through. This was the sensible thing to do as the house then offered little resistance. The waves, however, swept a trunk from the house. It was found the next morning, quite a distance away, resting in the marsh that bordered the place. Maulsey also found her umbrella sticking up in the mud. My father had just finished building her house. It suffered no real damage except for smashed windows."

As stated above, the 1885 storm destroyed Edingsville Village. The location of the original village is now far out in the ocean.

In 1911 a storm took out the remaining large sand dunes on Edingsville Beach.

There is also an account of the 1911 hurricane in Chalmers Murray's book "Turn Backward 0 Time in Your Flight" that I thought was interesting. These details tell you why you should leave Edisto when a hurricane is predicted to hit Edisto.

A story by Chalmers S. Murray

"The hurricane of 1911 was the first severe storm that I remember. It came up on a Sunday just as we were getting ready for church, so we had to call off the trip. I watched grey, dishrag clouds scurry across t he sky and felt the house tremble with the wind, which had by then reached gale force.

My father went outside for several minutes and came back shaking his head. If the wind kept up, it would be the end of the cotton crop, he said. He shook his head again. 'I'm afraid that will mean that you can't go back to the Citadel.' He told me. I thought he was talking through his hat. Somehow, the Murray family always managed to come through every crisis. My father (up to now) had always been good for a loan.

The wind was making a weird sound: sometimes it whistled, sometimes it roared and sometimes it howled. The house seemed to be doing a kind of dance. I looked out at the creek and marsh in front. In a little time all of the marsh was covered with water and I could see breakers rolling in. My mother managed to cook some kind of dinner on the kerosene stove. The wood was too damp for a wood fire.

My father went upstairs and returned with a dazed look on his face. 'The minute I opened the parlor door, all the window panes crashed.' he said. 'I'm afraid all the panes upstairs have been broken. We will have to spend the night down here.'

Ina started to cry and nothing my mother could do would comfort her. The wind was now blowing higher than ever, and I expected to see the roof fly off but, despite my fears, this did not happen. The howling gale kept up all day and all night. My mother had made a bed on the floor and I lay down with the rest, but couldn't sleep for a long time. Ina, however, went to sleep almost at once. I think my parents caught cat naps.

Monday dawned at last, but the heavy rain clouds obscured the sun. My father remarked that luckily, the hurricane had struck at low tide, otherwise the yard would have been flooded. He looked out gloomily. The cotton had been stripped from the bolls and lay in white patches in the fields. What had been a promising crop had been completely destroyed."

Mr. Murray's house was located on Frampton Creek. Across Frampton Creek there was a large area of marsh grass and then what was left of Edingsville Beach. The area that was covered by water in his story was that large area of marsh grass between Frampton Creek and Edingsville Beach.

The comment that was made about a hurricane hitting on high tide was also the worry of my father when I was coming up. If a hurricane hit on high tide and the hurricane blew long enough a second and maybe a third tide would come in on top of the first tide. I am told this is what happened during the 1893 hurricane.

We started spending the summers on Edisto Beach in 1942. We moved to Edisto permanently in the fall of 1947. I remember riding down Palmetto Blvd. when we first arrived and seeing that there were no houses on the front beach down to about the sixth block. When you are leaving the beach you will notice that the sidewalks stop at about the sixth block at an old beach house. The number of this old beach house is 602 Palmetto Blvd. I have included a picture of this old beach house as a reference point so you can easily see where I am talking about. From this point on there were no houses. There was one house standing out in the ocean near the pavilion when we first arrived. It soon gave way to the ocean's pounding. We later learned that the 1940 storm took these houses out. I also later learned that everyone left the beach before the 1940 storm hit. One man stayed down where Palmetto Blvd. goes into two lanes. The ocean came in so far that waves were breaking all over this area and it looked like a bay. The house he stayed in held together during this storm but I am told it was such a horrible experience that the man really never got over the ordeal. It must have been awesome to be in a house that seemed to be in the middle of St. Helena Sound during a northeaster with waves breaking all around you.

Another story that I heard was about a man that had just bought a new outboard motor and had it on the porch. As he was making preparations to leave the beach before the 1940 storm he decided he'd better put his new outboard motor in the house. When he came back the house was gone and the porch was still standing.

It was quite some time before this end of the beach was re-nourished and houses were rebuilt.

This is the house I talked about.

When we moved to Edisto to stay in 1947 there was a hurricane in the next three or four seasons. It seemed that every year there was at least one hurricane. Living on the coast you got used to northeasters and just learned to ride them out. But back in the late 1940s there were no advanced hurricane warnings as Chalmers Murray stated. One day the wind would start blowing and it just kept on blowing. I remember that during our first hurricane in 1947 a policeman came to our door and told us we had three hours to get off the beach because a hurricane was about to hit Edisto. We rode that storm out at the Hopkinson's plantation house. As I talked about earlier, the eye of the hurricane came right over us. During another storm we rode it out at Buck Fisk's grandparents' house. I remember the same kind of weird sounds caused by hurricane force wind as sounding just like Chalmers Murray described. At this time I am having a hard time remembering all that happened during these late 1940s hurricanes that we experienced.

I do remember one time coming back to the beach after leaving for a storm and finding four feet of beach sand all the way from the entrance to Edisto Beach down about eight blocks. The highway department had to remove the sand before we could get our car to the house.

Another time when a small storm was about to hit we went up to the Edistonian and stayed in the car until the storm passed. The sea water came almost up to the Edistonian. They said that the causeway leading to the beach was covered by four feet of water during this storm.

Once we left the beach, came back home and had to leave again because the hurricane came over us, went back out to sea and them came back over us again all in one night.

On several occasions the storm water did not come over the sand dunes in front of our house but came in from the marsh off Scott Creek and flooded our downstairs with about two feet of water. The water did not come from the front but filled the creeks so much that it flooded Palmetto Blvd. A couple of blocks on each side of our house at 1207 Palmetto Blvd. seem to be a little higher than the rest of the beach. In my lifetime I have never seen the storm water come over this part of the beach.

After one storm I went back in the woods and the hurricane had lifted a house off its piers and floated it back into one of the lagoons. I went in this house and pictures were still on the wall and chairs were still standing upright.

The 1954 storm damaged all but one of the houses Daddy had bought or built and I thought he was going to die trying to get all these houses put back together.

One thing that many forget is that northeasters (Noreasters) cause major problems for the beach. They blow for one, two or three days. The three day blow is the most common. I can remember that it seemed that the wind would never stop. You did not dare go on the beach or try to swim in the ocean during a northeaster. The blowing sand would sting and the waves were big and dangerous to swim in. I did not dare go out in the sound with my sailboat during a northeaster.

There was a large pier built in the 1950s where the present short pier is. I personally saw a northeaster take it apart during one northeaster. I watched as large waves came in and each time a large wave hit the pier another board or piling would break off. Therefore northeasters are not to be taken lightly. They can cause major erosion to the beach especially when there are several close together.

After I was married and had children of my own many times I'd have a dream of gathering up my children in blankets, putting them in the back seat of the car and heading for high land. This is what Daddy and Mother did when we left the beach when a hurricane was approaching.

The last major hurricane Edisto experienced was in 1959. I was in the U.S. Coast Guard's Office Candidate School in Yorktown, Virginia and did not personally experience it. It also did major damage to many of the houses Daddy owned and it was costly. If it had not been for the Athletic Grant in Aid David had been offered by The Citadel to play football Daddy might not have been able to send David to college. I graduated from The Citadel in the spring of 1959 and he entered in August of 1959.

A major hurricane has not hit Edisto since 1959. When the next one will hit is anyone's guess. But one will probably hit Edisto again. My advice to you is if one is forecast to hit anywhere near Edisto you should head for high land. Don't take a chance on it not being bad and try to ride it out. Be especially aware of any hurricane that is forecast to hit below Edisto from about Savannah, Georgia on up toward Edisto. The front of the storm is where most of the damage is done. If one hits above Edisto it will probably not do much damage because there is less force in a hurricane below the eye. But don't sit on edge wondering if Edisto will have a hurricane this season. Just enjoy your stay on Edisto and pay attention to the birds. If one morning you wake up and there are no birds to be found then get your tail off Edisto. You may not believe in God but He has built into his birds the ability to know when a major storm is coming. They head for high land to get out of the way of strong winds that could cause them great harm. Also when you see very large waves begin to hit the beach and they are very far apart, then cut the radio on and listen to the weather channel because there is a storm out in the ocean causing these waves and the storm may be headed for us.

From my observation it seems that when the storm surge hits the beach it flattens out and the water does little damage to the second row of houses. If a house is built very strong on the second row it is likely to ride out a storm. Front beach houses are at the mercy of God. But no building anywhere close to the ocean, whether on the second row or not, will stand a strong hurricane under the right circumstances. Therefore get your tail off the beach and take your family and pets with you when it is forecast that a storm will hit anywhere near Edisto, especially south of us. Hugo in 1989 was a powerful storm and hit just north of Charleston but did little damage south of the Stono River. But north of the eye it tore up everything.

Oh, there is an indication that the sea level on Edisto has risen a few inches over the past several years and if things continue there maybe a cycle of warming that will cause our sea level to continue to rise. Therefore keep this in mind and plan accordingly. As I have written early on in this book, there is real evidence that the ocean went up to Peach Tree Rock near

Columbia, SC and the seashore off Edisto has gone out to the continental shelf due to the warming and cooling of the earth from time to time. Therefore our Earth has been under constant change from its creation. This should tell us to enjoy the beauty of Edisto as much as we can but we should also watch the birds and the sea level for changes over time. Slight changes over time add up to big changes. As changes take place there comes a point of no return and those that have not keep an eye on these changes will be left short. Man and God's other creatures can adjust to whatever changes come if they keep their eyes on what is going on around them. Only fools never adjust or change when change is required of us.

Don't be like the people that try to ride out a storm and were never heard from again. Don't be like the Vikings that settled Greenland and failed to take notice when the climate got colder and killed them off because they did not adjust to the changes. Greenland was green at one time and was a great place to raise sheep. But it did not last. Let us hope that Edisto stays as beautiful as it is now for us to enjoy for many generations to come. But let us all remember that the only constant on earth is change. Sometimes change comes with one storm but remember Fig Island which I talked about earlier? That was 4,500 years ago. Therefore Edisto has not had that much change since then because people were living on Edisto that long ago. So watch for change but don't sit and worry about it. Therefore get off Edisto if a storm is headed this way.

Rabbit Trail: While they were building the pyramids in Egypt the people living on Edisto were building a large shell ring called Fig Island. This gives us some idea of how long people have been living on Edisto. Therefore Edisto is not an upstart place. People have been living on Edisto for longer than we can imagine. Fig Island has also stood all the hurricanes nature can throw at it untouched during its 4,500 years of history. Likewise people keep coming and discovering Edisto. Many come and are refreshed by what they find. I keep discovering something new in my paradise every time I look. The Edisto ("Edistow") experience is a never ending experience of discovery and enjoyment.

Talking about change -- This is what happens when the tide and wind get together. The tides come way over our dock. If you look closely you will see that we have our johnboat high above our dock level in case the tide and wind get together and bring in an unusual tide. --- Keep your eyes open.

CHAPTER ELEVEN

"The Lord is far from the wicked: but he heareth the prayer of the righteous."
Proverbs 15:29 KJV Chapter 11

The previous chapters are about all I can remember about Edisto worth writing down. I have others stories but they are minor and I tried to only hit the high spots to paint a picture of the true Edisto Island in order to give my grandchildren some idea of how I spent my time as a child. Their parents can fill in what we did as a family when they were coming up. I hope you have enjoyed my stories and items I borrowed from others that I thought did a good job of describing Edisto and what has happened to it over the years.

Allow me to end this rambling by telling you my impression of what I saw early this morning while Joyce and I were sitting on our front porch overlooking Store Creek.

I had just sat down with my first cup of coffee trying to get waked up when I heard a dolphin blow. I looked up over the freshly greened marsh grass to the other side of the creek and saw the fins of several dolphins pushing mullet against the mud bank with mullet jumping everywhere as the dolphins had their fill of them. As I strained to see the commotion two laughing gulls flew close down over the live oaks on the creek bank telling us that they were there also. Joyce brought my attention to a large white egret that was getting in on what the dolphins had stirred up by picking up small mullet. Off to our right at the marsh edge were several marsh crows also trying to get a meal. While sitting there drinking our coffee a yellow throated Warbler began singing his heart out in the palmetto tree out by the creek bank. A few minutes later we were pleased to hear a towhee and a bob white quail that we had not heard in a long time.

As we continued to sit there a light cool breeze began to gently blow across us and almost put me back to sleep to dream dreams and see visions of how our world should be and how we all should try hard to take care of each other by loving each other as Christ loved and died for the church.

While I was dozing away Joyce called me to breakfast and fed me grits with butter and cheese. Sometimes she puts shrimp in the grits which I especially like. Most of the time we have a freezer full of shrimp and fish we caught in the creek in front of our house. Often I come in and Joyce is preparing fresh vegetables from our garden for dinner. With a little work and imagination you can live well and inexpensively on Edisto Island with a little land and taking advantage of the bounty found in Edisto's many creeks and waterways.

What a life!

Let me leave you with this. Edisto is a place that has been in the midst of everything that went on shortly after Columbus discovered the New World. But he really discovered what thousands of human beings just like us had known about for eons of time but they called them Indians. There is real evidence that people have been depending on Edisto for its bounty for more years than we can count. The ocean has come and gone over Edisto and the climate has been very hot on Edisto and very cold in the past. Thus there has been constant change since the piece of land called Edisto (Ed-is-tow) came into existence.

A lifetime could be spent learning all there is to know about Edisto and what went on throughout the ages. If you become bored with life then come to Edisto and spend the rest of your life being amazed at what happened on Edisto as the years have gone by. As you have noticed I love to hear what others had to say about the same experiences I had coming up on Edisto throughout my life. St. Helena Sound has been pleasing many over the years and has been a horror to others.

Therefore come to Edisto, read about it and then go find the places that are written about it. The books that I credited at the beginning of this book are worth reading because they will fill in much of what I left out. My objective in writing this book is to let my grandchildren learn about what their grandfather was all about and what he liked and did coming up on Edisto.

Companion Book

I have researched and written another book that dove tails with this book. It is about my ancestors and how the Lybrands fit into the Edisto Story. My original intent was to include both of these books into one book. But I began to see that this would make this book too large. Therefore I divided it into two books.

Both covers look alike. This book is called volume one and the one on my ancestry is called volume two. Therefore if you want to find out the real and full story you need to read both volume one and volume two. I believe you will enjoy both books.

Over my 75 years I have come to understand who controls our universe and whose commandments and precepts we must follow to live a contented and productive life. Over the years I have seen many people lose their creativity by being mad with the world or holding grudges and thus living miserable lives. I personally believe that you will miss the greatest part of life here on Planet Earth if you don't live by the standards found in the Holy Christian Bible. I have included two passages that I think sum up how we should live. If you will dwell on the following two scripture passages and really try to understand and live accordingly, I truly believe you will live a more contented and productive life.

Psalm One
King James Version

Blessed is the man that walketh not in the counsel of the ungodly, nor standeth in the way of the sinner, nor sitteth in the seat of the scornful. But his delight is in the law of the Lord; and in His law doth he meditate day and night. And he shall be like a tree planted by the rivers of water, that bringeth forth his fruit in his season; his leaf also shall not wither; and whatsoever he doeth shall prosper. The ungodly are not so; but are like the chaff which the wind driveth away. Therefore the ungodly shall not stand in the judgment, nor sinners in the congregation of the righteous

For the Lord knoweth the way of the righteous; but the way of the ungodly shall perish.

1 Corinthians 13
King James Version

Though I speak with the tongues of men and of angels and have not charity (love), I am become as sounding brass, or a tinkling cymbal.
And though I have the gift of prophecy, and understand all mysteries, and all knowledge; and though I have all faith, so that I could remove mountains, and have not charity (love), I am nothing.

And though I bestow all my goods to feed the poor, and though I give my body to be burned, and have not charity (love), it profiteth me nothing. Charity (love) suffereth long, and is kind; charity (love) envieth not; charity (love) vaunteth not itself, is not pufled up, doth not behave itself unseemly, seeketh not her own, is not easily provoked, thinketh no evil; rejoiceth not in iniquity, but rejoiceth in the truth; beareth all things, believeth all things, hopeth all things, endureth all things.

Charity (love) never faileth; but whether there be prophecies, they shall fail, whether there be tongues they shall cease, whether there be knowledge, it shall vanish away.

For we know in part, and we prophesy in part.

But when that which is perfect is come, then that which is in part shall be done away.

When I was a child, I spake as a child, I understood as a child, I thought as a child; but when I became a man, I put away childish things.

For now we see through a glass, darkly; but then face to face; now I know in part; but then shall I know even as also I am known.

And now abideth faith, hope, charity (love), these three, but the greatest of these is charity (love).

(Note: The modern translations translate charity as love. That is why I have added love in parentheses. But when you really think about it charity is a thoughtful way to get across the point in this passage.)

Oh, one morning as I was wrapping up this book, Joyce called me to see if I knew what kind of large bird was standing on the sandbar out in front of our dock. We both noted that it was bigger than most of the sea birds we were familiar with. I looked and saw that it had a white head and black body. But I still did not know what it was. We got out our field glasses and realized it was a bald eagle. About the time we identified it, it flew off, showing its white tail feathers. Then we knew for certain that it was a bald eagle. This was the first time we had ever seen a bald eagle near our house on our creek. I have included this to make a point that things are constantly changing on Edisto and every day it seems that we unveil another mystery. I guess up until I die there will be another bird or something God created that I had never seen before that will excite me and I will go off into eternity with a smile on my face.

God bless you all — every one of you.
Sam Lybrand

Dream Dreams and See Visions

There is a place where you can get off by yourself in the midst of God's wonders and let your mind wonder about the mysteries of life.

There are plenty of places that are seldom visited where the pelicans and dolphin know.

Along the way the marsh hens make strong and wonderful sounds that are heard only in places like this.

The air is clear and free from the smells of the city where everyone is going aimlessly to and fro.

A johnboat, canoe, or kayak is all you need to explore miles after miles of beautiful marsh grass and creeks lined with live oaks extending their long arms to welcome you.

Eagles and osprey work these waters that go here and go there. There is no telling what you will see around the next bend.

Grand old plantation houses are seen along the way as a testimony of wealth long ago.

New elegant houses seen along the way are a testimony of the current success of many that chose this romantic place.

If you quietly go down the many varied creeks and take notice, you will see egrets, herons, wood storks, and belted king/ishers catching their daily bread. You will hear the march wren singing its sweet song but you will be blessed if you actually see him.

At the edge of the creeks blue crabs and the graceful stingrays will be noisily splashing around catching their meals for the day.

When you come to that quiet spot stop and let your mind dream dreams and see visions of how God meant man to enjoy His great creation.

You will be hard pressed to find a more peaceful and beautiful place on earth to dreams your dreams and see visions of thing as they are and are to become.

This lovely place is called Ed—is-tow.

Sam Lybrand 9/19/12

Going home after a great day fishing.

DEDICATIONS

These books are dedicated to my first wife, Ida Margaret Myers, who I was married to for 40 years. She gave me three wonderful children. She had an untimely death in early 2000 and is truly missed. It is also dedicated to my children, Jimmy, Amy and John and their children. Included in this dedication are my second wife, Joyce Hills Abrams, who I grew up with on Edisto, and her children who have taken me in and treated me so well.

My Children:

1. James Samuel Lybrand, my firstborn, born in Puerto Rico in 1960 while I was in the service. He married Melinda Jozette Starnes. Their children are Samuel Dugree Lybrand and Laken Jozette Lybrand. 2. Amy Margaret King, my second child. She was born in Orangeburg, SC in 1963 while I was working at my first job out of the service. She married Matthew King. Their children are Anne Harley King, James Oliver King, and Robert David King. 3. John Myers Lybrand, my third child, also born in Orangeburg, SC in 1965 while I was working at my first job. He married Elizabeth Hay. Their children are John Daniel Hay Lybrand, and Sarah Elizabeth Lybrand.

Joyce's Children:

1. Karen Abrams Peterson, who is married to Bill Peterson.
Karen's children by her first husband are Joseph Bradford Smith, and M Katherine Smith. 2. Pamela Abrams Welch, who is married to Kyle Welch.

Their child is Garrett Kyle Welch. 3. Marie Abrams Asbill, who is currently not married.

Her Children are Marsh Seabrook Elliott, Tide McTeer Elliot, and August Savanna Asbill from two previous marriages.

4. Josegh Scott Abrams, who is married to Josie Shimp. Their children are, Emma Louise Abrams and James Lucas Abrams.

It is my desire that all of the above live happy, contented and fulfilled lives. It is especially asked that my children and grandchildren warmly remember their mother and grandmother. Joyce's children and grandchildren are reminded what an unselfish, loving and kind mother and grandmother they have and should cherish her all the days of her life.

"Train up a child in the way he should go: and when he is old, he will not depart from it". Proverbs 22:6 KJV

CREDITS

The credits listed below are for both Volume One and Volume Two so that I have all those people that helped me in one place.

From the start I want to recognize those who have helped me put these books together and those books or other sources I have used to help put some color and flavor to this book. Without all this help these books would not have been possible. These are not listed in any particular order so that I am not giving anyone special recognition, except for my wife who worked tirelessly to try to help me write this story as clearly as possible. Just know that I sincerely appreciate all the help I have received.

Individuals that so kindly helped me with this book.

Joyce Lybrand, of Edisto Island, my wife, who has worked tirelessly editing and improving my sentence structure to make these books more readable. Without her this would not have happened. These books would be only a dream of mine without her. Thanks, Joyce.

Amy Lybrand King, of Summerville, SC, my daughter, who saved my family pictures for me to use in these books.

David Lybrand, of Edisto Island, SC, my brother, who provided a story or two and some great pictures of Rockville. He also helped me get pictures of White Shell.

Jim Lybrand, of Pelion, SC., my son. He did some fact gathering for me for this book.

Jack Lybrand, of Columbia, SC, a distant relative, who first sparked my interest in finding out about my ancestry and provided a copy of his own book on the Lybrands, of which I have used a portion. He also provided additional stories and pictures.

Jimmy Lybrand, of Sally, SC, a distant relative, who provided pictures and stories of my ancestors in the New Holland, SC area.

George Marion Lybrand, of West Columbia, SC, a distant relative, provided a great letter about my father's first real job as a teacher in New Holland, SC.

Bobby Lybrand, of Pelion, SC, a distant relative who told me how to get in touch with his sister, Frances Tyler, who in turn provided great information. LeMyra T. Young, of Wagener, SC, a distant relative, who provided what I would consider a vast amount of information and pictures that made this book come alive in some places.

Frances Tyler, of Wagener, SC, a distant relative, who provided a nice long letter with her experiences with the Lybrands.

Phil Hydrick, of August, GA. who told me how to get in touch with Marcia Hydrick Foreman, who provided invaluable information about my grandfather, grandmother and Thelma, my father's older sister.

Marcia Hydrick Foreman, of North August, SC, a cousin, who sent me pictures of my grandfather and grandmother. She also sent me a picture of Daddy's sister Thelma, who I had never seen. Without her a great hole would be left in this book. Thanks again, Marcia.

Doris Brittain, of California, a distant relative who I talked to in 1985 and who sent me a book she had written called Lybrand Oaks. I have used some of her material in this book. William B. Rauch, of Chapin, SC, a distant relative, provided invaluable information about John Lybrand, Sr. and John (Jack) Lybrand, Jr. His family married into the Lybrand clan in the 1800s. Bill is the President of the Dutch Fork Chapter of SCGS, Inc. (South Carolina Genealogy Society)

Shirley F. Trotter, of Lexington, SC, a distant relative, provided letters from and about Wesley Allen Lybrand and several pictures of my great, great aunts. I have a section inserted called "Shirley's Extra" in volume two that includes all the information she provided. She is also a member of the Dutch Fork Chapter of the SCGS, Inc. as the State Representative.

Jamie Dalhousie, 17'" Earl of Dalhousie, gave me permission to use the portrait of Governor James Glen who signed Hendrick Lybrand's land grant in 1755. Thanks again, Jamie. What a find.

Tide Elliott, of Edisto Island, SC, Joyce's grandson. He allowed me to take a picture of the mammoth leg bone he found on Edisto.

Marie Asbill, of Edisto Island, SC, Joyce's daughter. She allowed me to take a picture of the mammoth tooth she found on Edisto.

Matthew Kizer, of Edisto Island, SC. He gave me the picture of Deveaux Bank that I have used in this book.

Elizabeth M. Johnson, Deputy State House Preservation Office, SC Department of Archives and History. She gave me permission to use the pictures of Fig Island. Credit for obtaining these pictures goes to The National Register of Historical Places program at the SC Department of Archives of History. I thank them for providing these pictures.

Susan Roberts, of Edisto Island, SC who gave me permission to use her pictures of the Painting Bunting and the Bald Eagles. She is a professional photographer who works out of Edisto. She is a well know photographer and I greatly appreciate her allowing me to use these two beautiful pictures.

The Post and Courier, of Charleston, SC. I have used several old articles that my wife, Joyce, had saved over the years that came from The Post and Courier.

The sunset photograph on the last page was taken by one of our neighbors when Joyce and I were coming back from fishing in Store Creek. This is a once in a lifetime opportunity when everything came together at a moment in time that may never happen again.

Unknown helper or provider of information. Being the old man that I am I am sure I have left someone out. Therefore if you are reading this and contributed something to this book then I also thank you.

Books I found that had interesting things about Edisto that I thought worth repeating in this book

Turn Backward 0 Time in Your Flight by Chalmers S. Murray, published by the Edisto Island Historic Preservation Society. P.O. Box 393, Edisto Island, SC 29438. I used several stories out of this book. As far as I am concerned this book has some of the best descriptive stories of Edisto and its past.

Edisto. A Sea Island Principality, by Clara Childs Puckett, published by Seaforth Publication, Johns Island, SC. I also used several of her stories about Edisto. Mrs. Puckett was well known to me. She rode my school bus to high school when I drove it in 1954/1955. When she got on the bus she sat directly behind me while I was driving. A very refined lady in anyone's book.

Tales of Edisto, by Nell S. Graydon, published by R.L. Bryan Company of Columbia, SC. I used a quote or two from this book.

Rumbling of the Chariot Wheels, by I. Jenkins Mikell, published by R. L. Bryan Company of Columbia, SC. As far as I am concerned Mr. Mikell tops all with his brilliant and descriptive use of the English language. I used several stories out of his book.

Thanks again for all who so kindly helped me with this labor of love, Sam Lybrand

Fishing pole, fresh shrimp, net for the big ones and a nice clear day — What else would you wish for?

> Fishing pole, fresh shrimp, net for the big ones and a nice clear day. What else would you wish for?

Made in the USA
Columbia, SC
21 June 2018